AMERICA
THE
ANXIOUS

AMERICA
THE
ANXIOUS

How Our Pursuit of Happiness
Is Creating a Nation of
Nervous Wrecks

RUTH WHIPPMAN

ST. MARTIN'S PRESS
NEW YORK

This is a work of nonfiction. However, the names and identifying characteristics of certain individuals have been changed to protect their privacy, and the author has reconstructed dialogue to the best of her recollection.

www.stmartins.com

Designed by Ellen Cipriano

Library of Congress Cataloging-in-Publication Data

Names: Whippman, Ruth, author.
Title: America the anxious : how our pursuit of happiness is creating a
  nation of nervous wrecks / Ruth Whippman.
Description: First U.S. [edition]. | New York : St. Martin's Press, 2016. |
  Includes bibliographical references and index.
Identifiers: LCCN 2016016272 | ISBN 9781250071521 (hardcover) |
  ISBN 9781466882669 (e-book)
Subjects: LCSH: National characteristics, American. | Happiness—
  United States. | United States—Civilization—21st century. |
  United States—Social conditions—21st century.
Classification: LCC E169.12 .W455 2016 | DDC 306.097309/05—dc23
LC record available at https://lccn.loc.gov/2016016272

ISBN 978-1-250-07152-1 (hardcover)
ISBN 978-1-4668-8266-9 (e-book)

Our books may be purchased in bulk for promotional, educational, or business use. Please contact your local bookseller or the Macmillan Corporate and Premium Sales Department at 1-800-221-7945, extension 5442, or by e-mail at MacmillanSpecialMarkets@macmillan.com.

First published in Great Britain under the title *The Pursuit of Happiness: And Why It Is Making Us Anxious* by Hutchinson, Penguin Random House UK

First U.S. Edition: October 2016

10 9 8 7 6 5 4 3 2 1

For Neil.
And for Solly and Zephy.
With love.

CONTENTS

1.

COMING TO AMERICA: OBSESSED WITH HAPPINESS, BUT NOBODY'S HAPPY

I'm at the gynecologist for my Pap smear, feet in stirrups, idly wondering what Emily Post might have suggested as appropriate small talk for those moments when the person you are speaking to will be replying to your vagina. We've been living in America for a few months now, having moved here from London for my husband's job, and in theory, Britishness should be good preparation for these kinds of occasions. After all, our national social specialty is the denial of glaring intimacies, soldiering on with weather pleasantries to avoid acknowledging any form of nudity, either physical or emotional.

Unfortunately, even at the best of times, making casual conversation with a British accent in America feels a bit like being a librarian in a nightclub, or wearing a set of iron tongue calipers. Now we're living here, I'm doomed to lug this paralyzing verbal awkwardness around with me for the next few years until we move back to England and I can stop attempting to sound convincing saying things like "awesome!" and "good job!" and "ass" (this last, genuinely technically impossible to pronounce with a British tongue without sounding utterly ludicrous or as though you're talking about a donkey).

This time however, I needn't have worried—the doctor is doing all the talking. Delving deep with her speculum, she delves deeper into matters of the heart. Apparently, she is reading Gretchen Rubin's best-seller, *Happier at Home*, and finding it very instructive. I've read that book too and am suddenly overcome with crippling self-consciousness. I hope desperately that my gynecologist is not currently reading the part about how in order to achieve true happiness, it is advisable to give total mental focus to how everything around you smells.

Six months ago I would have found it hard to believe that I would be discussing the path to everlasting bliss with the ob-gyn, but after a stint living in California, it feels almost routine. Since arriving here, I feel as though I have had more conversations about my own and other people's happiness than in the whole of the rest of my life put together.

We moved to the States from the UK when my techie husband, Neil, was offered a job with a software start-up in Silicon Valley. A lifelong Americanophile, he had jumped at the chance, and I had quit my fre-netic job making television documentaries to be a stay-at-home mom to our toddler son, Solly. Although I got a fair amount of mileage from the clear moral advantage of being the one who "gave up everything for her loved one's dreams," in reality I was ready to ditch my lifelong codependent relationship with surly gray London and embrace the sun-drenched beauty of California.

But a few months in, I'm feeling displaced and lonely. I have gone from being desperate to spend more time with Solly, to having vast unbroken vistas of togetherness that are sending me slightly crazy. He is, of course, the very delight of my soul, but he only knows ten words, and five of those are names for different types of construction vehi-cles. Desperate for adult conversation, I am sidling up to anyone and everyone—moms pushing swings next to me in the playground, the dry cleaner, the man in front of me in line at the grocery store, and a range of random local contacts scratched together for me by friends back in London. Oddly, the same topic comes up time and time again. Happiness.

The conversations tend to fall into two broad categories: the agonizing kind and the evangelical kind. As a compulsive overthinker myself, the agonizing ones feel more familiar to me. These conversations are all about questions. Am I with the right person? Am I following my passions? Am I doing what I *love*? What is my purpose in life? Am I as happy as I should be?

As a Brit raised on a diet of armchair cynicism, the evangelical-style conversations are newer territory. In these, people claim to have found the answers. They enthuse about their chosen paths to bliss, convinced, at least temporarily, that they have found the definitive *thing* that will pin down the happy-ever-after.

Their answers range from the mundane to the mind-boggling. Yoga and meditation. Keeping a "gratitude journal." A weekend seminar on how to Unleash the Power Within. Keeping your baby attached to your body for a minimum of twenty-two hours out of every twenty-four, and, most bafflingly, not least on a practical level, the drinking of wolf colostrum. A friend of a friend that I meet for coffee livens up a rather dull conversation about what time her husband gets home from work with the observation that it really doesn't matter one way or the other, as the most important person in her life is actually Jesus.

It seems as though happiness in America has become the overachiever's ultimate trophy. A modern trump card, it outranks professional achievement and social success, family, friendship, and even love. Its invocation deftly minimizes others' achievements ("Well, I suppose she has the perfect job and a gorgeous husband, but is she really *happy?*") and takes the shine off our own.

It all feels a long way from the British approach that I was brought up with. Jefferson knew what he was doing when he wrote that "pursuit of happiness" line, a perfectly delivered slap in the face to his joy-shunning oppressors across the pond. Emotionally awkward and primed for skepticism, the British are generally uncomfortable around the subject and, as a rule, don't subscribe to the happy-ever-after. It's not that we don't want to be happy. It just feels embarrassing to discuss it and demeaning to chase it, like calling someone moments after a first date to ask if they like you.

Self-help books and yoga classes and meditation all exist in the UK, of course—there is no shortage of people willing to take your money in return for the promise of bliss—but they somehow don't have the same magnetic pull, our inbuilt cultural skepticism providing a natural check.

Part of this is that Americans seem to have a deep cultural aversion to negativity. This can be a welcome change, but the pressure to remain positive at all times often results in some complicated mental gymnastics. My son's report card at preschool divided his performance not into strengths and weaknesses but into strengths and emerging strengths. American problems are routinely rebranded as "opportunities," hence the filthy bathroom in our local supermarket displays a sign saying: "If this restroom fails to meet your expectations, please inform us of the opportunity," as if reeking puddles of urine are merely an inspirational occasion for personal growth.

Cynicism is the British shtick, our knee-jerk starting point. I think back to a time a few years ago when I was working at the BBC in London, and our managers booked a motivational trainer to come and attempt to galvanize the dispirited employees in my department. The trainer identified the problem. We were all far too negative, and would be much happier and better motivated if we would just stop saying no all the time. He suggested that next time someone put forward an idea, instead of responding with the words *"no, but . . ."* (insert mean-spirited objection to other person's creativity), we should instead force ourselves to respond with a *"yes, and . . ."* (insert positive-spirited, constructive comment building on other person's idea). He made us try it out, kicking things off himself with an initial sample idea, then throwing it over to the next person in line to pick up. *"Yes, and . . . that's bollocks,"* said the next person. This pretty much sums up the British attitude.

It feels good to be away from this sometimes life-leeching negativity, but I also find it hard to throw myself full tilt into the American approach to hunting down bliss. Happiness over here has its own vocabulary: *mindfulness, empowerment.* Whenever I hear the word *empowerment,* it always makes me feel slightly edgy, as if at any moment I might be asked to take my clothes off. If someone suggests that a given activity is going to be "empowering," I know that is almost certainly going to be undignified, mildly humiliating, or involve heights. As a rule, "empowerment" appears to be the consolation prize for those of us who will never have any actual power, and you can safely assume that no one in any position of genuine authority will be joining in. Creating a Tumblr of photos of your post–C-section wobbling and scarred naked stomach? Empowering! Creating a Tumblr of photos of your post-prostate surgery rectum? Not so much, Senator.

Mindfulness is everywhere, the hugely popular zeitgeist theory that in order to be happy we must live fully in the present moment, with total mental focus on whatever we are doing or experiencing Right This Second. *Time* magazine publishes an eight-page spread, featured on the front cover entitled "The Mindful Revolution," that opens with the author, an impressive and decorated journalist, bringing the full force of her considerable mental capacity to bear on a raisin. The raisin "glistens." I can't help thinking that, as a rule, food shouldn't glisten.

During my first few months in America, I come across mindful parenting, mindful business dealings, mindful eating, and even mindful dishwashing, complete with a detailed set of instructions on the *Huffington Post*, in printable format, to pin above the sink. According to the practice's thought leaders, in order to achieve maximum happiness, the mindful dishwasher must refuse to succumb to domestic autopilot and instead fully mentally engage with every piece of congealed scrambled egg and clump of oatmeal on the saucepan.

I find mindfulness a hard theory to embrace. Surely one of the most magnificent things about the human brain is its ability to hold past, present, future, and their imagined alternatives in constant parallel, to offset the tedium of washing dishes in Pinole with the chance to be simultaneously mentally in Bangkok or Don Draper's boxer shorts or finally telling your mother-in-law that despite her belief that "no one born in the seventies died," using a car seat isn't spoiling your child. I struggle to see how greater happiness could be achieved by reining in that magical sense of scope and possibility to stare down some oatmeal.

Although I'm probably just being defensive. As a person who is ridiculously distractible, the whole philosophy of mindfulness comes across almost as a personal attack, an intervention from some well-meaning body to compel me to stop doing the "Which Brunch Entrée Are You?" BuzzFeed quiz and go read *Llama Llama I'm a Self-Harmer* to my son for the nineteenth time this morning. (Anyhow, I'm convinced that the idea that distraction is a product of the modern age and that our foremothers spent their days in a state of total mindful focus on their children is a myth. The desperate urge to escape the more grinding realities of childcare was surely just as strong for our mothers' generation; they just used Valium instead of iPhones.)

I start to wonder whether the high-octane approach to the pursuit of happiness that I'm seeing here in middle-class California is in any way representative of American culture more widely. California has always been the headquarters of the Great American Search for Happiness, and the people I am meeting, although generally not rich or part of any kind of mega-elite, do tend to be college-educated professionals, a similar bracket to me and most of my social network back in the UK. Is all this joy hunting just the ultimate luxury for a privileged bunch of high-income Californians?

A bit of digging suggests not. Although the poverty stricken are unlikely to be wandering into Barnes & Noble for a book about mindfulness, a little research reveals that the explicit and focused quest for happiness as a goal distinct from the rest of life is seeping through virtually all sections of American society. Oprah Winfrey, the reigning queen of the happy-seekers, is widely considered to be one of the most influential people in America, having brought her signature brand of self-improvement and spirituality to hundreds of millions of Americans. Yet around half of Oprah's audience had a household income of less than fifty thousand dollars, the US median, and a similar proportion had no education beyond high school.[1]

Mindfulness is seeping into the public education system throughout the nation. In Ohio, Congressman Tim Ryan recently received a sizable federal grant to bring mindfulness classes into the state's elementary schools[2] (although at least one school discontinued the program after parents complained that they were "taking valuable time out of education to put students in a room of darkness to lay on their backs").[3] Americans buy a billion dollars' worth of self-help books and audiobooks each year.[4] Meanwhile the Internet bursts with links to motivational happiness seminars all across the country aimed at the unemployed, rebranding destitution as "an exciting opportunity for personal development."

As the perfect blend of the pioneer spirit and the perky one, the Great American Search for Happiness is a characteristically American struggle, a "wagons west" of the soul. This is the emotional face of the American dream and the faith in meritocracy that underpins it. The belief that if you put in enough emotional elbow grease, if you slog out the hours in yoga classes and mindfulness seminars, parachute jumps and self-help books and megachurches and therapy sessions, then eternal happiness will be yours. It's an inspiring promise, but for something that's supposed to be pleasurable, it can also feel like an awful lot of hard work.

It occurs to me that all these happiness pursuits often don't seem to be making people particularly happy. When a new American friend persuades me to try out a yoga class, you can almost smell the tension and misery in the room. Although it's a little hard to determine cause and effect, as anyone who was already feeling happy would be unlikely to waste the sensation in a fetid room at the YMCA, contorting their body into uncomfortable positions. The happy person would be more likely to be off doing something fun, like sitting in the park, drinking.

Before moving to America, I didn't really give a whole lot of dedicated thought to whether or not I was happy. Like most people, in any given day I will experience emotions and sensations including (but not limited to) hilarity, joy, irritation, ambivalence, excitement, embarrassment, paralyzing self-doubt, boredom, anxiety, guilt, heart-stopping love, resentment, pride, exhaustion, and the shrill, insistent buzz of un-eaten chocolate somewhere in the house. It's hard to pin one definitive label on all this clattering emotional noise, but I'm confident that if you add them all up and then divide by the number of emotions (or whatever other formula they use to calculate the statistics in all the research studies on happiness that I start to notice in the press), then you reach an average falling squarely into the box marked contentment.

But the more conversations I have about happiness, and the more I absorb the idea that there's a glittering happy-ever-after out there for the taking, the more I start to overthink the whole thing, compulsively monitoring how I am feeling and hyper-parenting my emotions. *Am I happy? Right at this moment? What about now? And now? Am I happy enough? As happy as everyone else? What about Meghan? Is she happier than me? She looks happier. What is she doing that I'm not doing? Maybe I should take up yoga.* The whole process starts to become painfully, comically neurotic. Workaday contentment starts to give way to a low-grade sense of inadequacy when pitched against capital-*H* Happiness. The goal is so elusive and hard to define, it's impossible to pinpoint when it's even been reached, a recipe for anxiety.

To an outsider, it can sometimes feel as though the entire population has a nationwide standardized happiness exam to take, and everyone is frantically cramming the night before to get a good grade. Like a stony-faced "that's hilarious" after a joke in place of laughter—another mildly unnerving staple of conversation in this country—it appears that somewhere along the line, the joy has been sucked out of American happiness.

Oddly, even adjusting for emotional openness, my new happiness-seeking American acquaintances seem no happier, and often more anxious, than my cynical joy-slacking British ones. My instinct is that this is because happiness should be serendipitous, the by-product of a life well lived, and chasing it in a vacuum just doesn't really work. I want to dig a little deeper and find out whether or not this hunch stands up to scrutiny.

After some initial research, I find a couple of somewhat surprising studies by psychologists from the University of California, Berkeley. In the first, participants were given a questionnaire and asked to rate how highly they valued happiness as an explicit goal and also how happy they were with their lives.

Surprisingly, the higher the respondents rated happiness as a distinct personal ambition, the less happy they were in their lives generally and the more likely they were to experience symptoms of dissatisfaction and even depression.[5]

This in itself doesn't prove cause and effect—after all, it makes sense that people who are unhappy would be likely to value happiness more highly—so the researchers designed another experiment to determine which way the effect was going.

This time, they gave one group of people an article to read about the importance of happiness, and then afterward showed them a happy film. A second group of participants were shown the same film but without reading the article first. The group that had read the happiness article reported feeling less happiness from watching the happy film than the group who watched without reading first. The authors of these studies concluded that paradoxically, the more people valued and were encouraged to value happiness as a separate life goal, the less happy they were.

Like an attractive man, it seems the more actively happiness is pursued, the more it refuses to call and starts avoiding you at parties.

Americans as a whole invest more time and money and emotional energy in the explicit pursuit of happiness than any other nation on earth, but is all this effort and investment paying off? Is America getting happier and happier? Are Americans more content than people in other countries? Is this Great American Search for Happiness actually working?

The answer appears to be a pretty clear no. Somehow, this great nation that included the pursuit of happiness so prominently in its founding principles has been shown by various international comparison studies to be one of the less happy places in the developed world. Although these studies are not without their problems, with different methodologies producing different results, Gallup's 2014 Positive Experience Index, an international comparison study of the moment-to-moment happiness of people living in different nations, ranked America at an underwhelming twenty-fifth in the world, two places behind Rwanda.[6]

For all the effort that Americans are putting into hunting down happiness, they are not actually getting any happier. According to the General Social Survey, a large-scale project that has been tracking trends in American life since the early seventies, there has been almost no change in American happiness levels since 1972, when records began. Every year, with remarkable consistency, around 30 percent of Americans report that they are "very happy." It's a fair chunk, but a figure that remains surprisingly constant, untouched by mindfulness or megachurches, by yoga or meditation or Gretchen Rubin or attachment parenting.

According to the World Health Organization, as well as being one of the least-happy developed countries in the world, the United States is, by a wide margin, also the most anxious, with nearly a third of Americans likely to suffer from an anxiety disorder in their lifetime.[7] A 2012 report by the American Psychological Association warned that the nation was on the verge of a "stress-induced public health crisis."[8]

There are many reasons why life in America is likely to produce anxiety compared to other developed nations: long working hours without paid vacation time for many, insecure employment conditions with little legal protection for workers, inequality, and the lack of universal health care coverage, to name a few. The happiness-seeking culture is clearly supposed to be part of the solution, but perhaps it is actually part of the problem. Perhaps America's precocious levels of anxiety are happening not just in spite of the great national happiness rat race but also in part because of it.

My journalistic curiosity kicks in, and I become full of questions. What is causing this strange paradox? Has something gone wrong with the *way* in which Americans are pursuing happiness? Or is the hunt for happiness counterproductive and damaging in and of itself? Am I just a meanspirited enemy of joy, or is a bit of British-style skepticism not such a bad thing? What really makes people happy in life? And most important, is there a more effective, less self-involved, and less *stressful* way to find happiness? If so, what is it?

To get some answers, I decide to investigate the Great American Search for Happiness rat race in all its many forms. I've been a journalist for most of my career both in television and print, so I have the background to investigate, but my interest is just as much personal. I will look more closely at my own life and the lives of the people I know. I will sample some of the bliss-promising offerings and find out what the research really says about this great national obsession. What is it that really makes us happy? What doesn't? All being well, we will be living in the United States for a good few years. During this time, I will make it my mission to work out just what is going on here.

Is it possible to hunt down a happy life, or is the Great American Search for Happiness creating a nation of nervous wrecks?

2.

PERSONAL JOURNEY? IT'S NOT
ALL ABOUT YOU

There should be a government information campaign, like the anti-drunk driving ones: Don't Drink and Update. It's 10 p.m., the bottle of wine next to me has a well-used look about it, and I'm recklessly updating my Facebook status. It's back in the odd brief era when we were all using that stilted, slightly self-important third-person format on Facebook. "Britney Jones loves her kids." "Bryan Smith is eating a sandwich," as though we were drafting our own Wikipedia entries or live-blogging our obituaries. You could always tell the grammar pedants because they kept the third person thing going for the second sentence: "And she loves her hot man too . . ."; "but he's removed the ham from it. . . ."

This time, though, the format is perfect for what I'm about to write, helping me pretend that I'm not actually referring to myself at all, and that rather than being about to make a full frontal public declaration of loserdom, I'm merely raising awareness of a good cause, even engaging in an act of philanthropy. "Ruth Whippman . . ." goads Facebook's prompt. I type: "has no friends. Can anyone help her find some?"

Our first few months in the States have been tough. Inasmuch as I had given it any real thought, my vision of how life in California would be was sketchily drawn from a mixture of Hollywood, *Baywatch*, and paradise. Overfocusing on beaches and weather, I hadn't really considered what it would feel like to be living without any of the usual scaffolding of my life at home—my job, my family and friends.

For all this talk of American happiness, the truth is I'm not very happy myself, which is compounded by feeling guilty about this unwarranted lack of bliss. The upside of first world problems is obviously that they are first world problems, rather than, say, Ebola or starvation. The downside is that they condemn you to a life lived to the strains of a looping mental sound track of your own subconscious jeering "first world problems!" on endless repeat and thereby invalidating your every emotion. But despite being in the world headquarters of self-actualization, my general state is a kind of sluggish loneliness, a lack of belonging that eats away at my days.

This isn't helped by the fact that if the many happiness articles and advice blogs I'm reading are to be believed, I'm missing out on a supersize, star-spangled brand of happiness available only in America, like some kind of four-animal McDonald's menu item, sold only in select outlets in Texas. The overriding message is that I should be dragging myself out of this slump and seizing it with both hands. The whole thing is making me feel like a bit of a failure.

It's hard not to get sucked in. I've caught myself scanning the *Huffington Post*'s "GPS for the Soul" pages before reading the news section in the morning. My Google searches have slowly shifted from my usual "Am I dying?/Is this cancer?/Is my child meeting milestones that I only knew existed through previous unhealthy googling?" toward "how to be happy." Google (and presumably the NSA) quickly pegs me as a happiness seeker, popping up spooky personalized ads whenever I log on, urging me to sign up for "daily inspirational content delivered direct to your inbox."

The "inspirational content" tends to offer up a vision of the happy-ever-after somewhere between ashram and Barbie Dreamhouse. "How to Get Everything You Want!" promises the subject heading of one e-mail. I assume this is going to be the kind of wisdom gimmick that will tell me how to get Everything I Want simply by realizing that what I want is, by magical coincidence, *exactly what I already have!* or by adjusting what I want away from "a lottery win and a night with Ryan Gosling" toward "truly knowing the love of Jesus." But, no, a click reveals it to be a straightforward, moral twist-free guide to getting Everything I Want, whether a pony, a castle, a signed photo of the Dalai Lama, or a one-way ticket to Everlasting Joy.

Secretly though, I prefer this high-end happiness fantasy to the uncharacteristically depressing pair of advice e-mails that land in my inbox a few days later that make me paranoid that Google's marketing algorithm has decided I'm beyond hope. They read:

1) Happiness Is: Lowering Your Expectations.
2) Time to Get a Cat.

But none of the advice is really taking the edge off the basic feeling that I don't quite belong here. In elementary school—while never quite the least popular person in the class, with my National Health Service glasses and Saturday mornings spent at Junior Orchestra—I was certainly in the remainder bin, usually around two weird kids away from total social isolation. This experience brings it back.

So I'M THRILLED when my Facebook plea pays off. A couple of days after my post, a friend from London e-mails me to say that her old college roommate is living nearby, and that she is also the mom of a toddler boy. She introduces us over e-mail and sets us up on a "friend blind date." After a few messages back and forth, Allison and I arrange to meet one morning with the kids in our local park.

I like Allison immediately. Fizzing with energy, she is smart and funny, in that warm American way of engaging first and judging later, rather than the British way that generally means only getting on board when all options for cynicism are fully exhausted, and then only with a kind of grudging, embarrassed irony. She instantly dispenses with small talk, and we get stuck straight into a long rangy conversation that covers everything from potty training to the meaning of life.

Having given up the promise of a high-powered career to raise son Ryan, and feeling underwhelmed with the day-to-day reality of toddler herding, Allison is on a mission to find happiness. She isn't unhappy as such, but being a lifelong overachiever, thinks she can do better.

She does yoga and meditation. She sees a therapist weekly. (She tells me that she once couldn't talk to her sister for two weeks because both of their therapists were on vacation and the relationship couldn't withstand unmediated socializing.) She practices mindfulness and reads Gretchen Rubin and is a devotee of a German self-help guru named Eckhart Tolle. I am embarrassed to have had never heard of Eckhart Tolle and surreptitiously google him on my phone while Allison is in the bathroom. A quick search turns up a beige-clad, gnomelike mystic offering brain-scrambling insights such as: "The secret of life is to 'die before you die'—and find that there is no death." It all feels a bit like being trapped in an elevator with a mystical self-help version of the Microsoft Word paper clip. "It looks like you're writing a letter. Can I help?" or in Tolle's case: "It looks like you're struggling to transcend your ego-based state of consciousness. Can I offer you some verbose pseudo-Buddhism?"

Although we are poles apart on many subjects, I really like Allison. She's good fun and I admire her intelligence and good-natured willingness to tolerate my cynicism. I enjoy talking to her and she tells me she feels the same way. We agree we must meet up more often.

It is later that I realize that Allison is very, very hard to get hold of. She is almost always busy. We text back and forth a few times trying to arrange another meeting, but it never quite pans out. During her relatively rare free time, she is almost always at yoga or meditating or on a retreat or at a workshop or blogging about her experiences. It makes me feel exhausted just hearing about it all. As she tells me regretfully, "I hardly have time to see anyone at the moment." Apparently Allison is so busy trying to be happy, friendship has gone to the bottom of the list.

IT MAY WELL have just been an elaborate ruse to avoid me, and frankly who could blame her in my current state of toxic neediness, but Allison's approach to finding happiness feels a bit back to front. After all, isn't spending time with friends and other people exactly what makes life happy?

But the more mainstream self-help type advice I read, the more I start to notice just how much of it pitches finding happiness as a personal journey that is best pursued alone.

"Happiness comes from within" declare a thousand blogs and articles, positive psychology books, and Facebook memes. Variations include: "Happiness comes from within, not from others"; "Happiness is determined not by what's happening around you but what's happening inside you"; "Happiness should not depend on other people"; and the perky and social media friendly "Happiness is an inside job." One e-mail I receive, advertising a new local yoga studio, even doubles down on the idea with the turbocharged word mash-up "withinwards." (Although when I first see the subject heading "Go Withinwards," I briefly think it's a review for a new nose-to-tail offal restaurant.)

I see what they're all getting at, I think. But after a while, the whole philosophy starts to sound like a strange kind of emotional isolationism.

"When you stray from the idea that happiness is inside of you, you start turning to people and things to make you happy," writes one prominent psychologist on *Oprah.com*, a site that devotes large chunks of space to the pursuit of happiness and the idea that we must dig deep into our own souls to find it. His tone is disparaging enough to suggest that he could just as well substitute the words *people* and *things* with *child pornography* and *human trafficking*. "Following your joy should be an internal activity," he concludes firmly, although providing no real explanation as to why.

This conviction that happiness cannot be found via other people or the outside world has trickled down to become so basic and uncontroversial that it even forms the basis for an article on the For Dummies Web site, the series which has made its name taking complex subjects and stripping them down to their universally accepted bare essentials. Entitled "Considering the Four Happiness Myths," the piece says definitively: "Just as money can't make you happy, other people can't make you happy either."

Given my own current social isolation, the revelation that other people can't make me happy, and that I should be pursuing happiness within and alone, feels odd. As an experiment, I try a Google image search for "Inspirational meme: Happiness is other people."

This is what shows up:

Hell is other people.

If happiness depends on other people, you're gonna
have a bad time.

Fuck you and your happiness.

And, most perplexingly, a picture of Hitler and another unidentified Nazi guffawing at a shared private joke with the caption: "Life is about doing the things that make you happy, not the things that please other people." I'm not entirely sure what the inspirational take-home from this is supposed to be. Genocide?

WHETHER CONSCIOUSLY OR not, people are clearly buying into the idea that happiness should not be sought through other people.

Increasingly, Americans are chasing happiness by looking inward into their own souls, rather than outward toward their friends and communities. Nearly half of all meals in America are now eaten alone.[1] The average American has fewer close friends than he or she did twenty years ago.[2] According to the General Social Survey, in 1974, nearly half of the American population had socialized with their neighbors in the last month. By 2008 it was less than one third and that figure has declined every year since.[3]

In another factoid that I secretly find oddly validating, helping keep a lid on my nagging, high school–inspired paranoia that everyone else is always at a Fantastic Party that I haven't been invited to, the American Time Use Survey shows that the average American now spends less than four minutes a day "hosting or attending social events," a category that covers all types of organized hosted social occasions apart from the most spur-of-the-moment informal.[4] *Four minutes?* Added up over a year that barely covers Christmas, Thanksgiving, and your own kids' birthday parties.

Perhaps even more surprisingly, the same surveys show that people in this country spend just thirty-six minutes a day doing any kind of "socializing and communicating" *at all*, where this is their main activity and not an incidental part of something else like working. This is in comparison to three hours watching television and even, for women, an hour "grooming."

The figure sounds so low that I call the Time Use Survey's help line just to check what it includes (feeling mildly relieved as I do so that no one is surveying my own Time Use). As it turns out, not only is the thirty-six-minute figure correct, it also doesn't just cover the good kind of socializing and communicating, but any form of communication at all when more than one adult is present, including arguing, nagging, bitching, and trying to convince your husband that For the Love of God, Being Born with a Y Chromosome Should Not Mean a Biological Inability to Search Inside a Fridge.

But at the same time that American socializing has taken a nosedive, there has been an explosion in the uptake of solitary "happiness pursuits," activities that are carried out either completely alone or in a group without interaction, with the explicit aim that each person stays locked in their own private emotional experience.

Meditation has seen a dramatic breakthrough in the last few years, with more than twenty million people across the country now regularly meditating.[5] *Time* magazine reports that Americans spend around four billion dollars a year on "mindfulness products."[6] Yoga has seen a similarly spectacular ascension, with the country now spending ten billion dollars a year on yoga classes and accessories,[7] making yoga the fourth fastest growing industry in America.[8] These figures are significant enough that savvy marketeers have even designated a whole new category they are calling "spiritual spending."

The self-help industry—with its guiding principle that the search for happiness should be an individual, self-focused enterprise—is also booming, with Americans now buying a billion dollars worth of self-help books and audiobooks a year[9] to help guide them on their inner journeys.*

And in what sounds like a extended metaphor from a midlist 1970s sci-fi novel, in which all human emotions are contracted out to soul-sucking personal microcomputers, there are now close to a thousand different options for smartphone apps to help us locate happiness deep within our cell phones.

I THINK I'M probably not the target market for these happiness apps. I assume the makers are pitching them more at some kind of

---

* There is some disagreement among experts over what, or rather whom, we are likely to find as a result of this search within. Conventional wisdom favors an inner child, although, in his seminal 1992 work, *Awaken the Giant Within*, self-help magnate Tony Robbins made a forceful case that it is in fact more likely to be an inner giant. I have a horrible feeling that it's both, and I left my inner child unsupervised around my inner giant and he swallowed her. They are probably both still in there, like a set of motivational matryoshka dolls.

superstressed Ayn-Randian tech billionaire firing off abusive e-mails from his yacht, or the mythical mean career-mommy from the magazines prying the wailing infant from her leg so she can hotfoot it to her arena of corporate cruelty. (Although my baby does cling to my leg and wail, when I selfishly attempt to "have it all"—both a child and a pee.)

But in a particularly lonely moment, after my husband sets off for work one morning leaving me with a gaping ten hours before my next adult conversation, I attempt to fill the void with a spot of happiness retail therapy in the app store.

Some of the options are mind-bogglingly complex, using sensors inside the phone to measure my happiness levels and then, if they are found wanting, attempting to correct the problem by showing me a range of sub-Upworthy-style Internet memes ("Chivalrous Goat Tries to Save His Friend!" "This Draping Wisteria Will Leave You Dazzled!") plus photo montages of sunsets, beaches, cute puppies, and my own family. (It doesn't occur to me until later that spending the time with my actual family rather than staring at my phone might bring me more happiness.)

In the end I opt for a lower-tech offering, a positive-thinking app called Positive. I obviously need it. My hardwired negativity means that my instant mental association with the word *positive* is not *affirmations*, but *HIV*.

Positive texts me every few hours with an inspirational statement that I am supposed to repeat over and over to myself until I start to believe it. The problem is, that whenever my phone buzzes, I get a Pavlovian jolt of excitement, thinking that it's a message from an actual person. The crushing disappointment I feel when I realize that it is only Positive, urging me to chant the phrase "I am enough" until bliss descends slightly spoils the effect. "I am enough," I snarl, sarcastically tacking on a muttered "which is lucky, because I haven't spoken to another adult apart from my husband in the last nineteen days."

• • •

PERHAPS THE CLEAREST example of the trend toward the solitary pursuit of happiness is the recent stratospheric rise in popularity of meditation, and its secular sidekick, mindfulness.

In his *New York Times* bestseller *Waking Up: A Guide to Spirituality Without Religion*, one of an influx of recent books on the topic, "contemporary philosopher" Sam Harris writes:

> Is there a happiness that does not depend on having one's favorite foods available, or friends and loved ones within arm's reach, or good books to read, or something to look forward to on the weekend? . . . I can attest that when one goes into silence and meditates for weeks or months at a time, doing nothing else—not speaking, reading, or writing, just making a moment-to-moment effort to observe the contents of consciousness—one has experiences that are generally unavailable to people who have not undertaken a similar practice. I believe that such states of mind have a lot to say about the possibilities of human well-being.[10]

A few years back, when meditation practiced anywhere outside of Tibet or adolescence still had the vague whiff of patchouli and dysfunction about it, it would have been hard to believe that Harris's words were being addressed to a mainstream audience.

But now the idea of seeking out solitary confinement to explore your inner consciousness is firmly at the heart of the establishment. Meditation's cheerleaders now include known radicals like the US Marine Corps, McKinsey & Company, and Deutsche Bank. Google runs a wildly popular seven-week mindfulness and meditation course for its workforce called Search Inside Yourself (unironic curriculum description: Success, Happiness, and World Peace).

In his number one *New York Times* bestselling meditation memoir, *10% Happier*, ABC news anchor Dan Harris chronicles his journey from cynic to committed meditator who goes on lengthy silent meditation retreats where even eye contact with other participants is discouraged.

He credits the practice of meditation with a 10 percent increase in his overall happiness (although in the book's acknowledgments section, Harris thanks his wife, Bianca, for "making me 100% happier before I was 10% happier," which begs the question as to whether he might have seen a ten times higher happiness return from spending his vacation time with her instead).

Meanwhile, for those who balk at meditation's quasi-religious overtones but still see happiness as something best pursued inside our own heads, there has also been the parallel rise of the secular "mindfulness."

The Moment is having a moment.

The idea that in order to be happy, we should constantly police our thoughts away from the past, the future, or the imagination in favor of a total mental focus on whatever is happening Right Now has gained traction in corporate boardrooms and public schools, in therapy sessions and universities and residential spa retreats. Within our first few months in America I see references to mindful eating, mindful business dealings, mindful sexuality, mindful parenting, mindful commuting, and even a Facebook invitation to a workshop in mindful butchering.

I realize I need to try it.

It's a Tuesday evening, and I'm standing outside what looks like a suburban church hall, except with a sign on the door urging me to "Please Enter Mindfully." I try to approximate what I think this might mean. It's roaringly quiet inside, in that uncomfortable, reverberating-reverence way that amplifies every tiny noise I make to a clattering obnoxiousness and stops me asking where the bathroom is. I try to reframe the need to pee into a spiritually enriching mind-body awareness.

I've come to an introductory mindfulness meditation session and seminar at the local Buddhist center, and I'm oddly nervous.

There only seem to be two possible narratives that people fall back on when describing their experience of discovering meditation. Either:

(A) I loved it with full-throttle enlightenment right from the
   first om . . . or . . .

(B) I hated it, railed against it, found it made me anxious and
   miserable before achieving a cataclysmic breakthrough
   which catapulted me directly to Response (A).

Knowing my own basic repertoire of neuroses, I fear I will be (B)
but without the breakthrough.

I'm naturally twitchy, I'm a fidget, I randomly suffer from claustrophobia, and strangely quiet places in which it would be Very Embarrassing to leave are among my worst triggers. I am naturally suspicious
of new things and hypercritical of anything that could even vaguely be
described as bullshit. Potentially even more worrying is my deep-seated
suspicion that mindfulness is just another word for "I judge you for playing on your iPhone when you should be interacting with your child."

I somehow end up in the right room—shoes off, mindfully assessing
the grossness of my feet—sitting in a large circle of people on cushions,
headed up by two monks in classic orange robes and cute little footie
pajamas. (If I gain nothing else from the experience, at least I will now
know what Buddhist monks wear on their feet.) The first monk is
straight out of central casting: Tibetan, beatifically Buddhist, round and
transcendent, speaking only in occasional, heavily accented wisdom
nuggets. The other monk is clearly Buddhism 2.0, midtwenties and
American, wearing a digital watch and peppering his conversation with
references to Google Alerts and video games.

The room is packed. A couple of attractive hipsters eye each other
up through their pious semiclosed eyes. A clutch of gray-haired grand-
mothers in leisure suits take advantage of the row of chairs at the
back. Only one person is talking, a commercial real estate agent named
Trenton, who has now been recounting a slightly bitter anecdote about
his ex-wife for an uncomfortably long time. Eventually Digital Watch

Monk interrupts him, telling us that we will have a group mindfulness meditation first, followed by an hour-long talk on the principles behind it.

He encourages us to get into the lotus position, which feels like an undeserved shortcut to the top, like going to a beginners' kung fu class at the YMCA, then being asked to step in to defend the honor of the Shaolin Temple. I yank my feet onto my thighs in an ungainly and unspiritual manner, then the monk rings a little bell and we get going.

And . . . kaboom.

It feels . . . mildly pleasant and slightly boring. Not terrifying or life changing or remotely revelatory, but remarkably unremarkable. Relaxing, but not as relaxing as a pedicure. Pleasant, but not as pleasant as a good book or getting stuck into a bottle of wine with a friend. I can honestly think of a sizable list of things that would make me happier, both in the short and long term. Not to write off a 2,500-year-old religion or anything, but so far, for me at least, meditation: *meh*-ditation.

The talk afterward unsettles me more. The monk runs through some of the basic ideas behind mindfulness meditation. He tells us that suffering is an inevitable part of life, and that our suffering is caused by our attachments to things, ideas, and people that bring about a state of anxiety. By a regular practice of meditation, we can free ourselves from these unhealthy attachments, and from the thoughts and anxieties in our own minds that spring from them. When we stop hitching our happiness to people and things in the wider world, we will be able to find it within ourselves.

Although so deeply associated with a hippy-commune aesthetic, with its insistence that happiness must be found independently of relationships with other people and the outside world, meditation sounds like a deep expression of emotional individualism.

This is compounded by the total and utter anonymity of the experience. Unlike most religious services or get-togethers, there is absolutely no social element to this event, no coffee and stale pastries, no sense that a co-meditator would ever pop round with a casserole if you have the flu or a baby, no sense of human connection of any kind. We arrive in silence and leave in silence, with not a word exchanged (unless of course everyone is secretly meeting up for a giant meditation after-party that they haven't told me about). I want to talk to people and ask them about their experiences, but when I hand a woman her purse from the rack afterward and ask "Is this yours?" rather than a friendly gesture, it feels like a clanging intrusion into her spiritual space.

A SINGLE MEDITATION session is never going to give me a very full picture of what the practice can achieve, and I realize that I am unlikely to go back anytime soon, so I am keen to take a closer look at what the research says about all this.

Meditation's advocates throw around some pretty hefty claims for its scientifically proven benefits, suggesting that the practice has been shown to be highly effective in helping a wide range of conditions ranging from low-grade unhappiness to severe anxiety and depression.

When I start looking into it, I find that there have been literally thousands of studies done on the effects of meditation and mindfulness in recent years. Clearly I won't be able to go through them all myself, but fortunately, I soon find that the US Agency for Healthcare Research & Quality has done the job for me. In 2014, they conducted a massive meta-analysis that looked at pretty much every reputable piece of scientific research published on the benefits of meditation and mindfulness–type techniques, taking into account more than seventeen thousand separate studies.[11]

But when I read it through, the results of this meta-analysis are underwhelming, at best. It looks as though many of the claims about meditation's almost miraculous effects have been quite heavily exaggerated.

Some studies do show that meditating or mindfulness exercises might bring some small benefits to people compared with doing nothing, but when they are compared against pretty much any general relaxation technique at all, including exercise, muscle relaxation, "listening to spiritual audiotapes," or a fake control that gives equal time and attention to the person, they perform no better, and in several cases, worse.

BUT WHETHER OR not the evidence for meditation's benefits has been overhyped, there's something deeper about all this that bothers me.

Social life in this country is going through a crisis. Research suggests that a full quarter of American adults now feel that they do not have a single friend or family member they would consider close enough to confide a personal problem to, and when family members are not counted, that number doubles to a staggering half of all Americans who claim to have no one to confide in at all.[12] Meanwhile, 40 percent of all adults over forty-five say that they are lonely.[13]

Yet in the midst of this near epidemic of social isolation, we are getting the message that the key to happiness is everyone sitting in a room in total silence, with each individual plodding his or her own solitary inward path to bliss. While time use surveys suggest that we are apparently too stressed and busy to see our friends or have a conversation with our families, we are managing to make the time for self-help books and yoga classes and mindfulness meditation.

Perhaps my own lack of a social life is clouding my judgment, but I start to wonder whether maybe if we really want to be happy, wouldn't we be better off spending less time trying to perfect our own inner lives and more time with other people?

AS IT TURNS out, the science backs this up.

The more happiness research I read, the more it starts to look as though we might all get a better happiness return from sitting in the pub with our friends, bitching about meditation, rather than by actually practicing it.

Quite an extraordinary number of scientific studies have been done in recent years about what makes people happy. Between them, they contain many anomalies and contradictions, but if there's one point on which practically every piece of research into the nature and causes of human happiness is consistent it is this: *our happiness depends on other people.*

Study after study shows that good social relationships are the strongest, most consistent predictor there is of a happy life. As Dr. Christine Carter, a leading academic at UC Berkeley's Greater Good Science Center, put it in an online article:

> The upshot of 50 years of happiness research is that the quantity and quality of a person's social connections—friendships, relationships with family members, closeness to neighbors, etc.—is so closely related to well-being and personal happiness the two can practically be equated.[14]

What's more, according to the research, if we want to be happy, it looks as though we should be spending less, not more, time alone.

One of the seminal research experiments of the positive psychology movement, entitled Very Happy People, identified a group of people who were much happier than average.[15] The aim was to examine the lifestyles, habits, and values of this golden group of emotional overachievers, and then work out what they did differently from the rest of us, information the researchers could then use to somehow "reverse engineer" happiness.

As it turned out, on the whole, the lives of these Very Happy People were virtually indistinguishable from the lives of anyone else. They didn't have more good things happen to them. They didn't exercise more or attend more religious services. The only substantial thing that the researchers were able to pinpoint that differentiated the VHPs from anyone else was that they had the "most satisfying and fulsome inter-personal relationships" of any group and crucially they spent the most time socializing and the *least time alone.*

The idea that we are significantly happier moment to moment when we are around others than when we are on our own has since been backed up several times by other studies. And surprisingly this effect is not just true for people who consider themselves extroverts but also equally strong for introverts.[16] (Other research has even shown that when introverts are told to behave like extroverts, even when they think that they will hate every second of it, they actually end up feeling hap-pier as a result.)[17]

On the flipside, not only is nurturing our social relationships cru-cial for our happiness, neglecting them can be shockingly dangerous. When I catch up on a Skype call with Professor Emma Seppälä, the science director of Stanford University's Center for Compassion and Altruism Research and Education, she tells me that strong social rela-tionships are the only "necessary condition for happiness"—meaning that humans actually can't be happy without them and shockingly, also that a lack of social connection carries with it a risk of premature death similar to that of smoking and is roughly twice as dangerous to our health as obesity.[18]

So is the solitary way in which many of us are now pursuing happi-ness more than just a poor allocation of time in our busy lives? Is it also, in and of itself, so self-absorbed and individualistic that it's actually com-pounding the problem of our increasing isolation rather than fixing it?

I need someone to help me put the pieces together. And by happy coincidence, it turns out that there is a world expert on exactly this sub-ject a ten-minute walk from my front door.

I TRAVEL UP to the third floor of UC Berkeley's Psychology Depart-ment in the elevator feeling hyperself-conscious. There's something about the fluorescent sterility of the place that screams "human experimentation!" making me paranoid that I might unwittingly be part of a study of elevator behavior that will somehow expose me as a person capable of unspeakable cruelty, or a racist.

I've come to see Dr. Iris Mauss, the academic psychologist who conducted the original groundbreaking series of laboratory studies showing that the more actively people value and pursue happiness, the less happy they become. I was already well-disposed toward Iris Mauss because of her name, which sounds like a visiting German relative in a Beatrix Potter story. I became even more well-disposed toward her when she told me over e-mail that although she gave birth to her first child less than three months ago, she is coming in especially from her maternity leave to meet me.

I arrive at Mauss's office to find her locked in a half-wrestling, half-bashing match with the door handle. I ask her if there's anyone we can get to come and open it for us. She shakes her head in resignation. "There's no one to call," she tells me. "All the maintenance has been centralized. I think the university is trying to make things more efficient."

Eventually she manages to find the magic, finely calibrated combination of twist, pull, and shove that opens the door, and we start talking at high speed to make the most of her forty-five minutes of childcare.

Mauss first moved to California from Germany as a young graduate student in psychology. The culture shock she experienced when she arrived sounds uncannily similar to my own.

"It was very striking," she says. "It's like a standard—you are supposed to be happy and it's seen as being under your individual control. Happiness is not seen as something that comes out of living a good life, but an achievement you aim for, like it's the individual's responsibility to be happy. It got to the point that if I was in a bad mood, I would feel almost guilty, as though I was falling short of the ideal. It was making me anxious."

This nagging anxiety led Mauss to a research specialty in happiness, in part with the aim of finding out whether the way she was feeling could be part of some kind of wider phenomenon. After her first series of experiments confirmed that explicitly valuing and pursuing happiness does indeed lead people to feel less happy, Mauss's next quest was to try to work out why.

She had a hunch that there might be a clue in some interesting research recently completed by one of her doctoral students, a woman named Brett Ford.

Ford's research had focused on cultural differences in approaches to happiness across the world. Conducting surveys in various countries across Europe and Asia, as well as in the United States, Ford had asked people a range of questions about happiness—how they defined it, how actively they pursued it, and how happy they were.

The results were revealing. In the United States, people tended to define the pursuit of happiness as an individual quest. Among her American subjects, the more intensively people claimed to pursue happiness, the less happy they were, replicating Mauss's initial findings. But in other countries, particularly in East Asia, people generally defined happiness in a different way, as a more socially oriented endeavor, and pursued it by engaging with other people. In these countries, where happiness was defined in this more collective way, the more actively people pursued happiness, the *happier* they became, the exact opposite of the American pattern.[19]

These findings led Mauss to wonder whether there might be something about the individualistic way in which Americans were pursuing happiness that was actually making them feel lonely and distant from other people.

She and her team set up a new series of experiments to examine whether there was any relationship between the explicit pursuit of happiness in America and feelings of loneliness or low social connection.

"We wanted to find out whether there was something about the pursuit of happiness in this country that is so self-focused that it actually isolates people from others," she explains.

Mauss came up with an innovative design for two related studies. In the first, her team asked a group of people to fill out a questionnaire designed to determine how highly they valued happiness as a goal. They then asked the participants to keep a diary of stressful events for two weeks and in particular to record their feelings of loneliness. The results were clear. The higher the participants claimed to value happiness in the initial questionnaire, the more often they felt lonely.[20]

Initially, it wasn't fully obvious which way this effect was working. Does valuing happiness make people lonely, or do feelings of loneliness lead people to place a higher value on happiness? So Mauss and her team embarked on their second experiment to find out.

This time, with a new cohort of participants, the researchers split them into two groups. They primed the first group to value happiness more highly from the start. These people were shown the following extract from a bogus article:

People who report higher than normal levels of happiness experience benefits in their social relationships, professional success, and overall health and well-being. That is, happiness not only feels good, it also carries important benefits: the happier people can make themselves feel from moment to moment, the more likely they are to be successful, healthy, and popular.

"We tried to make it read as much as possible like one of the kinds of happiness articles you read all the time," Mauss tells me, with just a hint of mischief in her voice.

The other group in the study was shown a different extract, identical, except that instead of the word *happiness*, it substituted the phrase "making accurate judgments." Both groups were then shown a carefully selected film clip, known to elicit strong feelings of social connection.

After watching the clip, all the participants in both groups were asked to rate the extent to which they felt lonely and distant from other people. The researchers also took a sample of the subjects' saliva to test for the presence of progesterone, a hormone known to be associated with feelings of intimacy.

The group that had been primed to value happiness more highly by reading the happiness article, responded to the film by rating themselves as more lonely than the other group, and their saliva showed lower levels of progesterone.

"Lab studies are itty-bitty analogues of what happens in real life," explains Mauss. "If this is what happens as a one-off in the lab, you have to think about what is the cumulative effect of the bombardment of all these messages about happiness on people in real life.

"It all comes back to this idea of self-focus," she says. "People monitor themselves. Am I happy yet? Am I happy enough? They are so focused on their own self and their own happiness that it comes at the expense of social connection. You can spend so much time focusing on what you are feeling that you just don't have time to focus on others. And when you are with other people you find you don't enjoy social activities as much because you are constantly worrying about your own emotions and not getting as engaged."

I ask Mauss whether her research means that we should all just give up on happiness completely. She thinks for a minute, then gives a careful reply.

"If people pursue happiness in a less self-focused, and more other-focused way, they might be able to circumvent the paradoxical effects of valuing happiness."

I think this is a nice way of saying, "It's not all about you, you know."

MAUSS MAY HAVE science on her side, but hers is almost a lone voice. She is up against a highly profitable and massively influential industry whose existence is dependent on pushing almost the exact opposite message. This is an industry with tentacles stretching widely through American culture and deeply into the collective psyche. An industry devoted to the Great Project of the Self, whose message, as I was soon to discover, is deeply seductive, even for the most committed skeptic.

3.

HAPPINESS FOR SALE:
SELF-HELP AMERICA*

"Ninety-two point five percent of people have a transformative breakthrough as a result of the course," an earnest Landmark Forum volunteer named Dave tells me confidently. Dave knows a lot about transformative breakthroughs, averaging about three a year following each of a series of personal development courses he has attended, one of which involved paying a company to abandon him in a forest without food for four days until he started hallucinating. The sheer rogue bonkers-ness of what he is saying is offset by his almost aggressively normal appearance. With his ironed button-down shirt and firm handshake, Dave looks a little as though he has been selected from a stock photo catalog's "young male businessman" section. Even his name sounds like it was chosen by a focus group. He, along with everyone and everything else in the room, appears to be operating under the guidance of a heavily enforced mission statement: "Don't Be Weird."

I'm sitting with a hundred or so other happiness seekers in a corporate conference room downtown, listening to a woman named

---

* All names and identifying details in this chapter have been changed, as well as the details of any personal stories told.

Claire with a powerful orange-tinted haircut telling me how to be happy.

So far, the gist seems to be that I need to accept that everything bad that has ever happened to me in life is entirely my own fault.

"Stop pointing fingers at everyone else! Point them back at yourself!" shouts Claire.

This is a free introductory evening for the Landmark Forum, the vastly successful self-help program that has trained more than a million Americans in the dark arts of contentment, as well as another million or so internationally. Encouraging participants to bare their naked souls to one another with the promise that they can "redefine the very nature of what's possible," the company has had its fair share of controversy. The mythology surrounding the organization is intense, and rumors abound, but so far, I'm slightly disappointed by the lack of Waco-style insanity. The general impression is less "apocalyptic mass murder" and more "Human Resources Department away day." The whiteboard is covered in flowcharts. Three hours to go, and Claire may well bore us all into happiness.

By the time she starts channeling Donald Rumsfeld, sketching out an intricate pie chart on the whiteboard segmenting the human experience into known knowns, known unknowns, and various combinations of the two, I've pretty much decided against signing up for the course.

But Dave has other ideas. He has clearly singled me out as someone in urgent need of personal transformation; and for him, "no" is just an opening gambit.

"What do you think it is that's holding you back?" he asks.

"The money, for one thing." The course costs five hundred and eighty-five dollars. "I could spend that money on a weekend away with my husband and a babysitter. Or on shoes."

"Shoes aren't transformative," says Dave. I look at him. He quickly changes tack.

"Something made you come tonight," he continues. "There must be something in your life that's not working. Otherwise you wouldn't be here."

He's right. I have made some progress, but I do still feel lonely and awkward in America, as though I might never quite fit in and be able to build a fulfilling life here. I've had a few pity playdates with kind local moms who have felt sorry for me, but nothing much has really stuck. If I'm totally honest with myself, I'm not particularly happy, and every time Claire says "transformative breakthrough," my inner happiness consumer pops up like a prairie dog.

It's been this way ever since I started delving into the world of happiness. I've been veering wildly between detached curiosity and getting sucked in myself. One moment I'll be totally on board with Dr. Iris Mauss's research that chasing after happiness is a one-way ticket to a lonely and miserable life. The next minute I'll be worrying that my cynicism is standing in the way of achieving some kind of glittering joy that everyone else is experiencing; and I'll start secretly hoping that while I'm researching, I'll be able to hitch my own sneaky free ride to bliss.

Maybe it's Dave's powers of persuasion. Maybe it's emotional greed. Or maybe it's all that stuff Claire is saying about pointing the finger away from everyone else and back at myself, and that, as a Jewish mother, the prospect of an entire weekend devoted to self-flagellation is just too enticing to pass up; but somehow, not long afterward, I find myself dialing Landmark's head office and booking myself on a three-day course starting the following weekend.

"WHAT DO YOU hope to get out of the program?" asks the slightly intense-sounding woman who answers the phone. I mumble something vaguely incoherent about becoming happier.

"You want happiness?" she intones with rote call-center efficiency, as though enquiring as to which department she should direct my call.

"Um, yeah, I guess so. . . . I mean, I guess we all want to be, you know . . . happy," I fumble Britishly. I don't want to sound greedy.

"Well, as it happens, Happiness is actually benefit number seven on our official list of key benefits of the Landmark Forum!"

She starts to reel off this list like an infomercial narrator racing through a list of drug side effects. "Number one: Courage. Number two: Self-confidence. Number three: Freedom from Resentment and Regret." I half expect the last one to be "death."

"But actually the benefits will start before you even attend the course," she continues breathlessly. "Now you've signed up, your happiness levels will actually start to increase *immediately*. Let me give you an example. One man registered on a Tuesday for a course for the following weekend. By Thursday, before he *even started the course*, his daughter, who he hadn't seen since birth, turned up on his doorstep." She pauses, waiting for the enormity of this information to sink in.

I give her my credit card details.

LANDMARK EDUCATION IS a key player in a vast and influential self-help industry. The systematic packaging and selling of happiness in the form of books, DVDs, webinars, and courses was last estimated to be worth around ten billion dollars,[1] roughly the same size as Hollywood, the other great purveyors of the happy-ever-after.

As our lives become increasingly isolated, with little time for friends and socializing, we have professionalized contentment, paying experts to give us the advice that used to come from our confidantes and communities. In a culture that loves consumerism, happiness has become the ultimate consumer product.

Individuals are getting rich. Landmark Education brings in more than eighty-four million dollars a year,[2] while the five thousand or so motivational speakers currently operating in the United States earn around one billion dollars between them. Mustachioed happiness grandee Dr. Phil McGraw pulls in around seventy million dollars annually while Tony "Unleash the Power Within" Robbins is reported to earn around thirty million dollars.[3] And the American public's appetite for neatly packaged happiness solutions is only growing.

Gretchen Rubin's bestselling superblockbuster *The Happiness Project* inspired a new generation of the worried-content to slave over Excel spreadsheets of carefully enumerated personal happiness goals. Those who remain bliss-poor after decluttering their closets and embracing good smells at Rubin's urging can choose from more than eighty thousand other titles on Amazon promising a road map to contentment.

There's an entire subgenre of self-help devoted to relationship advice. During one particularly toxic breakup in my early twenties I think I read the whole canon. The advice across the board can be pretty much summarized as Women: Pretend you don't care. Men (in the unlikely event that you are reading): Pretend you do care.

The principle that we can empower ourselves to radically improve our own happiness levels is used to sell us everything from luxury cars to dishwasher tablets. Politicians now employ self-help's characteristic language and principles so routinely that it can now be almost impossible to distinguish the words of a senior politician from a motivational speaker. When Nelson Mandela died, Twitter went crazy re-tweeting a quote from one of his speeches. "Our deepest fear is not that we are inadequate. Our deepest fear is that we are powerful beyond measure."

But Mandela never said those words. The quote actually came from bestselling self-help book, *A Return to Love: A Reflection on the Principles of "A Course in Miracles"* by "spiritual teacher" Marianne Williamson. It is a mark of just how far self-help culture has seeped into the mainstream that people were unable to tell the difference.

Although perhaps it's not surprising. Self-help guru Tony Robbins has worked with both presidents and presidential candidates across the political spectrum including Bill Clinton and 2012 Republican candidate Mitt Romney. (Robbins also apparently approached Romney's rival Barack Obama at the time with the offer of his services, but the future president turned him down. It is a tribute to the power of positive thinking that when Robbins tells this story, Romney somehow emerges as the victor and Obama the loser.)

FRIDAY IS ONE of the most beautiful days of the year so far, and out-side, the early spring air shimmers with golden light. I am sitting deep in the bowels of Landmark Education's climate-controlled conference facility, waiting for my Landmark Forum course to begin, staring at a retractable vinyl banner printed with the following words:

Transformation: "The Genesis of a New Realm of Possibility."

I have rarely heard the word *realm* used outside of science fiction, the outer reaches of the British aristocracy, or the prophecies of a fringe religious group. In this particular Realm of Possibility, the lighting is fluorescent, the gray venetian blinds are down, and the heavy steel fire doors are firmly shut. Several rows of identical midrange confer-ence chairs face the whiteboard.

We won't be finished until 10 o'clock tonight, and according to the slightly scary contract that a Landmark assistant asked me to sign the moment I entered the building, we will be having a meal break only in the "late afternoon to early evening." (The contract also flags up that a tiny proportion of the participants claim to have suffered from symptoms ranging from diminished sleep to psychotic behavior after the program.)

I do a quick mental calculation. Between the hundred and ten or so people in the room, we have paid Landmark almost sixty-five thousand dollars and we are eagerly awaiting our respective transformative break-throughs. By the sounds of the conversation buzzing around me, this is a crowd that's already well versed in self-help. Before the teacher has even arrived the air is thick with talk of "empowerment" and "authen-ticity." The slightly sweaty air-conditioning contractor sitting to my left uses the word *self-love*. I shift my chair a little to the right.

The only people looking more ill at ease than me are two Japanese administrative assistants in the row behind who have been sent on the course by their boss. Next month he's sending them to Tony Robbins. Apparently Landmark is about "being," while Tony is about "doing."

THE LANDMARK FORUM is the direct successor to the notorious 1970s program, est, the brainchild of a former car salesman named Werner Erhard. Contemporary accounts of the est courses describe participants being shut in hotel ballrooms for fifteen hours at a stretch, forbidden from taking bathroom breaks, branded *assholes*, and yelled at them until they accepted that all their problems from cheating spouses to divorce to assault were all their own fault.[4] Despite its controversial methods, est was hugely popular in the 1970s, including with several celebrities who claimed it had transformed their lives. In the 1980s, Erhard reinvented his course in a gentler, more corporate incarnation as the Forum, which later became the Landmark Forum. In 1991 he sold the "technology" of his program to his employees and quit. The course has been toned down in various ways from the est days, so I am keen to see to what extent the basic driving philosophy and principles have stayed the same.

At nine o'clock exactly, the doors open and the leader bursts into the room, Oprah style, to wild applause. Valerie is heavily back-combed, and wearing a burnished gold vest that gives off a vibe that is less "time to party" and more "tactical body armor." As she introduces herself and takes a few questions from the floor, her shtick is a kind of plain-speaking take-no-prisoners down-home directness. She uses the word *highfalutin* a lot, in a way which I start to suspect might be passive-aggressive.

LANDMARK'S IMPRESSIVE CAPACITY to sell its products with little mainstream advertising has been well documented, and maybe it's difficult for Valerie to transition from sales mode into teaching mode, because the first few hours of the day seem to be devoted to a frenzied sales pitch for the very course for which we have already paid.

Valerie outlines the many gifts that the Landmark Forum has brought to her own life and tells us again and again about the glittering changes we too can expect to see in our lives and personalities by the end of Sunday night. We watch a promotional video full of Landmark alumni ballet dancing, beach frolicking, and cello playing that has the slight feel of a tampon commercial. We hear about the Landmark Forum's commercial arm, the Vanto Group, which assists corporate America in enabling personal transformation among its workers. We study various Landmark promotional materials, like a group of yeshiva students poring over the word of God.

"Anything you want for yourself or your life is available out of your participation in the Landmark Forum . . ." Valerie reads from a vast banner stationed at the front of the room. She repeats the word *anything* several times with intense gravitas, fixing the room with a stare of cosmic significance, as if to say "in this Realm of Possibility, the laws of physics are not obstacles but opportunities." I glance at my watch. More than two hours have gone by. I wonder when we are going to get to the specifics.

Perhaps part of the reason why this extended sales pitch is taking so long is that Landmark Education has its own painfully contorted corporate language, so stuffed with mind-boggling verbiage that everything takes about four times as long to say as it needs to. One of the regular criticisms of self-help is its tendency to reduce complex human experiences to oversimplistic sound bites, but Landmark appears to be aiming for the complete opposite effect, taking relatively simple concepts and weighing them down with so many subclauses, qualifiers, and grammatical contortions that they become almost impossible to follow. It gets to the point that whenever I start reading one of the sentences in their course material, I feel like I need to pack a lunch and a water bottle to make it to the end.

After three or so hours of dizzying promises, but little substance, by now everyone is either in a pumped-up state of transformative readiness or a grammatically induced stupor. Either way, we are all begging for something different. Mercifully, Valerie temporarily suspends her sales pitch, and the "sharing" begins.

A pretty Eastern-European woman in her early twenties is first up at the microphone. She starts to tell her life story to the room, a story which, like many of the personal histories of the people present, is so full of heartbreaking tragedy it makes me feel like a fraud to be sharing a personal development course with her.

Valerie stands at the whiteboard, marker pen in hand. She draws two large circles on the board, labeling the first circle WHAT HAP-PENED and the second one NEVER HAPPENED. Each part of her history that the young woman reveals, Valerie delivers her personal ver-dict on whether it was fact or fiction by placing a large X in one of the two circles.

Young Woman (to the room): I was born in Poland.

(Valerie draws an X in the WHAT HAPPENED circle. "Born in Poland" is a verifiable fact.)

Young Woman: My parents abandoned me.

(Valerie draws a gleeful X in the NEVER HAPPENED circle. Un-like Poland, abandonment is not a fact but an interpretation.* Young woman bursts into tears.)

Young Woman: The people working at the orphanage were cruel to me. They didn't love me like a parent would.

(Two X's go into the NEVER HAPPENED circle in quick succes-sion.)

Young Woman: All through my life I've struggled with forming lov-ing relationships.

(Valerie draws a triumphant X in the NEVER HAPPENED circle, rapping the marker on each word on the board for added dramatic effect.)

---

* Historically, certain world leaders have also considered Poland to be an interpreta-tion. This view has now been discredited.

Buried deep within this unpleasant showpiece is an interesting idea. It is true that all of us are constantly constructing interpretations of the events in our lives and failing to recognize that these are not facts. I mentally scan through my own life and see that many of the beliefs I hold dear are indeed stories of my own invention. "I am homesick and lonely in California" is an interpretation, as is "5:30 p.m. is unreasonably late for a lunch break." (Thinking about it, time itself is just an interpretation, although I fear that diving too deeply into this particular philosophical rabbit hole might result in us never, ever breaking for lunch.) I suspect that Valerie's wariness of story and interpretation might be a little less acute when the story in question concerns, say, the transformative potential of the Landmark Forum, but I can see that being able to differentiate fact from interpretation is a valuable life skill.

But I can't help thinking that the stories we tell ourselves are built up over years, crafted for complex psychological reasons. Is three minutes with a marker pen on the whiteboard really the best way to dismantle them? Valerie, by her own admission, is not a mental health professional, and watching her take a sledgehammer to a vulnerable woman's natural defenses feels not just deeply uncomfortable but also quite worrying.

Then suddenly Valerie turns to the room at large and launches into a full-scale verbal tirade at all of us about our inauthenticity and all-out fraudulence. The young Polish woman whose story provoked this spew of vitriol is still standing at the microphone, now weeping openly.

The whole thing is like a grotesque piece of theater, but for some strange reason, no one objects. If anything, people are having the opposite reaction. When Valerie asks for another volunteer to come up to the microphone to share, a sea of hands shoots up.

Over the next few hours, several more people volunteer to come up to the front of the room to have Valerie divide their life stories into fact and fiction. Between them, according to the whiteboard circles, they have invented parental abuse and neglect, lackluster romances and narcissistic husbands, and bullying bosses and racism.

After the "circles," Valerie then coaches each sharer, picking away until she pinpoints their personal weak spot, then debunks whatever story it is she feels they have been telling themselves until they finally crack and cry. Sometimes she is uncannily perceptive, homing in on a truth about a person's life that they have been denying even to themselves. Other times she seems scarily wide of the mark. To watch, it feels less like therapy than a cross-examination at a murder trial. Afterward, Valerie is all smiles again, congratulating the sharer warmly and inviting the room to applaud. It's a bizarre and disorienting spectacle.

Finally after Valerie has fully convinced us that story and spin are egregious aspects of the human experience that are eating away at our happiness, she takes a moment to pass round some promotional flyers for the Landmark Forum's advanced course. According to the flyers, "THERE'S SIMPLY NOTHING LIKE IT." The course is being offered at a $290 discount from the regular price of $875 if we pay in full before Tuesday.

BY 5:45 P.M. WE have yet to break for lunch, immobile in this airless, fluorescent-lit room for hours on end, like passengers stalled on the runway after a long-haul flight. The air is stagnant with breath and need. My back hurts, my head hurts, and my contact lenses are burning two gritty circles into my eyes. I feel as though my brain has been forcibly removed and replaced with a miniature air-conditioned conference suite, and I have a horrible suspicion that all of this is The Point.

When we finally do get a break, in the long line for the women's restrooms I am surprised to find that those of us who are finding this whole thing a powerfully unpleasant experience are in the minority. One woman runs out of the building in floods of tears and doesn't come back for the rest of the course, but many more claim that they are already having life-changing breakthroughs. A woman in her early fifties speaks to her mother on the phone for the first time in three years and repairs a vicious, long-festering argument. Another, who to my mind went through one of the more brutal grillings at the microphone, is full of nothing but glowing praise for the experience.

Our homework over the meal break is to get into small groups and "share" some more with our fellow participants about what we are hoping to get out of the course. We head to the local Safeway to grab some limp refrigerated sandwiches and hurry back to Landmark's dreary break room to bolt them down in time to get the sharing and eating finished in time for the evening session. Something tells me that Valerie won't take kindly to lateness.

For me, this is easily the best part of the day so far. There is so much genuine goodwill in our little group—an odd-looking crew aged nineteen to seventy with sartorial choices spanning crocheted shawls to facial skull tattoos—all thrown together in this peculiar pressure cooker of an emotional quest. The youngest, a boy of nineteen weighed down with body piercings and suppressed rage, starts to tell us about how his deeply religious father had convinced him as a child that God hated him. The whole group gets caught up in his story, and we lose track of the time. Suddenly, we realize with alarm that we are five minutes late for our evening session with Valerie.

We slink into the back of the room, hoping to slip past unnoticed, but no such luck. Valerie turns on us and makes us an example, launching into an antilateness tirade, during which somehow a "few minutes late back from the break" becomes unassailable proof of our total lack of integrity in all areas of life.

By 10 p.m., when the steel fire doors finally open, I feel both mildly humiliated and physically and emotionally depleted. Our homework, which is supposed to somehow be completed before tomorrow's session, is to make a phone call or write a letter to a person in our lives with whom we have been "inauthentic" (and to invite them to the Landmark recruiting session on Tuesday night). The volunteers distribute a handout with a sample script for this task: I glance at the first line. "What I came to the Landmark Forum to accomplish is . . ."

With the high billing of the phrase "Landmark Forum," the whole thing feels like some kind of horrific corporate sponsorship deal where a company shoves its name into something that used to be considered a shared human experience—the Barclays Premiership, say, or the Sleep Train Mattress Traffic Report. The "Landmark Forum Relationship with Your Mother."

I try, and fail, to think of a single person in my life with whom I could use this script who wouldn't think that either (A) I was casting them as an extra in my Personal Emotional Journey and therefore making it All About Me, or (B) that I had been abducted by aliens. My mother would be horribly concerned.

I think back to a story a friend told me a few years ago, about how she had been lying in bed asleep with her boyfriend at seven o'clock one morning, when the phone rang, waking them both up. It was her boyfriend's ex from several years back, calling to tell him that she was at the Landmark Forum; she had no hard feelings about their relationship; and she was completely "over him," a fact that he had never doubted until exactly that moment.

I chicken out of calling anyone, convincing myself that probably no one wants to hear from me anyway at this hour. By the time I get home, it is nearly midnight, and everyone in the house is fast asleep. I creep into my son Solly's bedroom. His little body is sleeping fiercely, and I realize just how much I've missed him all day. I whisper in his ear that I love him and how sorry I am that I have spent the entire day out looking for happiness. He doesn't wake up.

I sleep fitfully, with Valerie appearing periodically in my dreams as a gold-clad velociraptor, to tell me I'm a liar and a fraud, that my life is a sham, and that I am one of the nasty ones.

THE NEXT DAY is Valentine's Day. Solly is up early. He pads into our bedroom in his blue airplane pajamas and proudly hands me a box of chocolates that he picked out himself for me the day before. The box has a cartoon picture of a dog on the front. The caption reads: Have a Pawfect Day!

"Don't go to Happy School today, Mummy," he pleads. "I missed you yesterday. Stay here with me instead."

I ignore him. After all, "missing" is just an interpretation. Instead, I choose to "restore my integrity" with the Landmark Forum. I am rewarded. When I pick up my name badge on the way into the room, underneath is a little preprinted Valentine's card from Valerie. She has even personalized it by filling out my name in red marker. My husband sends me a frosty text saying he has canceled our dinner reservations.

If yesterday's theme was "You Made It All Up," today it seems to have shifted to "It's All Your Fault" or, in Landmark jargon, "Taking Responsibility," an idea at the very heart of the organization's philosophy.

Over the next few hours, several people come up to the microphone to share their stories, the vast majority of which are utterly heart-wrenching. This time, Valerie's coaching is focused on getting them to see that their situations are entirely of their own making.

A divorcée learns that, contrary to her belief that her husband was callous and emotionally cruel, she should be assuming the entire responsibility for the failure of their marriage. Another woman finds out that the struggle that she is having feeling at home in a new city is really just because she herself is incompetent. Valerie berates an elderly African American woman at length after she shares with the group that her long-term male companion gave her a fur stole as a Valentine's Day gift, despite knowing that she is a committed animal rights activist. As it turns out, her boyfriend is not inconsiderate or thoughtless. She, on the other hand, is a nasty, nasty woman. Afterward, this nasty nasty woman sits back down next to me, head bowed, with tears in her eyes.

I WAKE UP on the morning of Day 3 with an odd sense of foreboding and dread. My head is pounding, my back and knees ache, and I feel oddly disoriented and tetchy, jangling with nonspecific anxiety. I profoundly do not want to go back inside that room. When I arrive at the center, I approach one of the Landmark assistants patrolling the hallway. I tell him I feel sick and anxious, and I am nervous about the effect that the course is having on me. He smiles enigmatically and mutters an incomprehensibly gnomic Landmarkism. I have no idea what it means but imagine it is probably something along the lines of "You're the one with the problem, not us; now sign up for the advanced course."

But I've made it this far, and I'm sticking it out. Especially because we've been told that our own personal transformations will be arriving "right around" 4:52 p.m. tonight.

At the appointed hour, Valerie, now sporting a boxy purple jacket and a chunky statement necklace, delivers the big reveal. Strip back the jargon, and it amounts to more or less this: our lives have no inherent meaning, and so we are free to create our own.

The sheer anticlimax hits me hard. After all that? After all the soul-searching and name-calling? After all the tears, the exhaustion, and sheer physical unpleasantness of sitting in a conference chair for thirty-six hours straight? This high school philosophical riddle is our happy ending? Simply decide to see things differently and instantly magic away your entire emotional back catalog?

But it seems I'm the only one. Suddenly, as promised, transformation is everywhere. The atmosphere has shifted from corporate conference to tent revival. The room swells with energy, people laugh and clap and cry and hug. I feel a strange mixture of vicarious emotion and utter disassociation. Then, as the excitement reaches fever pitch, Valerie turns the whiteboard over. On the back is a prewritten list of dates and prices. The advanced course costs $895, or $585 if we pay in full before Tuesday.

WHY DID LANDMARK'S "technology" fail to work on me?

For a while, I'm obsessed. For a good two weeks afterward, I can't stop thinking about the course, rattling Valerie's words round and round in my head, questioning myself over and over, like a crack team sweeping the room for bugs. Is this thought that I'm having an interpretation or a fact? Am I failing to take responsibility for the fact that my husband hasn't unloaded the dishwasher in three weeks? I become sick of the inside of my own brain, exhausted by the constant self-monitoring.

This must be what Dr. Iris Mauss meant when she talked about obsessive self-focus making it harder to get as engaged with life and other people. My husband also clearly isn't keen on this new hyperintrospective incarnation of his wife, pleading one night as we sit down to dinner, "Can we talk about something else tonight apart from the Landmark Forum?"

But I have to acknowledge that the majority of people at my Landmark Forum course found the experience transformative, or at least that's how they said they felt immediately afterward. So why did it leave a nasty taste for me?

At first I assume it's a cultural thing. Maybe my British cynicism was getting in the way, and the style is simply better suited to an American audience. But I soon find out that Landmark Education in London is doing a roaring trade, with thousands of Brits signing up every month. An old friend from back in the UK, who I would never have pegged as a self-helper, tells me that she did the Forum and loved it, saying that among other things, it helped her make peace after a bitter, long-running quarrel with her father.

A big factor was that a key part of the basic philosophy just didn't sit well with me. The whole notion of "taking personal responsibility" for your own happiness or, as Claire had put in the original introductory session, "Stop pointing fingers at everyone else! Point them back at yourself" seemed to easily veer off into a basic lack of compassion and even into victim blaming.

IT'S NOT JUST Landmark. This kind of blame-tinged rhetoric is surprisingly common in the self-help movement more generally.

The more I immerse myself in the Great American Happiness Machine in all its various incarnations, from mindful dishwashing to Tony Robbins, Eckhart Tolle to the *Oprah Magazine*, the more I realize that once you get past the fist pumping and the platitudes, there's a steely and anxiety-inducing underlying thread to the message.

If there is one idea driving the consumer happiness industry, it is this: forget other people or life circumstances—cheating husbands and unfair bosses, sex or race discrimination, cancer, poverty, losing both your legs or your job, or the fact that they've discontinued the peppermint cookies at Trader Joe's. There is only one thing that has the power to make you happy, and that is . . . YOU! (Self-help tends to capitalize the word *YOU* in much the same way as the Bible capitalizes the word *LORD*.)

Happiness Is a Choice! shout a thousand inspirational virtual photo cards. Even the dictionary agrees. Although the word *happiness* originally came from the Middle English word *hap*, meaning "chance" or "good luck" (think *happenstance* or *perhaps*), any idea that our own well-being may be outside our direct control has been firmly squashed. Merriam-Webster's online dictionary now declares that the old definition of the word *happiness* as "good fortune" has become obsolete.

The financial success of the happiness industry relies heavily on the idea that circumstances matter little, that we are in complete control of our own mental state and can simply choose to upgrade it at will.

On the face of it, this is a seductive, even inspirational, promise. But it doesn't take long to realize that the flip side of this logic is that, if I am not happy, then it is All My Own Fault.

The reasons given vary a little. "Resources are never the real problem. The real problem is a lack of resourcefulness," declares Tony Robbins, teeth agleam, in his Ultimate Edge course. Eckhart Tolle gives a blanket condemnation of my wrong-thinkingness, covering any potential life eventuality with the simple explanation: "The primary cause of unhappiness is never the situation, but your thoughts about it." The late Jim Rohn, a right-wing motivational guru, summed it up: "Don't wish it were easier! Wish you were better!"

There's the whole "Women Who . . ." subgenre of self-help, a surprisingly large range of books whose titles begin with the words *Women Who . . .* and end with a character flaw that then blames us for our own failure to be happy. *Women Who Love Too Much*, *Women Who Think Too Much*, *Women Who Worry Too Much*, and *Women Who Do Too Much*. (Perhaps some of life's problems might be better explained by the alternative titles *Men Who Love Too Little/Think Too Little/Worry Too Little*, and *Do Too Little*, but these seem to be oddly absent.)

Embedded in the voice of inspiration is a hefty scoop of blame. The central message driving the sales of ten billion dollars' worth of happiness products and services is clear. The problem is YOU!

On a personal level, relentless self-criticism doesn't seem like the most effective path to contentment. But beyond that, I can't help thinking that this constant focus on individual responsibility for our own happiness seems to run counter to the evidence about how happiness actually works.

A large and consistent body of research points to the idea that strong social relationships and community are the keys to well-being. But surely being part of a supportive community means acknowledging that we are all interdependent and taking responsibility for one another's happiness as well as our own? Self-help's individualistic narrative of blame seems like the exact opposite of how a nurturing community would think and act.

AFTER A COUPLE of weeks of exhausting hyperself-awareness, the Landmark Forum somehow just vanishes from my brain. It's like it never happened. When I meet up for a drink with Matt, a guy from my course, he tells me the same thing happened to him. "I thought about it pretty much all the time for about a week," he tells me. "It all felt like a bit of a revelation. But then a few days later, everything just went back to normal, and I've basically forgotten everything they said." Perhaps Matt's and my shared reaction is one of the more common pitfalls of the happiness quick fix.

I've almost forgotten about Landmark completely, until a few weeks later, when I'm browsing through some Web sites looking for volunteer opportunities in the local area. Ever since learning just how important community is to happiness, I've had it in the back of my mind to look for ways to get more involved.

I come across a post from a nearby middle school, advertising for volunteers for something called Challenge Day. I don't know what Challenge Day is, but I like the sound of volunteering in a middle school. I used to work with teenagers a fair amount in my old life making TV documentaries and I miss being around them, so I click on the link.

I learn that Challenge Day is a self-help-type program run in public middle and high schools across the country. According to the Web site, more than a million students across forty-seven American states have taken part.

Oprah is a fan, with a tub-thumping endorsement emblazoned across the Web site's "Evaluations & Research" page. "I'm not kidding when I say this is the way we change the world," she says.

"Changing the world" seems like a big ask for a one-day program with some teenagers in the school gym. Curious, I start trawling around for some more information, finding a handful of articles online and a couple of YouTube videos.

The videos show what looks like a day-long mass confessional, with a hundred or so eighth-graders in a room together, taking turns publicly revealing their innermost secrets about their sexuality, family abuse, neglect, addiction, and bullying. The more I watch, the more it starts to remind me of something. The Landmark Forum, but for kids.

A bit of digging reveals that although not linked formally with Landmark Education, several members of the Challenge Day leadership do indeed claim to be heavily influenced by Landmark's techniques and approach. One member of Challenge Day's Global Leadership Council was a former Landmark leader.[5] In interviews, a few of the council's other members have referred to Landmark as a major influence in their way of thinking, with one of them even claiming to have been an enthusiastic graduate of Landmark's asshole-yelling, bathroom break–discouraging predecessor, est.[6]

Although Challenge Day doesn't appear to be driven by Landmark's philosophy of individual responsibility or have its victim-blaming tone—apparently more about just publicly revealing problems rather than trying to fix them—it still all feels like a lot for kids to handle. It makes me wonder whether something fundamental has changed about the nature of children since the mideighties when I was in middle school and quite possibly the worst thing anyone keen to make it through adolescence with a functioning psyche could do would be to announce their most personal secrets to their entire grade.

It seems like a mark of just how far the commercial happiness movement's influence has spread that children are being put through self-help programs in middle school. Challenge Day is not a fringe experiment—with more than a million participants to date, it is fast becoming a mainstream part of public education. I'm surprised that it is not considered more controversial to be putting teenagers through this kind of mass public ersatz therapy at the taxpayer's expense. Like at Landmark, the Challenge Day leaders are not mental health professionals. How do they deal with these complex and difficult problems without that kind of training? How do the kids meaningfully consent to this?

For something that is being rolled out in public schools across the country, I'm surprised at how little there is written about Challenge Day. Just one article from the *Seattle Times* from a few years back, criticizing the program for being overexposing, and a blog post from a evangelical Christian mom whose main problem with the whole idea was that it encouraged kids to think that it was "okay to be gay." I feel as though my instinctive unease might be putting me on the wrong side of this. I decide to reserve judgment.

THERE ARE SEVERAL schools in our neighborhood looking for adults from the local community to help out at Challenge Day. I call the first one on the list, and leave a voice mail saying I'd like to volunteer. Within an hour, I get a call back. The conversation goes like this:

> VERY POLITE MAN FROM SCHOOL: Hello, is this Ruth? You left a message saying you'd like to volunteer at Challenge Day on Monday?

> ME (mentally scrambling for any credentials that might qualify me to do this): Yes . . . I . . . used to work with—

> VPMFS (interrupts): Great! I'll put your name down on the list. You'll be facilitating a group of seventh graders. Please come to the gym by 8 o'clock.

That's it.

Not a single question about my background, my motivation, my qualifications for dealing with emotionally distressed young people, or whether or not I might be, say, a registered sex offender. (For the record, I am not a sex offender, either registered or unregistered. There are limits to gonzo journalism.) It is, quite literally, the easiest gig I've ever got.

Before I go, I read up a bit about the school. It's a challenged urban middle school in a tough part of town. The student population is 99 percent nonwhite. Test scores are low. I think about what it must be like to work in a place like that, with so many obstacles in your path, where every day must seem like an uphill struggle. Can these kinds of problems be self-helped away?

. . .

DESPITE ITS MANY challenges, when I arrive at the school the following Monday, it feels like pretty much any middle school in the Western
world. The discount paint colors and battered lockers, the ancient over-
shined linoleum and posters urging respect and tolerance, their edges
curled up with neglect.

The disgruntled receptionist harrumphs at my incompetent navi-
gation of the signing-in process, and then an impeccably polite and un-
assuming man walks me over to the gym where I pick up my name
badge. I later find out he is the principal. During this time, no one asks
me who I am, what I'm doing there, or if I am in any way qualified to
navigate the innermost emotional traumas of a large group of twelve-
year olds. I guess they assume that someone has already asked.

Over in the gym, the atmosphere is buzzing. The kids have yet to
arrive, and it all feels a bit like they're setting up for a One Direction
concert. The Challenge Day leaders, Sarah and Casper, a charismatic
and highly professional duo, hook up speakers, tap on microphones, and
hang giant Challenge Day–branded banners. A handful of other adults
are also there to help out—mostly teachers and guidance counselors
from the school. They all seem a little surprised that I'm there, though
no one really probes much further.

Sarah and Casper give the adults a breathlessly quick induction before the kids arrive, in which they inform us several times that we are
awesome, instruct us to "bust out our dance moves" and "hug as much as
possible" (with the hurried disclaimer that we should stop hugging if a
child looks obviously uncomfortable), and alert us to the two giant crates
of tissues hidden discreetly under the speaker system, because apparently at Challenge Day, although tears are not the goal, "crying happens."

There's a quick reminder to report anything a kid tells us that
suggests that they might be in immediate danger, and then the music
is cranked up and we're off.

The kids file in to the gym, around a hundred of them, in a long

snaking line, contorted with middle school awkwardness and complicated orthodontics. We have been instructed to whoop and cheer and
high-five them as they go past, but situations like these always make
me feel paralyzingly un-American, my vocal cords and limbs turn instantly to British steel, and I find myself physically unable to whoop.
"Show us your MOVES!!!!" shouts Casper, cranking the music up. He
busts out his own moves, and the whole room starts dancing. These are
not prime dancing conditions for me. It isn't even 9 a.m., we're in a
school gym, and I haven't had coffee yet, let alone alcohol. I shuffle
around a bit, feeling uncomfortable.

Most of the morning is taken up with various warm-up-type exercises. We play a game involving an oversize beach ball, for which everyone seems to instantly understand the rules except me (although this
could probably describe my relationship with any given sport at all).
Sarah calls on a few kids to stand up and describe their "dream life,"
using the present tense, as in "I *am* a . . ." rather than "I want to be
a . . . ," because apparently, the more you say it, the more likely it is to
become real. The kids' ambitions are predictable. Lots of future pro
footballers and NBA stars, except for one girl who hollers with perfect
cheerleader pep: "I *am* a middle school math teacher!" then, when the
room quiets down, "and . . . I'm writing my autobiography!"

"It will be a bestseller!" shouts Sarah.

All this is just preamble, though, to the main event—the sharing.
Sarah and Casper divide the kids into groups of five or six, each with
one adult. My group consists of the good-looking guy clearly uncontested for the position of "coolest in the class," three girls who all look
as though they would rather be almost anywhere else, and a nonverbal
boy from the special needs program.

Sarah turns on some music and, almost in a singsong hypnotic voice,
starts to suggest a long list of problems that the kids might want to share
with the rest of the class.

"Are you unpopular? Are you popular and feeling unbearable pressure keeping up your image? Do you feel like you aren't good enough?

Aren't pretty enough? Are you struggling with your sexuality? Are you suffering abuse or violence? Is someone hurting you?" Soon we are all laid bare, emotionally raw and bursting to share. Tightly coiled springs.

Finally, Sarah and Casper open the giant crate of tissues with studied solemnity and hand boxes out ceremoniously from group to group.

Then Sarah issues the instructions: "Each one of you will have two minutes to share. I want you to start with the words 'If you really knew me, you would know . . .' I will set the timer on my iPhone. When the timer goes off, please wrap up your share. Now, can I have a volunteer from each group to be person one? . . . No, no, not an adult. It works much better if it's a student. Anyone?"

A sweet, previously quiet girl named Chelsea in our group tentatively puts her hand up. "Okay, person one," says Sarah. "I'm setting the timer on my iPhone. Start your share . . . NOW."

"If you really knew me, you would know that . . . my dad thinks that my brother is turning gay," begins Chelsea, then immediately bursts into tears. "He won't let me play with him anymore. Now my dad is angry all the time and he keeps throwing things."

"How old is your brother?" I ask.

"Nine," says Chelsea. I have absolutely no idea what to say. I look around for some other adult who might be qualified to deal with this sort of thing, but they are all deeply immersed in their own groups. I decide the best thing to do is just to let Chelsea talk, and listen as best I can, but Challenge Day runs to a strict schedule, and a tearful thirteen-year-old with a complex family issue isn't going to stand in the way.

"Okay, person one, start wrapping up your share," interrupts Sarah.

But having broken the seal, and finally found an adult willing to engage with her problems, Chelsea isn't ready to wrap up. "Yesterday," she continues, now talking faster, "when I got home from school, my dad—"

"Okay, person one, bring your share to a close," says Sarah, firmly. Chelsea looks wounded. I feel as though we have just opened up a giant can of worms and sent them crawling all over the gym.

"Okay, person two, I'm setting the timer on my iPhone," says Sarah.

Person two is Kayla, a pretty African American girl with a mouthful of multicolored braces. Unlike Chelsea, Kayla looks deeply uncomfortable with the whole idea of sharing, shifting in her seat and staring longingly over at her best friend in another group. "What's the beginning bit again?" she stalls.

"'If you really knew me, you would know . . .'" prompts Sarah.

"If you really knew me—Hang on, what's the next bit?" Kayla says, clearly buying time. Eventually, after she can hold out no longer, she mutters almost under her breath that her father has recently gone to jail. I feel totally and utterly unqualified to deal with this.

By now, we are all weeping, including me. Hearing what these kids are up against, at barely thirteen years old, with the music playing and sheer level of emotional rawness, it's almost impossible not to.

It's as though something strange has happened to me. The mood is so carefully manipulated, I am now sucked in. I have shifted slowly from skeptical observer to full-blown participant, suddenly in character myself, drunk on emotion. My voice has even taken on a slightly new register of showy earnestness. I had been prepared to make up something to share when it got to my turn, but instead I blurt out something real.

"If you really knew me, you would know . . . that I'm really worried about my son at preschool," I begin. "Another kid is picking on him." I even end with a plaintive and dramatic wail: "And I'm his *mom* . . . I'm supposed to be the one who knows what to *do*. . . ."

Later, on the subway home, I feel slightly dirty—embarrassed and overexposed. I can't imagine how I would feel if I were in middle school and had just offered up my darkest secret to a group of kids, who will then potentially use it against me for the rest of my school career. Yet again, I start to think that defenses are there for a reason.

THE GRAND SHOWPIECE of Challenge Day is an activity called Cross the Line. After everyone has had exactly two turns at "sharing" in our smaller groups, Sarah and Casper call everyone back together. They stick down a line of blue tape on the floor, across the length of the gym. Sarah instructs us all, adults and kids, to stand on one side of the line and tells us that she is going to call out a list of categories. Anyone who feels they belong in the category she calls should walk across the line, then turn around to face the rest of the group.

The categories start off easy. "Anyone here who is under the age of eighteen, please cross the line." All the kids walk across, then turn around to face the adults on the other side.

But soon, they start to get harder. "Anyone who has been discriminated against for their religion or beliefs." "Anyone who has lost a close family member or a parent." "Anyone who has been the victim of bullying."

So far, several people have crossed the line for each category. Then Sarah ups the ante again.

"Anyone who has been the victim of homophobic abuse, please cross the line." People look more uncomfortable. A few brave souls cross over. I wonder what this will mean for them later on, whether they will regret the public confession or find it empowering.

"Anyone who has ever considered themselves poor, worried about money, or become homeless," continues Sarah. I'm surprised to see that the kids seem to look more ill at ease with this category than the previous one.

"Anyone who has themselves or who has had a family member or friend with an addiction to drugs or alcohol," calls out Sarah.

More than half the kids and many of the teachers cross the line for this one, most of them openly weeping. Sarah probes deeper. "Did they choose their addiction over you?" she asks. "How did that feel?"

Then Sarah's voice rises to a swelling crescendo as she reaches her dramatic peak.

"Anyone here who has ever had thoughts of suicide, please cross the line and face the rest of the group."

One girl who has crossed the line for virtually every category so far and is now in floods of tears walks emphatically across again.

Suddenly, I snap out of my reverie. This feels staggeringly inappropriate.

AFTER THE KIDS leave, the adults have a ten-minute meeting in which we fill out a sheet asking us to flag anyone we think is in immediate danger or who might need some kind of follow-up with the school guidance counselor. Then we all head home.

On the way out of the building, I run into one of the girls who was in my group. I ask her what she thought of the day.

"It was amazing!" she replies, full of enthusiasm.

I smile. "Which part did you find amazing?"

"I had no idea so many of our teachers were addicted to drugs."

I HAD BEEN truly shocked by the extent of the challenges that these kids were dealing with—addiction, poverty, racism, family abuse, and serious mental health issues had all come up. It seemed as though what the school and community needed was some serious investment in offering genuine long-term help to these kids, rather than an expensive one-day piece of emotional theater.

Over the lunch break, I had asked one of the teachers who helped facilitate the program last year if she had seen any lasting change among the kids since then. "No, not really," she had replied. "It all kind of just went back to normal."

Perhaps one of the slipperiest things about self-help programs generally is the fact that it is almost impossible to verify any claims they might make. Usually the transformational benefits they promise are sufficiently vague that it is hard to prove or disprove them.

Challenge Day's basic philosophy is that if children only knew what their peers were going through, then understanding and empathy would flourish and that teasing and bullying and other forms of harassment would stop.

The organization publishes some figures on its Web site about the program's effectiveness, but the measures are pretty woolly. One evaluation survey claims that after the program, 90 percent of students reported being "more accepting and supporting of other students" and "more aware that their actions affect others." But students' own reports of their awareness, although not meaningless, are not really a clear evaluation of a program's objective success.

I am keen to see something a little more concrete. Fortunately, there is one source of more objective data as to whether the Challenge Day program stops school bullies in their tracks.

By law, all schools are required to report any incident of violence, bullying, or harassment on school property to the California Department of Education. The department keeps detailed records for each school, which are available to the public on their Web site.

I look up this school, and get a shock.

The year before the school hosted its first Challenge Day, there were a total of eight reported incidents of force or violence on school grounds. The next year, after Challenge Day, there were forty-six. Similarly, in the category of "harassment or intimidation," after Challenge Day was introduced at the school, incidents quadrupled from the previous year.

These figures should almost certainly be treated with some caution. It is always hard to determine cause and effect with something as complex as school violence, and it certainly can't be inferred from this data that Challenge Day somehow caused violence at the school to skyrocket. Perhaps incidents were no longer going unreported. Maybe a new teacher joined the school with a more rigorous approach to record keeping.

What the data does do, however, is throw real doubt over whether this type of middle school mass confessional has quite the transformative power that its champions maintain.

. . .

IT WOULDN'T BE the first time that self-help has overpromised and under delivered. One of the most quoted factoids knocking around the publishing industry is that the most likely customer of a self-help book is someone who has bought another self-help book in the last eighteen months,[7] a dreary reminder that something, somewhere, isn't working.

The self-help industry is wholly unregulated, with no requirement to demonstrate the effectiveness of any of its techniques before marketing them. A growing body of research is emerging that contends that many of its key interventions—such as positive thinking, affirmations, and the attempt to exert control over our own emotions—are, at best, unproven and in some cases can actually end up making people more unhappy rather than less.

But maybe it's not just that these programs can often be a waste of time and money. I start to think that there might be something more insidious going on here.

I think of the Landmark Forum, with its strangely angry, blaming tone. I mentally flick through some of the other happiness material I've been reading, the endless books and articles and courses and advice listicles with their subtle insistence that I am a problem that needs fixing. It seems as though the happiness industry is almost manufacturing a culture of anxiety, trapping us in a self-feeding loop of self-doubt. On top of this, the message that the real solutions to human distress lie within, rather than without, seems to actively encourage us to focus on ourselves and ignore the genuine issues out in the wider world.

WHEN MY HUSBAND gets home from work one evening, I mention these thoughts to him. He gazes longingly over at the TV. I can tell he's mentally weighing up whether it's worth trying to buy his way out of the conversation by admitting that I'm absolutely right and that all of society's ills are the result of a sinister conspiracy cooked up by Big Happiness.

"None of this is compulsory, you know," he says finally. "No one's forcing anyone to read self-help books or do the Landmark Forum."

It's a fair point. I mutter something slightly snooty and defensive about cultural narratives affecting all of us, whether we agree with them or not. But honestly I'm not sure that it is that simple to opt out. The fact that kids in seventh grade are having semimandatory self-help-style workshops at middle school shows just how far the happiness industry's influence has seeped into the mainstream. Several people on my Landmark Forum course were there because their employers had sent them, and although Landmark insists that everyone taking the course needs to be there of their own free will, when it comes to your boss's wishes, there's free will and there's "free will."

The more I start to look into it, the more I find out that this employer-sponsored happiness agenda is becoming more and more common. For an increasing number of workers in corporate America, dealing with the commercial happiness machine is indeed becoming all but compulsory.

4.

WORKAHOLICS

"Sit and enter into the goodwill that is the best of your intentions for being here," says Soren Gordhamer to the two thousand or so corporate seekers searching for their inner wisdom in the basement of the Marriott Marquis hotel in San Francisco. "Look around and offer that goodwill silently to others." A key event for Silicon Valley's tech elite, the combined wealth in this room almost certainly rivals the GDP of a medium-size nation. I offer my goodwill silently to the heavily perspiring venture capitalist sitting to my left. He can't seem to work out how to put his phone on silent. Siri starts talking loudly.

This is Wisdom 2.0, the high-profile annual conference where the business world convenes to explore the nature of wisdom and the profit potential of the inner journey. Talk topics on the agenda for the next few days include "Mindfulness in Business: Why It Matters," "Activating Starbucks Values: Being Present to Inspire and Nurture the Human Spirit," "Turning Inward and Reaching Outward: How Meditation Spread at the World's Largest Asset Manager," and "Business as Unusual: How a Leader's Healing Journey Is Transforming a Company."

Wisdom 2.0 is at the forefront of a wider trend, in which businesses are increasingly taking an interest in their employees' emotions and personal and spiritual growth.

People are swapping business cards. Chief Mindfulness Officer. Chief Happiness Officer. Mindfulness-Based Achievement Officer.

Listening to the lengthy introduction from the team of conference organizers ("Something I really love to be with is sound, and the unifying quality of sound. Please join me in 'sounding.'"), it strikes me that the mindful elite seem to have collectively adopted a kind of special mindful voice—drawn out, significant, full of pregnant pauses and slow intakes of breath. In the spirit of self-inquiry, I become mindful to an unpleasant truth about myself. This voice makes me inexplicably enraged. I clearly have a long path to enlightenment.

Out in the hallway, which has been repurposed as a kind of mindfulness trade show, a group of Buddhist monks creates an intricate mural out of colored sand, scraping away with a series of tiny funnels and tubes. At the end of the conference it will be ritually swept away to symbolize the impermanence of everything in life (including, in all likelihood, many of the jobs of the people present). Surrounding them are rows of stalls selling mindfulness books and handing out free pens advertising luxury corporate yoga retreats.

A lone inventor bravely mans a stall showcasing his invention, the Brainbot. His display table is scattered with a tangle of wires, exposed circuitry, and several types of screwdrivers. I approach him.

"What is it?" I ask.

"It's a wearable biofeedback belt. You wear it just under your bra, then it alerts you when you're getting stressed or unhappy."

"How does it alert you?"

"It starts to hug you more and more to help you relax."

"You mean it constricts?" I ask.

"I prefer to see it more as a pattern of hugs."

I look doubtfully at the large and complicated-looking tool kit sitting next to the Brainbot, and wonder if the mere act of assembling the thing might tip me over into uncharted waters of despair. He notices my expression.

"We're making another version that won't need pliers."

Unconvinced, I head next door to try out a couple of the "hosted conversations," smaller round table discussions, each on a specific theme, with a self-appointed host leading the conversation. I sit down at a table with a sign indicating that the topic under discussion is "Conscious Prosperity."

The host is an executive coach and, as he explains to the assembled group, a highly successful man. "I'm a rock star in my field," he tells us. "I've reached a point in my life where I never have to say 'I can't afford it.'

"But how do I use my money powerfully as a source of self-expression?" he ponders. "I took my family on a trip to Africa recently and we could have stayed in thousand-dollar-a-night hotels or in fifty-dollar-a-night hotels. We just didn't have scarcity as a navigator. People don't realize that scarcity makes life *easy.*"

The two women sitting on either side of him look skeptical.

He opens the discussion up to the group. "What are you all curious to discuss with others to support you in conscious prosperity?"

"I want abundance," says one of the women, clearly not fully sold on the idea of scarcity.

"Do you mean money?" I ask her.

"Yes," she admits. "But abundance sounds more Buddhist."

I try another table. At this one the discussion topic sign reads "The Most Important Principle in Business—I Love You."

The host is a trim-looking man in his late forties, wearing the name tag Mark. He glances at my own name tag as I sit down.

"Hi, Ruth. I love you," says Mark.

I must look slightly taken aback, so he explains. "Imagine a world in which every conversation started with 'I love you.' I go into businesses and run workshops on this principle. I have a hundred percent success rate."

"At what?" I ask, confused.

"At breaking down barriers around 'I love you.'

"Can you imagine a world in which that happened?" he continues.

"In which every time the president addressed the American people he started with 'I love you'? In which every debate in Congress started with 'I love you'? Every conversation in business?"

"Don't you think it might start to lose some of its meaning after a while?" I ask.

"I couldn't disagree more." The woman sitting on the other side of Mark, who has been quiet up until this point, leaps to his defense. "Let's not use this precious time for him to have to defend an idea that clearly doesn't need defending."

Mark looks happy. He and the woman start talking to each other animatedly, and ignoring me. I suspect they no longer love me.

"'I love you' is a can opener and catalyst," says Mark. The woman nods enthusiastically. I try to inject myself back into the conversation.

"Is there anyone you don't love?" I ask.

"No," says Mark.

But after a moment's reflection, he reconsiders.

"Well, there are people that I fucking hate and I wish God would take them. One of them is my business partner. I say to myself several times a day 'I love you.'"

I think this might be unplanned, but he recovers his sales spiel quickly.

"Imagine, Ruth, if you started your next business meeting with 'I love you.' How would your boss feel?"

"I don't have a boss, but if I did, I imagine he or she would probably be a bit uncomfortable if I did that," I say.

"But that's exactly my point. It's not about him. It's about you."

"Don't you think that when you say something you should take into account how it will make the other person feel?" I ask.

The woman steps in to answer on Mark's behalf, with the slightly pained tone of the enlightened trying not to lose patience with an obvious idiot. "I just don't see the world that way," she says. "I take care of myself; you take care of yourself."

"What do you do for a living?" I ask her.

"I work with businesses teaching compassion."

I LEAVE WISDOM 2.0 none the wiser.

It's not just in Silicon Valley that the corporate personal growth agenda is taking hold. Across the country, businesses are increasingly seeing it as their role to intervene in their workers' emotional and even spiritual lives, in the hopes that inner exploration will positively impact their bottom line.

The Wall Street Journal runs a piece on a new trend for companies to provide their staff with "happiness training" noting that high-profile blue-chip employers such as UBS, American Express, and KPMG are rushing to sign up in an attempt to boost worker productivity. Methods stretch from seminars in positive psychology to full-scale mystical spiritual retreats.[1]

The coverage of this phenomenon in the business press has generally been surprisingly positive, with journalists often throwing out some oddly specific statistics to make the business case for the inner journey. "On average, mindfulness increased by about 9.7 percent," gushes *Forbes* magazine in a ringing endorsement of one program.

"Can happiness be a $2bn business model? Yes! And we can show you how!" promises the Web site of workplace happiness consultancy Delivering Happiness at Work, while sought-after corporate spiritual guru Srikumar S. Rao—whose Web site advertises that his eight-thousand-dollar (excluding accommodation) residential Creativity and Personal Mastery course has been adopted by companies including McDonald's, IBM, and Merrill Lynch—makes even loftier claims for how he hopes his program will help dispirited middle managers answer the questions that have troubled philosophers through the ages. "This course is designed to help you discover your purpose in life . . . the grand design that gives meaning to all of your activities."

It's not just a novelty curiosity for the privileged; blue-collar bosses are also increasingly keen to cash in on their employees' emotions and souls. America's largest employer, Walmart, announced a thirty-million-dollar company-wide "personal development" program for its associates (the same workforce that is often reliant on food stamps to supplement poverty level wages[2]). *The New York Times* sent a reporter, who described the program as "equal parts self-help class, corporate retreat, and tent revival."[3]

McDonald's went for a more budget option in happiness promotion. After countrywide strikes from its workers protesting their low wages, the company offered "wellness advice" on its McResource employee Web site. "Complain less," the Web site McSuggested. "Stress hormones rise by 15 percent after ten minutes of complaining." Also "Sing more: singing along to your favorite songs can lower your blood pressure." If workers still found themselves experiencing subpar happiness levels when their wages didn't stretch to adequate food, the site advised them to "Eat less: Breaking food into pieces often results in eating less and still feeling full." After an outpouring of barely contained rage on the Internet in response, the company took the advice down, claiming that it had been "taken out of context."

PERHAPS KEEN TO evaluate whether they are getting their money's worth from all this happiness training, some employers have even taken to monitoring their employees' happiness levels with high-tech surveillance equipment.

"Get real-time access to all your employees' moods," advertises employee engagement software company Hppy, makers of a mobile and Web tool that "enables companies to track and manage employee happiness," requiring workers to record regular updates of their moment-to-moment emotional state, to be fed back in real time to their bosses.

Japanese electronics company Hitachi releases its "happiness meter," a wearable device for bosses to strap to their employees, that monitors workers' motions, posture, and body language, information which Hitachi then aggregates to give the employees a collective rolling happiness score between one and a hundred.

The happiness meter could almost be dismissed as something that might appear in a BuzzFeed listicle of "crazy Japanese inventions," corporate Japan's answer to the singing urinal or the toilet paper dispenser helmet, but this kind of dystopian emotional surveillance is taking hold in American firms too.

A group of researchers from MIT's Human Dynamics Lab launched start-up Sociometric Solutions to produce an even more Orwellian sounding device for widespread employee happiness monitoring. As well as similar features to the Hitachi device, the Sociometric Badge also includes a location tracker and microphone that can monitor an employee's tone of voice as well as who spoke and for how long. The data is then anonymized and fed back to the employer. Bank of America was one of the first to try the device, strapping the monitors onto its call center workers, apparently leading to "marked and sustained improvement in call handling productivity."

ASIDE FROM THE obvious privacy concerns that all this raises, this new trend constitutes a fundamental shift in the nature of the relationship between worker and employer. Until relatively recently, the contract between the two was straightforward. The former delivered their labor, and the latter paid them for it. While work has always brought people a number of additional benefits—dignity, self-esteem, and often friendship—those were the basics, and anything else that should happen to come of this arrangement were incidental perks. But with their recent obsession with their employees' moods and emotions, employers are now demanding not just their workers output but a share of their souls.

But is this sudden interest in employee happiness actually making anybody any happier? Do people really want their bosses inside their heads, constantly monitoring their mental state and emotions, then manipulating and tweaking them in service of company objectives? Are we entering a brave new era of labor relations in which workers are happier than ever before? To find out, I decide to pay a visit to a company where the happiness agenda is front and center.

THE HUMAN RESOURCES Department of the online shoe retailer Zappos looks as though it has fallen victim to an attack by a hit squad of guerilla taxidermists.

A life-size stuffed llama loiters outside meeting room C01. A slightly menacing gang of big game grazes on a display of potted indoor office plants. Next to them, in a bizarrely gruesome tableau, a toddler ball pit is filled with what looks like a pile of dead zebras.

I'm in Las Vegas, on my first overnight trip away from my son since he was born, but instead of spending my Sin City getaway stuffing my life's savings into a slot machine or a stripper's jockstrap, then rocking out at some kind of Celine Dion–Totalitarian State Circus megamash-up, I'm on a tour of the Zappos corporate headquarters.

Happiness is a serious business here at Zappos. The company is probably the nation's leader in a trend that has been dubbed "corporate fungineering," in which management attempts to turn office life into a dizzying parade of fun (or as many companies now refer to it, FUN!). Although Zappos is at the more extreme end of the spectrum, it is certainly no longer anomalous in the ranks of corporate America, and is often seen as a model for business leaders keen to build a similar funorama culture in their own workplaces. Zappos even offers consultancy services on how best to go about this.

The animals, which on closer inspection are not hunting trophies but a kind of bestial uncanny valley of realistic stuffed toys, are part of a workplace culture that includes a constant stream of corporate high jinks—office parades, costumes, wigs, Ping-Pong tournaments, and heavily encouraged out-of-hours socializing.

I'm not the only one spending their Vegas vacation like this. Around twenty thousand members of the public take the Zappos tour every year. Some are business leaders themselves, looking for tips. The rest are a mix of intrigued customers, tourists, and even the odd bachelor or bachelorette party. In our group, there is a married couple in navy business suits who run their own software company, a silent lone male tourist, and a mom and part-time library furniture saleswoman who buys her kids' shoes from the company, a fact which somewhat perplexingly made her want to check out their call center. She eyes the bloodbath in the ball pit doubtfully. "It's a lot different from where I work," she says.

Our tour guide is Dani, who introduces herself to us by her in-house company nickname, the Culture Kitten. They like nicknames here at Zappos. Dani has already christened us, the people on the tour, as her "Kitty Litter." She didn't specify whether she meant it in the sense of "sweet newborn kittens" or "feline toilet."

Dani gestures toward the big-game massacre. "Tony really likes llamas," she explains.

She doesn't need to tell us who Tony is. We all know that she is referring to Tony Hsieh, Zappos's charismatic CEO and high-profile happiness evangelist. Hsieh sees himself as being at the helm of a "global movement for happiness." As well as Zappos, he also started a consultancy business, Delivering Happiness, to spread the happiness gospel to the corporate world and beyond. His bestselling book of the same name is part memoir, part manifesto, describing how he built his business concerns with employee happiness as his driving philosophy. "It wasn't just about building a business," Hsieh wrote. "It was about building a lifestyle that was about delivering happiness to everyone, including ourselves."

Hsieh's mission was to make work such an endless source of fun and joy that his workers would stop drawing a distinction between work and life, which in turn would mean that they would never feel the need to call for work-life balance. Instead, the two would simply be merged together in his workers' imaginations, a philosophy he called "work-life integration."

THE TOUR LOOPS us back past the free cereal, the desks decorated with crepe paper streamers in honor of either something or just as likely nothing in particular, to the Royalty Room, a small side office dominated by a giant throne and a sign saying "You Are Royalty," the province of the Zappos resident life coach, Augusta Scott. Four half-hour sessions a year on the throne with Augusta, optimizing your personal or professional happiness, is a company-wide perk.

We hear about the nap room and see the wall of ties. "Corporate attire," as they call it, is discouraged at Zappos. Any unsuspecting tie wearer is liable to have the offending item cut off at the neck by Fun Enforcement and mounted on the wall, in service of the company's official Core Value 3: "Create Fun and a Little Weirdness." (Although I can't help feeling that for anyone wanting to try something truly weird or subversive in this environment, a neatly pressed business suit might be a good place to start.)

A FEW WEEKS ago, I sent an e-mail requesting an interview with Tony Hsieh. I phrased the message in my perkiest language. I even signed off with the words "have a GREAT weekend!" with both capitalization and exclamation point. I almost never use exclamation points. I even thought about upping the ante with a second exclamation point, but my Britishness kicked in and I deleted it.

I received a prompt and equally perky e-mail back from Hsieh's PR person. So perky, in fact, that it took me a moment to work out that the answer is a flat no. Tony doesn't have a spare hour in his schedule in the next six months to talk to me. By way of explanation, he attached Tony's personal priority list for the coming months.

The priority list is an interesting insight into Hsieh's mind, or at least a glimpse behind the curtain of corporate culture. The document itself is almost completely impenetrable, full of words I don't understand, like *holacracy* and *brand aura*, which, when I google them, only generate more phrases like "sentiment of the product" and "making the implicit, explicit" until my head starts to spin with ever decreasing circles of management speak.

Halfway down Tony's priority list, I spot something that feels closer to the real reason:

> In addition to the priorities listed above, I've also found that certain types of people or meetings are energy draining, while others are energy producing for me. I will prioritize the people who I generally end up feeling more energized by rather than drained by after I interact with them.

I should have used that second exclamation point.

INSTEAD OF TONY, I talk to some of his employees.

Mark Rowland is a fully paid-up Tony Hsieh devotee. The former CEO of a successful restaurant chain in Australia, he was fascinated by the corporate happiness agenda. A Google search for *happiness* led him to Zappos. He loved what he saw online and e-mailed Hsieh directly, telling him that he wanted to copy Zappos's entire culture and approach in a new business venture of his own. Expecting a cease and desist letter from Hsieh's lawyers, he actually received an invitation from Hsieh to come and spend some time at the Zappos headquarters in Las Vegas to experience Hsieh's happiness-based business model up close.

Mark was instantly hooked, and after some to-ing and fro-ing eventually managed to persuade his wife and young children to move to the

States permanently so he could work full-time on a range of Tony Hsieh's business concerns, including in the role of "Happy Cheerleader" for his Delivering Happiness consultancy firm.

Now, a few years on, Mark runs his own start-up, part funded by Tony Hsieh, that according to its Web site "unleashes the potential of entrepreneurial ecosystems to transcend awesome." I'm not quite sure what entrepreneurial ecosystems are, but the idea of "transcending awesome" makes me feel a bit tired.

When I looked up Mark's profile on the Delivering Happiness Web site before I came, next to his bio and grinning photo was a large purple stylized block quote from Ayn Rand, the notorious ultra–right-wing philosopher who rejected all notions of selflessness and altruism, in favor of a radical individualism based on "the virtue of selfishness," whereby "the achievement of your own happiness is the only moral purpose of your life." Rand's ideas have been influential among American conservatives, and in particular in Silicon Valley. Given that everything that I've learned so far about the nature of human happiness has pointed to the exact opposite of Rand's philosophy, I'm curious to know just how far Mark subscribes to her ideas.

"I see you have a quote from Ayn Rand on your profile page on the Web site," I begin. "Are you a fan?"

"Ayn Rand?" Mark looks blank. "Who's he?"

I can't help feeling a little bit disappointed that Mark is not a radical individualist, and realize that I had been mentally rolling up my sleeves for a vigorous debate. Feeling slightly deflated, I change tack and instead ask Mark to give me some examples of how he goes about delivering happiness to his employees.

"Well, for a start, I ban the word *don't*," he replies.

"I don't understand," I say, then catch myself, worrying that I might have entered some kind of positive-thinking mind-games casino in which the House Always Wins. Mark laughs.

"One of our core values is positivity," he tells me. "If I ask someone how they are, and they say 'not bad,' I say to them, 'I asked you how you *were*. I didn't ask you how you *weren't*. I didn't say, how *not* are you?'" He sits back in his chair and folds his arms with the infinite satisfaction of a middle manager with a new aphorism.

I ask him if this might make his staff feel more irritated than happy.

"No," says Mark. "They know not to say it more than two or three times."

He gives me another example. "We also like to add an *a* to the word *menial*."

My brain scrambles around trying to work out where the *a* should go. Amenial? Meniala?

"No, *MEAN*-ial," says Mark triumphantly. "As in . . . it's got *MEANING*."

He tells me a story to illustrate the point. On a walk through the Zappos distribution warehouse a while back, he had spotted a worker boxing up shoes in a manner suggesting little sense of wider significance.

"So I said to him, 'Let's put some meaning into this task,'" Mark begins. "I ask him, 'Who are these shoes for?' So the guy looks on the order form, and says, 'Rachel.' So then I ask him, 'And what kind of shoes are they?' He looks down at the form again and says 'Red stilettos.' So then I say, 'And where would someone wear a pair of red stilettos?' He thinks for a bit, and then he says, 'To a party.'"

Mark encouraged the warehouse worker to picture Rachel, excited for Saturday night's big event, eagerly waiting for her red stilettos to arrive to complete the outfit she has been planning for weeks. But Saturday morning's mail delivery arrives stiletto free, and Rachel is left shoeless and bereft for the big party. And all this because a warehouse worker in Las Vegas had failed to complete the order on time.

"Then this guy looks at me," says Mark, "and a tear starts rolling down his face. This great big six foot seven West Samoan guy, with these big fat tears." Mark looks wistful.

"I layered meaning onto it for him."

. . .

As I'm talking to Mark, I start to notice that he has a strange way of talking about the company and his job, as if somehow he doesn't really see it as a job at all but more as a kind of personal mission. "It's like a family," he says.

This is a phrase I will hear many times during my stay in Las Vegas. Workers are actively encouraged to refer to themselves as the "Zappos Family," a phrase that appears not only all over the company literature but regularly in general conversation too. (Unfortunately, whenever I hear it, my brain defaults instantly to "Manson Family," which slightly spoils the effect.)

But Mark's relationship with his employer turns out to be more like family in one other crucial respect too. Unexpectedly, he reveals something that shocks me.

For the first nine months that Mark worked for Tony Hsieh, putting in around sixty hours each week on Hsieh's various projects, Mark didn't get paid. At all. He doesn't seem to think this is a big deal, but I can't let it go.

"You worked for free?" I ask him, incredulous.

"I was volunteering," he says.

Volunteering seems like an odd word to use about a sixty-hour workweek for a multimillionaire on a series of profitable businesses.

"Was that a fair deal?" I ask. "Weren't they taking advantage of you?"

"A fair deal is whatever's fair to you," says Mark. "I was building options." He pauses.

"I got thanked, *a lot.*"

I look at him.

"They gave me a card."

In an environment in which your private emotions are not just your boss's business but part of his business plan, it's easy to see how quickly the lines can blur between a business arrangement and a personal cause and how open that can be to exploitation.

This ambiguity about what is part of the job and what isn't is written into the very philosophy driving Zappos, something that becomes clear when I talk to Christa Foley, the company's Human Resources manager, a woman of about my age, with a warm smile and an armful of tattoos.

"We don't talk about work-life balance," says Christa, after ushering me into a surprisingly average meeting room, without a stuffed llama or popcorn machine in sight. "We talk about work-life integration. If you love what you do, you don't need a line to distinguish between home and work."

Christa describes how, before offering someone a job at the company, she carefully screens them to make sure they buy into this philosophy.

"So an interview question might be—'Do you socialize with your coworkers outside of the office?'" she tells me. "If they say, 'No, I come in at eight and leave at five to go home' that would be a red flag for me. I don't want people who view work as other from their life. If they start asking lots of questions about what kinds of benefits they'll get, that's another red flag."

At the beginning of the Zappos tour, Dani the Culture Kitten had sat us all down to watch a video about the company, presented by Tony Hsieh, in which he discusses the thinking behind the Zappos official recruitment process. In the video, Hsieh tells us that when he is deciding whether or not to offer a potential candidate a job, the deal-breaker question he asks himself is, "Would I want to go grab a drink with this person?"

I ask Christa about this. She looks a little uncomfortable, like a long-suffering wife trying to rein in her husband at a party and stop him spouting off about his hilarious college drinking escapades to the elderly couple sitting opposite. I get the impression that Christa is keen to make the whole recruitment process sound a little more formal and less arbitrary. But when you strip back a couple of layers of human-resources jargon, what Christa tells me seems to amount to roughly the same thing.

She explains that for every potential new recruit, the company goes through two entirely separate hiring processes. The first is the conventional one, in which the department with the vacancy interviews the candidate to see if they are qualified for the actual job on offer. The other, and more important, part of the hiring process is usually done by Christa herself. This is the "culture interview."

This second interview seems to be essentially the formalized way of establishing whether or not Tony Hsieh would want to "grab a drink" with the candidate. Even if the interviewee is undeniably the best, most highly qualified person for the job in question, if they don't meet this criterion, they will be automatically rejected. "Preserving our culture is our top priority," says Christa.

"They don't know it, but the screening starts the moment they walk up to the front desk," she continues. "Even before that. On the shuttle on the way there. We'll ask the shuttle driver what the person was like. We'll ask the receptionist."

I ask her what kind of person might measure up.

"People who believe in a higher purpose for the company," she says.

"What higher purpose?"

"To deliver happiness to everyone we come into contact with."

Even after a candidate is given the job, they aren't off the hook. "We always say—we hire people slowly and remove them quickly," says Christa.

"What do you mean?" I ask.

"If people don't turn out to be a cultural fit, we move forward to exit them."

"You mean fire them?"

"Yes."

"It's like a family," she says.

IF "CULTURAL FIT" means funster crazy and lapses can potentially cost you your job, the pressure to maintain a state of constant upbeat hilarity sounds intense and exhausting. I start to wonder how I would feel having my emotional state and personal values be the subject of such close scrutiny by the person paying my wages.

When I put the question to her, Christa denies that going through a personal low patch can get you fired, but this seems at odds to the overall picture that is coming across. With a lifesize cardboard cutout of your boss holding a sign saying "Delivering Happiness" greeting you every day in the lobby, and a constant bombardment of messages about the importance of your happiness to company objectives, it's hard to imagine that having an off day wouldn't be a stress in itself. This all feels compounded by the not so subtle message that failure to continue the party out of hours with regular work-based socializing is another black mark on your "cultural fit" record. I'm all for fun at work, but this feels anxiety inducing.

BUT TONY HSIEH had no such reservations. For him, filling a single company with balloon hats and llamas wasn't enough. He wanted to take his happiness empire building to the next level, scaling up his vision of a world in which work and life were not separate to far grander heights, with an unprecedented social experiment. Hsieh embarked on a radical new project, a venture that would go on to expose some of the fatal flaws at the heart of the corporate happiness agenda. After selling Zappos to Amazon for just over one billion dollars (though he still runs the day-to-day operations), instead of buying himself a yacht or another company, Hsieh bought himself a city. Downtown Las Vegas.

A few miles from the outsize glitz of the Strip, most tourists would probably never know of downtown's existence. Previously a seedy cluster of low-rent casinos, vacant lots, and grimy motels, this was a place a person might venture to blow a welfare check, get in a bar fight, form a crack habit, or be murdered by the mob and stuffed under a motel bed.

Hsieh identified around sixty acres of this blighted real estate

bordering the Zappos offices, an area that on the map forms the shape
of a llama, and bought almost the entire thing, buildings, businesses,
and all. His aim was to turn the area into his personal start-up city, a
manufactured community in which he could take his "work-life integration" mission to the next level. Hsieh called this experiment in social
engineering the Downtown Project. He pitched the idea to reporters
and the public at the time as "Playing SimCity in real life."

Hsieh pledged $350 million of his own money to turn this llama-
shaped tract of human desperation into an entrepreneurial wonderland
of happiness and innovation. He pumped $50 million into investing in
new technology start-ups, luring would-be entrepreneurs to move to
his desert utopia from across the country. $200 million went to real
estate, buying up restaurants and bars and high-rise apartment buildings to house the influx of new entrepreneurs in various degrees of semi-
communal living.

He funded restaurants and bars and cupcake stores to service them,
a health center (or "wellness ecosystem," as it advertises itself online)
to take care of their medical needs, and a private school to educate their
children, accepting babies as young as six weeks and specializing in en-
trepreneurship. Everything, from the location of the buildings to the
density of the population (the aim was a hundred residents per square
acre) was based on Hsieh's detailed research on how to maximize innovation and happiness. A hefty Downtown Project administration,
similar in some ways to a city government, was set up to administer the
whole enterprise.

Hundreds of would-be entrepreneurs followed the money, upping
and leaving their families and communities across the country to set
up shop in Hsieh's new desert paradise. The idea was that it would not
just be a collection of businesses but a constructed utopian community,
founded on the principle that work and life should not be considered
separate. "I want to be in an area where everyone feels like they can
hang out all the time, and where there's not a huge distinction between

working and playing," Hsieh told *The New York Times* in the early days of the project. In a later speech he described his vision for the Downtown Project as "one big party."

INTRIGUED TO SEE how things have turned out in Downtown three years after it began, after I finish my Zappos tour I venture out to explore the project on foot, pounding nineteen blocks in the piercing midday desert sun.

While Zappos had a solidly corporate feel to it—less radical thought experiment than human resources in a revolving bow tie—the Downtown Project to me has a more volatile, unpredictable atmosphere. The whole area still has a fundamentally shady, bail-bonds feel about it but with a thin, fragile veneer of hipster.

Five years ago, before Tony Hsieh got involved, a typical purchase on Downtown's Fremont Street was probably a blow job from a desperate prostitute with no health insurance. Now it's "artisanal cheese plates, constructed from upcycled wine bottles."

Vacant lots and boarded-up motels sit alongside high-end wine bars and vintage vinyl record stores. It's barely lunchtime, but party music blasts out everywhere. It's hard to walk ten feet without stumbling on a place to buy a drink.

I walk past the Airstream trailer park, where Tony Hsieh lives. When he first started his Downtown Project experiment, Hsieh initially lived in one of his newly acquired high-rise buildings, the Ogden, in lavish quarters made from three separate apartments knocked together. But a year or so ago, he ditched this luxury lifestyle to set up home in a tiny trailer, taking his personal commitment to the communal-style living of his utopian vision to the next level. The park is encased with a high and snarly barbed wire fence, but I can just see Hsieh's Airstream over the top, one of a cluster of several. It has a tiny wooden house attached to the back, as if delivered via tornado, *Wizard of* Oz style.

Parked next to it is the distinctive blue Delivering Happiness tour bus, the vehicle that provided the transportation for Hsieh's original traveling "Global Movement for Happiness."

I walk down another few blocks to the Downtown Project's showpiece, the Container Park, a shopping, eating, and drinking plaza constructed from old shipping containers. Towering outside the entrance is a thirty-five-foot fire-spewing praying mantis made out of scrap metal. Rumor has it that Hsieh saw it at Nevada's Burning Man festival, bought it on the spot, and had it specially shipped to Downtown. Not far away, a woman sits with her two glassy-eyed toddlers behind a cardboard sign that reads "Need Money for Food and Diapers."

I AM ON THE hunt for some of the tech entrepreneurs that moved out to make their homes here as part of the Downtown Project experiment. I want to know what it's like to leave behind friends and family and live and socialize 24-7 with your colleagues, and what daily life is like in a place where the only grocery store appears to have more varieties of olives than household basics. Downtown's tech entrepreneurs were supposed to be the very foundation of Hsieh's new community, but I'm struggling to find many.

I had assumed the place would be buzzing with start-up energy, but in reality it's mostly deserted. The Container Park is empty, save a few stray Zappos employees and a group of off-duty waitresses enjoying a round of lunchtime cocktails. I ask one of them if she has any idea where all the entrepreneurs might be hanging out.

She points me in the direction of the Gold Spike, previously a seedy low-rent casino, now a Hsieh-owned bar and hotel complex with cheap apartments upstairs designated for Downtown entrepreneurs with shared kitchen and socializing space.

From the street the Gold Spike looks totally unmodernized, all faltering neon and shady backstory. But inside, it has gone the full hipster. A cavernous bar sports a double bed and a beanbag toss. Outside, on the large patio sit several oversize outdoor sofas upholstered in luxury Astroturf.

I order a drink, and then across the bar spy a group of intense-looking young people, deep in conversation, each with a MacBook open in front of them. I assume this must be a tech start-up having a company meeting and wander over.

I'm wrong. This is not a powerhouse of entrepreneurs, hard at work creating the next Google or Facebook, but a production meeting for an amateur TV show, filmed weekly down at Tony Hsieh's trailer park. A few months ago, the star guest was Sarah Jessica Parker, they tell me proudly. This week, it's a traveling petting zoo. As I start chatting to the group, it becomes clear that although many of them live upstairs in the housing earmarked for entrepreneurs, most of the group is either unemployed or cobbling together bits of freelance work. As far as I can tell, none of them is running a successful start-up, or even an unsuccessful one.

Dylan Jorgensen is the show's presenter and host, a handsome all-American guy in his early thirties, with a powerful Buzz Lightyear jawline but a slightly defeated expression.

Dylan looks down at the script he has open on his MacBook, and back up at the group for approval. " 'Festive lemurs.' That's funny, right?"

"No, sorry. It's not," says the man at the end of the table, who introduces himself as a local comedian who helps the team out with script writing. Dylan looks crushed.

I ask Dylan whether he would be willing to chat to me about life in Downtown, and he seems happy to step away from the meeting and follow me outside. Although it's still only early afternoon, the patio has filled up, with a crowd of young people playing a game of giant Jenga and knocking back imported beers. We sit down at a table away from the throng, in the shade of a ten-foot gilded statue of a serpent.

Dylan tells me that he was one of the original pioneers of the

Downtown Project, moving out to Las Vegas from Utah, leaving behind a strict Mormon upbringing when Hsieh funded his tech start-up, online ticketing company Ticket Cake.

"It was exciting. We all moved out here together. Like, sixty small businesses," he tells me. "We wanted to make it so work and life and play are all merged together. No one had family out here. We became our own family." By now I am used to hearing people describe their work colleagues as their family, and it has even lost its slightly cultish ring. But then Dylan starts using a whole new kind of vocabulary that I hadn't heard before.

"The city is curated. Tony curates the people," he tells me. I ask Dylan what he means. "It was the exact same philosophy as Zappos," he says. "It's the 'Do I want to have a beer with this guy' test. It's about cultural fit."

"Does Tony Hsieh meet all the people who move here himself?" I ask.

"No—he has a system to check people out—people are checked out by other people. It's less about 'Is the business a good idea?' It's more about 'Do you like this person, would you be a friend to her?'"

Dylan tells me that many of Hsieh's cash handouts to start-ups as part of the Downtown Project have gone to friends or acquaintances. At the very least, the people he chooses to invest in have to enjoy hanging out. The selection process usually involves at least one evening in a bar, if not a week or more's partying and shooting the breeze with Hsieh or his friends in the drinking spots of Downtown.

But perhaps "cultural fit" wasn't the best basis for determining which business ideas were likely to take off, as many of the new start-ups folded. One of them was Dylan's company, Ticket Cake. But by then, he was hooked by life in Downtown.

"I had layers of my shell taken off one by one," he tells me. "I had my first drink, I said my first curse word. It was liberating. It was exciting." Highly committed to the Downtown Project's philosophy and entranced by Tony Hsieh's vision, Dylan didn't want to go back to

Utah. "I'm fascinated by happiness," he tells me. "I had my heart in the project."

Instead of quitting, he got a job with the Downtown Project's administration as a "collision scientist" in the brand-new City Science Department.

Collision science was at the very heart of the Downtown Project's mission. Dylan explains that in Downtown-speak, a "collision" is any interaction between two or more people. Hsieh had read the research on the importance of community and human connection to happiness, and had become convinced that deliberately engineering as many of these collisions as possible was the key to delivering a happy community.

Right from the start, Hsieh had carefully planned every aspect of the layout and architecture of the city to maximize the number of collisions between people. Instead of talking about ROI, or return on investment, like the rest of the business world, he and his team developed a new metric they called ROC, or return on collisions (or sometimes return on community). The idea was that the more people could be encouraged or forced to collide, the more creative, productive, and ultimately happy they would be.

Dylan tells me in his new job in the City Science Department, he was tasked with keeping tabs on residents and visitors to Downtown, without their knowledge, tracking where they went and who they talked to, solely using data from their cell phones. He and his team then plotted their movements on a series of maps, with the aim of getting a measure of the total number of collisionable hours of the Downtown Project as a whole. Dylan explains the formula for exactly how one collisionable hour is calculated, but it's slightly complicated and I'm not sure I fully follow the explanation, partly because I'm still slightly creeped out by the idea that perhaps the City Science Department might currently be monitoring me.

According to Dylan, in the early days, there were even plans to take this collision surveillance a step further, and that in addition to tracking people via their cell phones, they would also encourage everyone to wear specially designed wristbands that would monitor the numbers of handshakes, hugs, and waves they were giving each other, although this upgrade never quite got off the ground.

The aim was that the City Science Department could use all this data about how the city's residents behaved to artificially engineer situations that would mean that people would collide more often. "We purposefully made it hard to get places, so people would have to bump into each other," Dylan tells me.

"The idea was that the structures of the city, like the Container Park and the Learning Village, were totally movable and interchangeable. We could rearrange them at any point. So if your favorite store was suddenly way over the other side of town, then you would have to walk a different way to get there, which would mean that you would bump into more people along the way."

I wonder if people might be so irritated by finding, when late for work one morning, that their usual coffee place had unexpectedly shifted nineteen blocks overnight that any collisions that might happen as a result might be more violent than congenial. But as it turned out, the plans for constant building reshuffles were a little harder to achieve in practice than in theory. "It never really happened," Dylan admits.

Dylan is sweet and a little nebbish. Hearing him talk about collisions is a bit like having a heart-to-heart with Siri or C-3PO about human connection. So far, he has been so evangelical about the Downtown Project, and his identity seems so wrapped up in the whole venture, it has been a little like hearing someone reading from a PR brochure or giving a TED talk. But I am keen to probe deeper, to find out the genuine emotional effects of living this way. It all feels to me like an oddly stressful environment—the claustrophobia of living around the same people you work with, with your daily movements under scrutiny. However much you love your colleagues, a life where you are expected to be constantly on with no emotional downtime sounds both exhausting and anxiety ridden. I voice these thoughts to Dylan and ask him whether he has ever found it stressful living like this.

"Oh yes, definitely," he replies, surprisingly emphatically. "There's a lot of social pressure here. I'm an introvert. I get a lot of anxiety around people. I sometimes feel like the biggest introvert in town." He gestures up to the high-rise towering over the Gold Spike patio that houses the entrepreneur apartments where he lives. "We share a kitchen and living space," he tells me, "but sometimes I just want to hide. I would be in my pj's and I would hear that there was some great entrepreneur in town and I would think, Now I have to not be stupid, to talk to that person."

I wonder whether this anxiety might be made even more acute by such a strong cultural emphasis on happiness, if living here would throw up a constant pressure to be happy and not to admit to any down days or shades of gray. I ask Dylan whether he ever felt like this.

"Definitely," he replies.

He glances over at the group of people crowded together on the patio. A guy in a multicolored jacket does a weird wriggly dance move. Everyone laughs and swigs their drinks.

"Logically I see how important it is to connect with people, but it's not my natural thing," says Dylan. "You're saying 'Let's use the power of relationships to be great.' But what are the pressures that come with those relationships? I get a lot of anxiety here."

DYLAN WASN'T THE only one feeling the strain of this strange pressure cooker of a social experiment.

A year or so after its inception, a strange and worrying trend had started to take hold in Downtown.

On January 27, 2013, one of the project's high-profile entrepreneurs, Jody Sherman, the founder of a baby product sales Web site called Ecomom, had plans to see a movie with a friend. He never turned up. Nearly twelve hours later, the Las Vegas Police Department found him. He was in his car, pulled over on the side of the road, about twenty-five miles from Downtown. Just five days before his forty-eighth birthday, Jody had shot himself in the head.

Jody's suicide came as a deep shock to everyone. In a community that prized happiness and positivity so highly, many speculated that he hadn't felt able to confide in anyone that his company had been struggling and that he had been struggling along with it. But even many of those closest to him had had no idea.

At first, this tragedy looked like a one-off coincidence. After all, the entrepreneurial life is a high-pressure one anywhere in the world. But then what looked like an alarming pattern started to emerge.

Matt Berman, a fifty-year-old former corporate executive, who had upped and moved to Downtown to start a whimsical men's barbershop funded by Tony Hsieh out of an old railway caboose in the Container Park, was found hanged in his home, another apparent suicide.

The project's youngest casualty was Ovik Banerjee, a fresh-faced twenty-four-year-old graduate who worked for Downtown's administration team.

Banerjee left behind a blog. His profile photo shows a young man in an interview suit, with an earnest, hopeful smile. Each week, he wrote a personal happiness review, measuring his progress against a set of happiness goals he had set for himself, the same sorts of goals that I have now seen in a hundred different advice blogs and positive psychology books:

Stay in touch with people better—Talked to Ethan after playing phone tag.
Get outdoors—Not this week.
Get 7 hours of sleep a night—Kinda sorta again. I've got to figure out a better sleep pattern. But sleep is important. . . .

With each blog entry Banerjee also shared an inspirational quotation. "If you aren't scared, you're doing it wrong," or "Life can only be understood backward, but must be lived forward."

Banerjee's last personal happiness review was in October 2013. Three months later, he jumped from the balcony of his Downtown apartment.

"ZAPPOS CEO'S LAS Vegas Dreamland Is Imploding," declared Gawker's Silicon Valley blog, Valleywag. "Zappos Chief Loses a Las Vegas Bet," wrote *Bloomberg View*. The influential tech publication *Re/code* ran a long article about the suicides and the project's troubled state, questioning the very nature of Tony Hsieh's philosophy, with the title, "The Downtown Project Suicides: Can the Pursuit of Happiness Kill You?"

The Downtown Project's team downplayed the suicides. When *Re/code* journalist Nellie Bowles asked Tony Hsieh about the tragedies, he brushed her off, saying, "Suicides happen anywhere. Look at the stats." (I do. It's hard to claim statistical significance with such a small sample, but three suicides over sixteen months in a group of this size puts the Downtown Project's suicide rate at around five times the Las Vegas rate, which is itself the highest in the nation.)

The project presented a unified Happiness as Usual front after the suicides. Less than two weeks after Matt Berman's death, the Container Park where he worked was packed with people for the Up Summit, a motivational conference for entrepreneurs from across the world, who gathered in the blinding desert sun to hear speakers blast out high-octane positive thinking messages. Many complained that the Downtown leadership was refusing to acknowledge the extent of the unraveling anxiety and distress at the heart of the community.

It's easy to see how, in a culture that prizes happiness as the ultimate goal and mark of success, it might be hard for anyone struggling with mental health issues to feel able to admit to them or discuss them. As one local speculated when talking to a reporter from *Las Vegas Weekly*, "Is it that everyone's so actively talking about how good it is, and how everyone is delivering happiness, that those who feel unhappy can't tell anyone about it?"

By that fall, the Downtown Project had hit the skids.

Hsieh announced that around thirty key members of the project's administration team were to be laid off. The project's Director of Imagination David Gould wrote a deeply critical open resignation letter to Tony Hsieh and published it in *Las Vegas Weekly*, describing the Downtown Project as a "collage of decadence, greed, and missing leadership." The City Science Department was disbanded. No more collision metrics. Dylan Jorgensen lost his job.

For the first time, the whole Downtown Project looked as though it might fall apart.

KIMBERLY KNOLL, A therapist who counts several Downtown Project entrepreneurs among her clients, did some crisis counseling in the aftermath of the Downtown suicides.

She has agreed to meet me, and has suggested this place, a Starbucks in a no-man's-land off the freeway, and although it has the smoggy, billboard dreariness that always feels like the worst of American cities to me, it's good to get out of Downtown. I was starting to find the project, with its constant blaring music and forced party atmosphere, slightly claustrophobic.

Kimberly is already sitting at a table outside waiting for me when I arrive, sipping an iced something, and exuding such a warmth of personality that I instantly want to give her a hug and engage her as my personal therapist for ever and ever.

She had told me over the phone when I had first contacted her a few weeks back that she was worried that I was going to misrepresent her views, and that I would somehow make it look as though she was blaming Tony Hsieh for the Downtown suicides. "Suicide is way bigger than anyone, or any one thing," she had said. "It's no one's fault." She seemed wary enough that I am surprised at how instantly candid she is about her concerns about the happiness *über alles* culture of many modern workplaces.

"For a company to come in and say 'We're going to make everybody happy,' it can be very harmful. It can be dangerous," she says, almost as soon as I sit down at the table. "Thinking that you have complete control over your emotions and if you don't feel happy it's your fault, that can make people feel shame. It's anxiety inducing."

Kimberly tells me about how in a culture that values happiness so highly, her clients often see feeling unhappy or having a down patch as almost a personal failure. "They say to me, 'I'm not okay because I feel bad,'" she says. "They feel shame for not feeling happy, like 'What's wrong with me?'"

Often her clients feel unable to admit to this unhappiness around their families or colleagues. "They come to me and say, 'Nobody knows I feel this way.' People go around saying 'Everything's great!' and I think *really?* Is everyone just kicking ass, because I hear that ninety percent of companies are failing. People can't share when they're not happy. It's a very lonely spot."

As Kimberly is talking, my mind wanders to various times in my own life when I have felt the need to pretend to be happier than I really was. Being devastated after a brutal rejection from an ex-boyfriend but believing that projecting a six-month fiction of joyous couldn't-care-less-ness was my best shot at winning him back. When I was single and deep in the giant poker game of the dating scene, where the most effective emotional strategy is "the one who cares the least, wins." After my son was born and I was falling apart with postpartum exhaustion and anxiety and a love that felt like a giant open wound, but felt compelled to answer any question about my mental state with some version of "never been happier."

Society would stop functioning if we didn't sometimes put a brave face on things, but even at this relatively trivial level, sustained emotional pretense can be profoundly corrosive. I can't even imagine the pressure of having that all wrapped up in my boss's business strategy or that even at the most indirect level, my job somehow depended on it.

"Experiencing emotions is extremely valuable," says Kimberly. "Emotions tell us things, and we need to sit with them for at least a bit. When clients come to me for therapy and ask me 'How do I get happy again?' I say 'It's okay to feel bad.' Negative emotions are awesome for telling us how to live. If we blunt negative emotions, we also blunt positive emotions."

After all the get-happy-quick schemes and self-help gimmicks I've seen so far during my research, it's a relief to talk to someone who is prepared to acknowledge the nuances and messiness of how human beings think and feel. Perhaps because she accepts that people are complex, Kimberly's whole approach feels kinder, more understanding, more fundamentally compassionate than the harsh narrative of personal blame that I'm getting so used to hearing from the mainstream consumer happiness movement. I wonder if Kimberly has pinpointed one of the root causes of the anxiety inherent in the whole happiness rat race—a kind of institutionalized emotional dishonesty that punishes people for experiencing the normal range of human feelings.

THIS IS WHAT happens when you leave your boss in charge of your happiness. Instead of human connection, you get "collisions." Instead of mutual support, you get "City Science." Community may be the key to happiness, but a manufactured community with financial motives lurking behind every interaction is not the same as a real, organic community, nurtured from genuine human empathy.

The Downtown Project is bouncing back. They have dialed back the rhetoric. When I finally talk to a spokesperson and ask her about the happiness agenda, she says that the Downtown Project's driving philosophy is not happiness but "enabling passion." She sounds sober and professional and somewhat defensive. The utopian language has been toned down from the early days. Happiness has become toxic.

· · ·

THAT NIGHT, BEFORE I rush to catch my plane back to California, I order a glass of wine and sit in the bar of the Gold Spike, at the same time desperate to get home and savoring my last hour of freedom before I hurtle straight back into the maelstrom of motherhood.

Across the bar, I see a man in his midthirties wearing a hat made out of a balloon animal. He is drinking alone.

I'VE BEEN BACK from Las Vegas for a few weeks when Brett, a local dad that I often bump into on the toddler scene, invites me to have lunch with him at work. I've been angling for this invitation for a while, issuing a series of not so subtle hints ever since Brett's unfeasibly intelligent two-year-old son Stephen gives me a *what can ya do?* shrug in the park and informs me proudly, "My daddy works for Facebook." (Solly could easily be forgiven for thinking that I work for Facebook too, given that every time I'm on my computer, browsing through some random person's baby photos when he asks me what I'm doing, I inevitably reply, "Work." Or if I'm feeling particularly defensive, "Important work.")

I am intrigued to see the Facebook offices, partly because I half expect the experience to be like a literal jumping into my own newsfeed, Mary Poppins-style, with the entire campus a live-action showcase of people staging flawless vacation photos and acting out angry debates about Israel or breastfeeding. But the main reason I want to visit is because it was in Silicon Valley that the whole culture of work-life integration got off the ground.

Tech giants like Facebook and Google famously ply their staff with free food and beer, video games and meditation gurus in an unwritten social contract that states that if the workplace agrees to meet its workers' every practical, emotional, social, and spiritual need, they in return need never go home.

.   .   .

I PULL UP outside Building 16 of Facebook's Menlo Park campus in time for my lunch appointment with Brett and hand my keys to the valet parkers. They spirit my car away with perfect, wordless efficiency. (Brett has warned me not to tip them. Apparently accepting tips might get them fired.)

Lunchtime is clearly peak time for visitors. Employees' families are encouraged to stop by and the cafeteria offers high chairs and free ice cream. In front of me are three or four slightly harassed looking women juggling toddlers out of the car, presumably hoping to catch a glimpse of Daddy. It all has the slight feel of a prison visit.

When I get inside though, I realize that if this is a prison, it is the prison of a hang 'em and flog 'em right-winger's fevered nightmares. If Tony Hsieh had taken a city and tried to run it like a company, this feels like an attempt to turn a company into a tiny exclusive city.

As Brett and I stroll through the leafy campus piazza, past the video games arcade, munching a salted caramel double scoop from the free ice cream parlor, he points out the hairdresser, dentist, and the doctor's surgery. There are restaurants offering most of the major world cuisines; and like some kind of crazed cruise ship buffet, almost all the food everywhere is free. As Brett explains cheerfully, "Everything here is designed so that you never need to leave."

He's right. When I go to the restroom, there is even a discreet bowl of wrapped toothbrushes next to the basin.

Right at the heart of the campus is an entire department, with its own printing press, dedicated to the production of motivational posters. They are on the walls everywhere. The Only Place Where Success Comes Before Work Is in the Dictionary. If I Was Interested Only in Earning Money, I Would Have Picked Another Business. The Greatest Risk of All Is to Do Nothing.

The posters are clearly having the desired effect. In the perfect metaphor for the overworked American, Brett tells me that the campus even boasts its own handful of treadmill desks, that let employees keep running to a never materializing destination and Never Stop Typing.

After a surprisingly delicious bowl of bacon-cheeseburger soup from the cafeteria, Brett walks me past the vast glass-walled offices belonging to Mark Zuckerberg and Sheryl Sandberg. He tells me not to act weird. No photos. In trying not to act weird, obviously I end up acting even more weird, sneaking furtive glances through the windows like a pervert. Mark's office is clinical. Sheryl's is homier but still achingly immaculate, the walls decorated with what look like customized pink *Lean In* posters.

The previous week, it had been in the news that Facebook was going to start paying for its female employees to freeze their eggs in order to delay having children. Strangely, there don't seem to be a lot of female employees around. All the women I see walking through the campus are wearing the bright orange visitors' lanyards, like the one around my neck. Maybe the whole female workforce is out the back having their eggs frozen. I picture a line of them, all with Sheryl Sandberg–perfect shiny hair, Leaning In, their eggs neatly labeled in the freezer next to the salted caramel ice cream and their childbearing years slipping away.

"WORKING 90 HOURS a Week and Loving It" proclaimed the T-shirts worn by the original Apple Mac engineering team. Facebook programmers still occasionally pull all-nighters in the office, ordering dinner and then breakfast as the sun rises over the foosball table. But Silicon Valley's vision that commitment to your job looks like an obsessively coding twenty-year-old software engineer with no family commitments or relationship with personal hygiene to lure him home is now creeping across corporate America. For the most part, they have stripped the free ice cream out of the equation, leaving only the notion that everyone should be working all the time.

According to one report from the International Labour Organization, American employees work more hours than anyone in the industrialized world, with longer days and less vacation time. The report points out that an average American worker works *two weeks* longer each year than the average Japanese worker, hardly a culture known for its slacker vibe.[4] The United States is also one of the only developed countries with no legally mandated vacation time for workers. Not that it would probably make much difference anyway. In a culture that prizes the total sublimation of the self to the company's needs, many American workers don't even take their allocated vacation days, with one study showing that in 2013, employees in the United States voluntarily forfeited more than fifty-two billion dollars' worth of paid time off.[5]

Some experts dispute the figures on American working hours, quoting government statistics that suggest that hours have not changed much in the last few decades. But this is an average that masks two opposing trends—white-collar salaried employees working increasingly punishing hours and involuntary low-wage part-timers scrabbling to cobble together enough hours to pay the bills from employers unwilling to fork out for the benefits that full-time workers require.

For many salaried workers, contracted hours are now more of an arcane legal curiosity than any remote guide to how a working week might actually look. Evening and weekend work is no longer the exceptional response to a crisis but a routine expectation of employees of all ranks. While a generation ago, an average office worker could expect to be home in time for family dinner most nights, now this is often considered a generous and rare exception.

One friend posts on Facebook about missing her son's first birthday for a work conference in another city. Another acquaintance, a lawyer, tells me about how she comes home from work at seven to put her daughter to bed, then stays up until midnight answering e-mails and finishing reports, a shift pattern her firm refers to as "flexible working." At first, I assume these kinds of hours must be a rarity, but then three more people I meet describe the exact same working schedule. I ask one of them what she does for a living, assuming it must be something hugely pressing and time sensitive. She tells me she is a medieval historian.

If there's one reason people in this country have so little time to socialize and connect with others, why Americans spend just four minutes a day "hosting and attending social events," and just thirty-six minutes a day "socializing and communicating" with the people in their lives, it is this. They are spending too much time at work.

IT'S NOT JUST at Zappos. Companies across America are rushing to sign up for "work-life integration," casting off the pesky notion of work-life balance, with its implications of protected free time for employees, in favor of a palatable-sounding slogan that ensures that workers will be constantly at the company's disposal, never off the clock.

The recent rush of interest in employee happiness is part of a trend in which the boundaries between work, leisure, and self have been almost totally blurred. There is now no hour in the day, personal emotion, spiritual question, or private thought that isn't considered to be the business or property of our employers.

The irony is, with this obsessive focus on our happiness, and rush to lay claim to our emotions and free time, our employers are actually providing the biggest hurdle to our genuine well-being, demanding so much of our time and emotional energy that we have little left for our relationships, families, and communities outside of work.

When the British journalist Oliver Burkeman wrote a humorously curmudgeonly article[6] in *The New York Times* about the creeping trend for corporate fungineering of the type that goes on at Zappos, the reader comments underneath the piece revealed a huge outpouring of distress from workers who felt that all this enforced company fun was starting to encroach dangerously into their genuine leisure time and private and family lives.

"I don't want 'fun' activities at work to distract me or the coworkers I rely on from the tasks at hand," wrote one commenter, "because that causes me to spend more time at work, reducing the time I have outside of work to have fun . . . my coworkers are not my friends and being made to socialize with them at company luncheons and parties etc. is a chore to me that takes time away from other things I'd rather be doing."

"Companies with Chief Happiness Engineers probably expect their employees to spend an unreasonable amount of time at work," wrote another commenter. "The solution is simple: hire more workers and let people work reasonable hours. Believe me, they'll find plenty of fun things to do with the extra time away from work, without their employers having to make work 'fun' for them."

Another distressed reader had a simpler solution for how to solve the problem of employee unhappiness. "If companies want to start making their employees happy, maybe they should focus on work-life balance, better benefits, more maternity/paternity leave, and better retirement programs instead of sugarcoating everything in a miasma of movie posters, balloon animals, and clowns."

THE WORKPLACE HAPPINESS industry has been relatively upfront that their motives are not fully altruistic. As positive psychology professor and happiness expert Chris Peterson admitted to the Cleveland *Plain Dealer* in 2008, "Hardheaded corporate culture is becoming interested in how to get more work out of fewer workers. They're realizing that if their workers are happy, they will work harder and more productively. So they're leading the charge."[7]

At the same time, a growing disconnect has developed between the happiness rhetoric that companies use with their staff and the increasingly grim reality of being an employee in modern-day corporate America.

No matter how much happiness training they attend, the reality is that the American worker now has a worse deal than at any point since the Second World War. Wages have stagnated while corporate profits have skyrocketed, and large numbers of full-time minimum wage workers now live below the poverty line, dependent on government assistance to get by.

Despite all the talk of employee empowerment, workers are losing what little genuine bargaining power they used to possess. Union membership, with the higher wages and better conditions it brings, is often methodically discouraged by these same happiness-pushing employers. (If businesses had a genuine interest in their employees' happiness, perhaps the single biggest thing they could do would be to encourage them to unionize. Wide-scale research shows that union membership is a large and significant predictor of happiness, with union members consistently reporting far greater well-being than their nonunion peers, independent of income.)[8]

Indeed many of the companies shouting the loudest about happiness and empowerment often have some of the worst records when it comes to genuinely looking after their workforce. Bank of America, who stuck high-tech happiness monitors on their call center staff, recently settled a huge-scale class action lawsuit brought by employees across the country alleging multiple wage and hours violations including failure to pay overtime and provide adequate rest breaks. The bank settled for seventy-three million dollars.[9]

Coffee behemoth Starbucks, whose Wisdom 2.0 talk I sat through was entitled "Activating Starbucks Values—Being Present to Inspire and Nurture the Human Spirit," was found by the National Labor Relations Board to have "mounted an antiunion campaign aimed at tracking and restricting the growth of union activities, during which it employed a number of restrictive and illegal policies."[10]

Meanwhile spiritually souped-up IBM and positivity-pushing Taco Bell (who refer to their low-wage workforce as "Champions") have both been implicated in lawsuits for allegedly failing to pay some employees appropriate overtime for the hours they have worked.[11]

As one former employee of another major corporation put it in an interview with writer Chris Hedges, "At my company, positive psychology is a euphemism for spin. They try to spin their employees so much that they forget they do the work of three people, have no health insurance, and three quarters of their paycheck goes on rent."[12]

Perhaps, rather than happiness, we would all be better off focusing on something less subjective, like rights and legal protections. Because, if you really want your employees to be happy, the answer is simple. Pay them fairly, give them good benefits and adequate vacation time, and most important, let them go home.

THE CRAZY HOURS that many middle-class Americans are now working have also had an unexpected effect on their home lives. Limited time with children has brought an added intensity to parenting when hard-pressed workers do finally get to go home. This heightened level of parental fervor is something I've been noticing more and more as I finally start to make some progress on the friendship front.

Life has been looking up for me recently. A new family has moved into the apartment downstairs, with a daughter the same age as Solly. The mom and I became instant friends, slogging out the long, toddler-heavy afternoons together in one or other of our apartments among the overflowing laundry baskets, interchangeable except that hers contains more pink. Then I meet Meghan when I start scouting around for a nanny share, and then Leigh at toddler kinder gym and things instantly feel much brighter. It turns out the research is right. Having friends to share my daily experiences with has made a huge difference to my happiness.

But the deeper I get into middle-class Californian parenting circles, the more I start to notice some rather strange behavior going on.

5.

"I DON'T CARE AS LONG AS HE'S HAPPY": DISPATCHES FROM THE PARENTING HAPPINESS RAT RACE

"I have a dilemma, and I need your advice," my friend Nicole confides. We are at her house for a social engagement that back in London would have been pitched as "come over for coffee and let's ignore the kids" but over here is called a 'playdate.' The children are jacked up on organic figs and running round in maniacal circles, screeching. In California this is called 'self-directed play.'

My ears prick up. I love dilemmas and Nicole's tone is similar to the one my friends and I used to use in the pre-kids dating years when our lives were full of them, and we could occasionally get a whole evening's discussion out of a three-word text message from someone's boyfriend. What does he *mean* by "see you later?" How *much* later? See me in *what way*? (After a while we stopped calling them texts at all and started referring to them as "subtexts." As in "Oh God, I just got a subtext from Neil. It says *'I'm on the train'* but it obviously means he's breaking up with me.")

"What's up?" I ask.

"I think my daughter's been breastfed by another woman."

This is mind-bogglingly weird, even for California. Apparently Nicole had left her daughter Morgan for an hour with another mom while she ran an errand and came back to find the woman doing up her nursing bra and remarking how different it felt when Morgan latched on compared with her own son. I can't begin to wrap my mind around this. For a start, Morgan is two and a half. By British standards, it's a little odd that even her own mother is still breastfeeding her, although living here I'm getting used to that kind of thing. But breastfeeding someone else's child? A starving newborn trapped in a snowstorm, maybe. But a preschooler whose mom has popped over to the bank? I look over at Morgan, so deceptively cute with her pigtails and pink sandals.

Adulterer, I think to myself.

Although the whole thing sounds like an ill-advised collaboration between the scriptwriters from *Sex and the City* and Child Protective Services, after spending a bit of time in new mom circles in California, it almost doesn't surprise me. Nicole's friend is an extreme advocate of a philosophy called attachment parenting, something that had barely hit my radar back in the UK, but is absolutely mainstream over here.

Attachment parents have taken the loosely metaphorical use of the word *attachment,* as in "I am very attached to my new kitchen blender" or "It is important that a child is well attached to its caregiver" and, like child-rearing creationists, unfathomably decided it is best applied totally literally, claiming that if children are to grow up happy and secure, they must spend as much of their early years as possible actually physically fettered to their parent (although for parent, read mother). Done to the letter, it is nothing short of an endurance test. But I'm finding that this is pretty typical of the increasingly extreme lengths to which American parents are prepared to go in pursuit of their children's happiness (or in this woman's case, other people's children's happiness).

The attachment gospel preaches that excessive crying in infancy can cause long-term emotional damage, and it is the parent's responsibility to prevent this. As a result, our neighborhood parks are full of exhausted-looking women shackled to thirty-five-pound toddlers, like a Dr. Sears chain gang. This is known as "baby-wearing," something which sounds as though it should be the next target for the anti-fur protestors at Milan Fashion Week, but is actually just an oddly politically charged way to describe carrying your baby in a sling and Never Putting Him Down.

Attachment parents shun basic baby conveniences like strollers, bottles, and cribs in favor of co-sleeping (although in my experience, more of a co-wriggling, co-insomnia hybrid) and breastfeeding, not just for the few months typical in Europe, but for as many years as their mothers can humanly withstand. One mom summed the ordeal up in a blog post entitled "How Attachment Parenting Nearly Killed Me":

> Reader, I did it! My baby didn't cry very often, or for very long. But I did. Constantly. By the time she was six months old, I was a complete wreck. I was 10 pounds below my pre-baby weight. My hair was falling out. My back and joints hurt from wearing her all day.[1]

My advice to Nicole over the whole boob-gate scandal comes from a place of deep Britishness. Whatever you do, don't confront it; act as awkwardly as possible when around the friend in future and continue to discuss the situation only behind her back. Perhaps as a result, Nicole will probably never find out the truth about what happened that day.

There is close to zero evidence to support attachment parenting's alarmist claims that failing to breastfeed a crying child might cause them emotional damage, or even that this style of parenting has any advantage over any other loving variety. Its advocates have instead co-opted unsurprising research showing that child victims of severe neglect suffer emotional consequences, and have heavily extrapolated from there. But when trapped inside this kind of absolutist high-stakes logic, the friend's actions make slightly more sense. With lifelong happiness itself on the line, sticking your boob in your friend's child's mouth is, at minimum, basic hospitality. At best, it's the heroic prevention of a life of heartache.

It is perhaps in the hothouse conditions of modern parenting that the American obsession with personal happiness is at its most acute. As soon as an American baby is born, its parents apparently enter into an implicit contractual obligation to answer all questions about their hopes for their tiny offspring's future with the words: "I don't care, as long as he's happy" (the mental suffix "at Harvard" must remain unspoken).

This is not just happiness as the vague guiding aim shared by all parents the world over but as a minute-by-minute project. In the same way that Americans see their own happiness as a state achievable through sheer hard slog, they appear to believe that with enough fevered effort, a parent has the potential and the responsibility to "build" a flawlessly happy child. As a result, happiness-seeking undertaken on behalf of children takes on an added frenetic intensity.

And much as I hate to admit it, I have a lot of these tendencies too. My son is the chink in my cynical armor. I may be able to remain skeptical of the happiness rat race when it comes to pursuing the Happy for myself, walking briskly past the personal development section of the airport bookstore to my gate without a backward glance. I can remain blissfully unmindful, disempowered, unactualized, and totally indifferent to my inner child, but when it comes to my actual child, the facade starts to crumble.

At some deep level, I am terrified that if I fail to maximize on every tiny happiness opportunity for Solly, he will grow up to be Not Happy. That his future memoir chronicling his mother's failure to give adequate praise to his cotton-ball Easter bunny will turn up in the Painful Lives section of the bookstore, next to the satanic abuse ones.

As a result, my approach to Solly's happiness can sometimes feel less like a by-product of living and more like a forced march. I just can't relax and leave it to play out naturally. A feeling of urgency and perfectionism creeps in, and I feel compelled to pursue it frenetically on his behalf.

I WAS ONE of the last of my friends to have kids. Shortly before turning thirty-five, after more than a decade of dating and overanalyzing and wrestling with the twin equally compelling but totally opposing terrors of never having children and actually having children, I met the man who would become my husband on an Internet date.

Just a few family-shaming months later, I was pregnant and strapped so tightly into a corseted wedding dress by my mother that I feared that my unborn child would come out with crystals embedded into his face. My wedding pictures are not a good look. I wasn't the pretty kind of pregnant, all empire lines and healthy glow. I was the gross kind, my skin a clammy film of pimples and my fat obvious but still unsourceable. I was thrilled to have found my life partner and to be having his baby so late in the game, but in truth, the highlight of my wedding day was the fact that it was the first time in ten years that the whole of my extended family had been in one room without anyone asking me if I was ever going to get married.

Four months later, after a down and dirty labor, so lightning quick that I missed my chance at either embracing my inner goddess or drugs (I hadn't fully decided which to aim for), Solomon was born, crystal free, fully alert, and shockingly, lavishly perfect. He stared me square in the face, and the rules of the game changed completely and forever.

Giving birth, for me, was like emerging from a car wreck to find myself inexplicably madly in love with Vladimir Putin. Babies are petty despots, blindly self-centered with megalomaniac life- and space-annexing aspirations. But I was biologically incoherent with adoration. Solly's happiness became my driving priority, and if it conflicted with my own, then so much the better, as it surely meant that I was doing an even more committed job.

After so much buildup, and so many years of theorizing about how perfectly I would accomplish the challenges of motherhood, I was aiming for a special kind of happiness for Solly. I wasn't just gunning for workaday contentment. I wanted him to be blissfully, outlandishly, obscenely happy.

Unlucky for him.

I instantly contracted every pathology in the Diagnostic Manual of Middle-class Parenting. I adopted the signature new-parent blend of sanctimony and guilt, misplaced self-righteousness and crippling self-doubt. I exhausted myself trying to optimize every aspect of his life. My voice took on a bizarrely overenunciated, syruped-up register I had never known myself capable of, somewhere between wartime BBC announcer and Julie Andrews, giving him a continuous running commentary of the tedious minutiae of everything we did. More often than not, his newborn face would contort into a tiny mask of pain in response, presumably just willing me to please, For the Love of God, Just Shut Up.

If I stuck him in his bouncer and took five minutes to check Facebook, I would then spend the next forty-five minutes compounding the problem by googling variations on: "Romanian orphans, emotional effects of caregiver neglect" and scour his behavior, hawklike for the signs. In short, I drove myself (and doubtless everyone around me) absolutely crazy.

Back when we lived in the UK, I always felt as though I was riding against the tide. I tried to play these aspects of my parenting down and conceal my helicopter tendencies as best I could. The overriding cultural tone among British parents is a kind of sardonic one-downmanship. Although the British middle classes can hyperparent with the best of them, it isn't the done thing to admit to it and instead, parents brag about their 'benign neglect' of their kids. Popular British parenting Web site Mumsnet, for example, is full of discussion threads with titles like "Tell me your worst parenting mistakes to make me feel better" in which parents pile in to confess to how they accidentally let their children chew on their own diapers, left them in the pub, or forgot to pick them up from day care (or in one woman's case, remembered to pick him up but rushed over and lovingly hugged the wrong child, explaining: "In my defense, they did look very similar.").

But living in coastal America, it's becoming clear that my slightly debilitating, and almost certainly counterproductive, desire to march my child forcibly in the direction of happiness whether he likes it or not is normal, even mild. Here in California, the happiness of the child is everything, and excesses that I am embarrassed to admit to in the UK are considered a badge of honor, codified into overarching and complex childcare philosophies.

This becomes clear when we finally decide it's time to look for a preschool for Solly. In the absence of any government-funded education before kindergarten for anyone except the lowest income groups, preschool in California turns out to be a highly charged, and highly expensive, affair. The range of choices is dazzling and all claim to be able to deliver lifelong happiness for my child. (Though apparently not the fun kind of happiness. "Birthday parties and holiday parties are strongly discouraged, and the consumption of refined sugar on the premises is strictly forbidden," admonishes one stern preschool Web site.)

But are we Montessori people or Kodály? Mandarin immersion? Do we subscribe to "the progressive model of education in which children learn most effectively through the demands of their social context?" We strike Waldorf off the list because of the creepy faceless dolls they have dotted around the classroom. Apparently faces limit children's imaginations, but I realize that I'm okay with that.

I'm nervous about leaving Solly, but my fears are set to rest when eventually we hit upon a small preschool of just ten kids, run jointly by four wonderfully kind, dedicated, positive-spirited women. I realize they will give my boy the kind of rarefied, special snowflake attention that I'm hoping for when I overhear another parent asking the director a question that had also been preying on my mind. How does she manage to be unfailingly in a good mood, no matter what's going on or what time of day you catch her? She replies, "How can you not be in a good mood when you work with toddlers all day?" which would probably sound to most people like both a question and an answer in one statement. We sign our child over to them on the spot.

The curriculum is incredible. They grow passion fruit and do shadow puppet shows. They play ukuleles and make collages using visionary combinations of dried pinto beans and old doorknobs. Of course, they learn both yoga and meditation. Solly comes home after a few weeks proudly showing off his Downward Dog pose; meanwhile posted on the school's Facebook page is a video of him with eleven other blissed-out toddlers sitting in a circle cross-legged, piously chanting the word *om* as the teacher taps a xylophone. Happiness seeking starts young in California.

It is when we get called in to the school for a parent conference to discuss Solly's first report card, that I notice a strange underlying trend to how the school operates. It seems as though negativity of any kind has been banned.

Neil and and I sit down at the tiny scaled-down table with his teachers, and they solemnly hand us the document. Although my rational brain tells me that report cards for two-year-olds are ridiculous, I can't believe my own hype enough not to care what Solly's says. Is he somehow failing? Is my rock-solid conviction about his complete and total wonderfulness in all areas of life about to be shattered by an unwelcome intervention from the Real World?

I needn't have worried. When I scan the document looking for bad news, I realize that there isn't any. He is apparently brilliant at everything. I look skeptically at the section entitled "gross motor skills," for which he has scored in the highest category, despite being unable to climb the rather small play structure in the yard. "You don't think he's a bit of a klutz?" I probe.

The teachers stare back at me, horrified.

"We don't like to use that word," one of them replies, restraining herself from adding, "you monster." "We prefer to call it 'self-directing toward the lower levels.'"

Over the next few months, I start to notice this aversion to anything that could even vaguely be construed as negative coming up more and more often.

For instance, in the classroom, the word "no" is used very sparingly, which makes discipline a somewhat contorted business. When I come to pick Solly up one day, I see a child clonking a classmate over the head with a wooden mallet. The teacher turns to the pint-size mallet wielder sympathetically and asks him: "Oh dear. Are you having trouble using your body safely?"

The whole place is like taking a trip to a parallel universe founded on my own personal value system, in which my child is brilliant at everything and bad at nothing. A magnificent arena in which he can do no wrong, and any transgression he might stumble onto will be deftly reframed with a swift dose of moral relativism. The whole experience is treacherously, gloriously enabling for me.

It's not just at preschool. The longer we spend in America, the more I notice a deep-seated cultural squeamishness about children experiencing negative emotions, with adults constantly intervening to prevent or reframe them.

When Solly hits the toddler tantrum phase full tilt and I'm feeling powerless in the face of it (representative example: full-scale reactor-core meltdown voicing his deep and urgent desire for a banana, while eating a banana), I'm on constant alert as to how other parents are handling the same issue.

Back in the UK, the overwhelming received wisdom on how to deal with toddler tantrums is to ignore the tantrumming toddler and not give the behavior any attention. My sister once told me that she actually enjoys her kids' tantrums as it gives her an officially sanctioned break, the only time when sticking on headphones and catching up on Facebook suddenly becomes high-performance parenting.

But not in California. One morning in the playground, I notice a child of a similar age to Solly deep into a fist-banging screamathon after being informed by his mom that it is time to go home for lunch. But rather than either ignoring him, or hauling him off under her arm like a surfboard (my default method with Solly), his mother pleads with him anxiously, "Tell me how I can support you through this."

Other parents attempt a running simultaneous translation of their children's tantrums, live commentating their emotions. "WAAAAAAH-HHH!!! I DON'T WANT TOOOO!!" "I see you are feeling very frustrated." "NOOOOOOOOOO, I HATE YOOOOOOOOUUUUU!" "Now you are feeling angry." I don't know quite what to make of it.

It's rare to hear a sharp "no" or a "stop that right now" directed at a child here. If two kids start to fight over a toy, they won't be told to "Stop it, or no one gets it." Instead a more convoluted scene plays out that I come to think of as the Californian Toddler Negotiated Peace Talks:

<u>EXT: DAYTIME. CALIFORNIA PLAYGROUND.</u>

Two toddlers fight over a toy dump truck.

TODDLER A: Miiiiiinnnnnneeee.

TODDLER B: Noooooooooooo. Miiiiiinnnnnneeeee!!! (Uses dumping feature of truck to shower rival with park detritus.)

(Parents A and B perform emergency landings of their respective helicopters and commence negotiations.)

PARENT A (to her child, using high-performance parenting voice): Can you tell us what it is about this situation that isn't working for you?

TODDLER A: I WANT IIIIIIIIIITT!!!!!!! WAAAAAAAHHH-HHHHH!!!!!!

PARENT A (passive-aggressively directing words more at other parent than her child): Would you like Carson to stop grabbing the dump truck from you because you *obviously* had it first?

PARENT B (ostensibly to her own child but simultaneously throwing other parent bone-chilling your-kid's-a-future-high-school-shooter look): Or, Carson, are you *understandably* upset because Wyatt always thinks he's entitled to the best toys?

(Parents continue to play out own psychodramatic subplot, while kids lose interest in dump truck and take advantage of adults' distraction to enjoy game of "baby brother annihilated in devastating natural disaster.")

I am intrigued by this technique, and I ask a few people about the theory behind it. Sarah, a local mom who I see around a lot in the nearby playgrounds, explains that it helps build kids' self-esteem to be an equal partner at the negotiating table. In her view, a sharp no can be damaging, knocking children's confidence and preventing them coming up with their own solutions to problems. She is convincing, and what she is saying makes sense to me. After all, the more self-esteem, the better surely?

But after a while, I become disillusioned. I try the technique out on Solly from time to time, and also see similar scenes play out many, many times in playgrounds and toddler groups with other children, but yet I never once see an example of toddlers coming to a thoughtful negotiated peaceable resolution of their own. It gets to the point where every time I hear the grammatically contorted phrase "Can you tell us what it is about this situation that isn't working for you," I want to scream "EVERYTHING!!" and grab my child and run.

Perhaps it's because although, on the face of it, this method is supposed to be all about helping children reach their own solutions to problems, in practice it seems to do almost the exact opposite. Rather than actually just staying out of it, letting the kids work it out on their own, and risking some pulled hair and hurt feelings, the parents feel the need to involve themselves in the situation, to *do something*, intervene, and fix. It all feels a bit like working for the worst kind of boss, the kind who micromanages without guidance, who has a single right answer in mind to any given problem, but rather than just telling you what it is he wants you to do, insists on setting a tedious series of psychological tests to see if you can come up with it yourself.

Much has been written in recent years about how American parents have become increasingly overprotective about their children's physical safety, but I've heard less about this similarly hovering, nervous approach to their psychological safety. The alarmist belief system propagated by attachment parenting—that crying in infancy can cause genuine long-term damage—appears to have set the tone for a much wider cultural fear about children's basic emotional fragility.

It's not just in California. I'm scrolling through my Facebook feed when I notice a post from my friend Anna in Wisconsin, a wonderful and devoted stay-at-home mother to her young daughter, Lily, whose frequent enriching craft projects and trips to the zoo always make me feel vaguely inadequate. But it turns out that she's feeling guilty too. Her status update says:

> Today I learnt a valuable lesson. Lily wanted to play but I had to clean up. So I said wait a minute. But then she cried and I realized that I had given her the message that I thought cleaning was more important than she was. I will never ever do that again. From now on, I will never make her wait, and will always put her first, no matter what.

My instant reaction to the post was to think that being made to hold on for a few moments while her mom unloaded the dishwasher certainly wouldn't do Lily any harm, and would probably go a long way in preventing her from turning into an insufferable adult. But it turned out I was squarely in the minority.

Several of Anna's friends joined the thread to comment that not to worry, she had caught her mistake in time, and one slipup like this probably wouldn't cause long-term damage to her daughter, but the point was definitely sound.

Anna had probably internalized the popular Internet homily: "Good moms have sticky floors, messy kitchens, laundry piles, dirty ovens, and happy kids." Versions of this motto turn up in wall decals and Pinterest memes, fridge magnets, and Etsy shop throw pillows. I try to unpick what it is that bothers me about its seemingly innocuous, even generous-spirited message (beyond the 1950s-style retro sexism, that is).

There's something about the way the statement disguises poisonously unachievable expectations behind a saccharine tone of relaxed forgiveness that reminds me of my elderly relative's reassurance when she's popping round to visit that I shouldn't worry, a "simple buffet" will suffice. The implication is that if a mother pauses her intensive child-rearing happiness program for even a moment to do the laundry (let alone get a pedicure or swallow a whiskey shot), she will somehow impair her child's happiness for life. Just the thought of it sends me into an exhausting tailspin of guilt.

Like dealing with the queen, who as urban myth has it, grew up believing that the entire world smells of fresh paint, the American parent's role has become to walk in front of their children sanitizing, reframing, and removing potential negative encounters, rather than allowing them to experience the normal ups and downs of life and then helping them deal with the consequences.

Therapists who work with older children and young adults are increasingly starting to voice concern about this parenting style and its impact on children's ability to develop the resilience necessary to deal with life's challenges. Paul Bohn, a psychiatrist at UCLA, told *The*

Atlantic that he believes that American parents are doing almost anything to avoid their kids experiencing even mildly unpleasant emotions such as discomfort, anxiety, or disappointment. When they turn up at his clinic later in life, they find themselves almost unable to handle difficult situations. "When they experience the normal frustrations of life, they simply can't cope and think something must be terribly wrong," he says.[2]

Child psychologist and Harvard lecturer Dan Kindlon agrees, writing in his book, *Too Much of a Good Thing: Raising Children of Character in an Indulgent Age:* "If kids can't experience painful feelings, they don't develop 'psychological immunity.' It's like the way our bodies' immune systems work. You have to be exposed to pathogens or your body won't know how to respond to an attack. Kids also need exposure to discomfort, failure and struggle."

But what is driving this frenetic edge to American parenting? Perhaps in part it's the fact that, as I'm increasingly finding, life here for young children is quite astonishingly socially segregated.

Apart from a few select low-income groups, prior to kindergarten, there are virtually no government-funded children's services here at all. When Solly was a baby back in the UK, we used to spend a fair portion of our time each week at the local children's center, hanging out at baby groups, toddler drop-ins and "stay and plays," all either at no charge or at heavily subsidized prices. Fifteen hours of preschool a week is free for all children from age three in the UK. Over here it can cost upward of a thousand dollars a month. Although the UK is notorious for its rigid class hierarchy, in reality, families of a wide range of incomes use the same services, attend the same preschools and music groups, and listen to the same fallen-on-hard-times-ex-members of eighties bands strumming the same defeated soft-rock versions of "The Wheels on the Bus."

But here in the States, apart from a twenty-minute story time at the local library and an uninviting-sounding offering called Godly Play at the Methodist church, there are very few structured activities for young children that don't cost money, and usually quite a lot of money.

Toddler classes start at around fifteen to twenty dollars a session, usually with a ten-session minimum sign-up. At these prices, the social mix
is extremely limited. It wouldn't surprise me at all, if in the whole time
we have been living in America, Solly has never played with a child
whose parents don't have a college education.

In this intense and rarefied environment of privilege, stewing in social similarity, middle-class child-rearing ideas that may have started
off as mildly useful tips become distilled and boiled further and further down to an overpowering strength and potency, like a balsamic
reduction, while parents whip each other up into a frenzy of anxiety
and guilt.

Meanwhile, in the absence of any government-provided services or
assistance with childcare, the free market has stepped in, providing an
ever more complex and often costly array of childcare theories, books,
classes, and Web sites. As a result, raising a child in coastal America
now appears to require a guiding philosophy, a quotable governing mas-
ter plan for the child's short- and long-term happiness.

The parenting section of the bookstore is vast and overwhelming.
As well as attachment parenting I come across natural parenting, positive discipline, mindful parenting, educaring, and even something with
a vaguely *Clockwork Orange*–type ring to it called unparenting. These
are just the beginning.

A friend in Seattle tells me about the popularity in her neighborhood
of a multimillion parenting advice empire called Love and Logic, incor-
porating advice books, courses, webinars, conferences, and playgroups.
I look it up to find that the basic package of early childhood Love and
Logic materials, including a book and CD to help me build my child's
self-esteem in those crucial early years, is currently on special offer
at $65.95, while a face-to-face Love and Logic parenting course will set
me back a mere $395 (and who would want to stint? The extra $329.05's
worth of self-esteem could be life altering).

Other parents reject name-brand parenting theories on principle
and go out on a limb to come up with their own. But sometimes the

rethinks of received parenting wisdom aren't necessarily an improvement on the original.

At a toddler playgroup we visit, in a moment of breathtaking cuteness, a two-year-old boy hands a little girl the fire truck he is playing with so that she can have a turn. All the parents gasp, like a group of birdwatchers marveling at a glimpse of a rare new genus of eagle, when out of nowhere, the boy's mom barrels in, grabs the fire truck off the little girl, and hands it back to her son. "We're teaching him that he doesn't always have to share," she explains.

A stay-at-home dad that we invite over with his three-year-old for a playdate and snack tells me that although he believes the words *please* and *thank-you* have their place, he encourages his daughter not to use them when asking for food, as this might somehow embed the notion in her head that eating was a privilege rather than a "basic human right."

Part of me envies these parents' certainty. I often feel out of control as a mother, and crave a unifying theory that will both guarantee Solly's complete and total happiness and make him Just Stop Whining and Get in the Car. In weaker moments, it's hard to resist the siren call of a well-marketed parenting philosophy.

The problem is, I don't have the courage of my convictions to actually choose one and stick with it. Within the course of a single one of Solly's tantrums, I veer wildly between totally opposing philosophies, lurching desperately from banishing him to the naughty step, to validating his feelings; from helping him "climb down his anger mountain," to packing a picnic and escorting him straight back up it again, to pretending we're all French and hoping that somehow if I start addressing him as Jean-Pierre, he'll magically discover some inner Gallic self-control.

But then again, maybe it doesn't matter. Although it is almost impossible to link any particular parenting style with any particular outcome in adulthood, the more I look into it, the more it seems that all this intense and focused thought devoted to the question of how best to create happy children is not really having the desired effect.

Dr. Robert Sears's *Baby Book*, the attachment parenting bible, was published in 1992, and has since sold well over a million copies, setting the tone for a whole new level of parental fervency. The first generation to be parented in this oddly intense way is now of college or recent graduate age. But research suggests that they might actually be *less* happy and secure than previous generations.

Experts have expressed mounting concern about a mental health crisis among college students. The 2013 annual National Survey of College Counseling Centers reported that 95 percent of counselors believed that the number of students with significant mental health issues was a growing concern at their campus, and that a full 44 percent of students using university counseling services are now classified as having "severe psychological problems."[3] Similarly, another survey by the American College Health Association in 2015 showed that around half of all college students had "felt things were hopeless" at some point in the last twelve months and over 35 percent had felt so depressed it was "difficult to function" over the same time period, while well over half had been "overwhelmed with anxiety."[4]

Young adulthood has always been an emotionally tumultuous life stage of course, but there is strong evidence to suggest that these levels of severe anxiety and emotional distress among young people have risen steeply over time. When Dr. Jean Twenge of the University of San Diego analyzed the results from college and high school students taking standardized psychometric tests for personality and psychopathy going back to the late 1930s, her results were shocking. Even after controlling for confounding factors, including the likelihood that modern-day students are likely to feel less of a stigma about reporting mental health symptoms, they still found that in 1938, between 1 and 5 percent of college students scored higher than the clinical cutoff for psychopathology. By 2007, that figure had skyrocketed to 40 percent. Twenge claims that the average high school student now has similar levels of anxiety to the average psychiatric patient in the 1950s.[5]

The driving hope of a generation of parents, that by their own intensive effort they could eliminate negativity for their children and guarantee their happiness, appears to have backfired.

As much as American children are becoming stressed and unhappy, it would seem that their parents are too.

American parents are increasingly preoccupied with the question of whether or not their kids are making them happy. Catering to a generation that has grown up prioritizing personal happiness above almost anything else and obsessing over its every nuance, the "Do My Children Make Me Happy?" parenting think piece has almost become its own subgenre of journalism, played out everywhere from mommy blogs to *The New York Times*. In articles with titles like "Love My Kids, Hate My Life," "Why Parents Hate Parenting," and "Is Having a Baby Really Worth It?" journalists tie themselves up in intellectual knots unpicking the semantics of the word *joy* to try and come up with a definition that somehow includes the sensation of changing four pairs of soiled Thomas the Tank Engine underpants in under two hours.

Heavily peppered with disclaimers about how deeply the writer loves his or her children, these blogs and articles chew over and over the same basic paradox: "This is *hard*. There is ground-up Play-Doh stuck to every part of my being, including my very soul. My child is not responding in the correct manner to the positive-parenting strategy in the book I ordered off Amazon and I'm exhausted. I thought having kids was supposed to make me happy, but I don't *feel* happy."

Popular science has also been nervously circling the same territory, with more academic research studies conducted in recent years into whether children make their parents happy than most of my mother's generation would have thought possible.

The overwhelming result of all this research has been a pretty clear "not really." Oddly—or not oddly at all for those of us who have spent the last hour stuck in traffic on I-580 with a three-year-old shouting "poo-poo nugget" on endless repeat—study after study has shown that people with children are less happy than the childless (or child*free* as they call themselves, while ordering another round of Bellinis).

One influential study from Nobel Prize–winning behavioral economist Daniel Kahneman showed that a large sample group of women in Texas were happier while engaged in almost any given activity other than caring for their own children, including housework.[6] In another particularly depressing piece of research, a group of German academics found that the average drop in happiness in the two years following the birth of a first child is greater than that after divorce, unemployment, and even the death of a partner.[7]

Research shows that the negative effect of having children on personal happiness is greater for women and for those whose children are still young, and declines sharply when they leave home; results which would certainly imply, if not definitively prove, that the more time you actually spend with your kids, the unhappier they make you.

So uneasily does this idea sit, that scientists keep repeating the studies, refining and spinning the methodology, desperately gunning for a different outcome, like a schoolboy repeatedly tossing a coin, then backtracking after each throw: "Best of three . . . no, no, best of five. . . ." After spinning it every which way, the most life-affirming answer researchers have managed to come up with to the question of whether having children makes people happy is a hedging "It depends on the person" (which, incidentally turns out to be the correct answer to every bizarrely universal question posed by academics about whether—insert life choice—makes people happy).

No one likes this result. It provokes profound unease in those of us with children both because it isn't true, and because it is. Most parents would agree that parenthood has opened up an otherwise inaccessible capacity for joy in their lives. But it's the niggling possibility that this data accesses some kind of deeper truth that makes it more unsettling. No one wants to feel that they have made an irreversible life choice proved empirically to be a one-way ticket to misery. These studies laugh in the face of the eternal social bargain between parents and nonparents: they get freedom, we get joy. They get cocktails, we get meaning. Without the coziness of that emotional certainty, parenthood becomes just guilt and feces.

However, none of this stops me from desperately wanting another baby.

Since we first arrived in America Neil and I have been hard at work trying to make one. But as we settle into life in California, my ovaries have clearly decided to retire to Florida for a life of canasta and the early bird special, because nothing is happening.

Every month I sidle sexily over to him, then seductively jab my finger at my iPhone screen, and purr: "For God's sake! What are you waiting for? Fertility Friend says it's a green day! Do you actually *want* Solly to be an only child?" When he follows me upstairs, it is more out of fear than lust. After a year of these joyless shenanigans and no pregnancy to show for it, my panic sets in. I am now thirty-eight and have done enough Google searches to know that the clock is ticking, loudly. We sign up with a fertility clinic.

WE ARRIVE NEARLY an hour early for our appointment, perching nervously in the waiting room, flicking through the chlamydia leaflets and trying to avoid staring at the walls, which are papered with a collage of the clinic's alumnae babies. Gummy babies smiling on blankets. Scarily translucent twins in incubators, bristling with tubes, and heavily accessorized newborns weighed down by outlandishly outsize floral headbands; all of them goading us with their sweet promise of bliss. Peer-reviewed scientific studies definitively proving parental unhappiness crumble to dust, powerless in the face of this carpet-bombing cuteness campaign. Perhaps more than anywhere else I've been on this entire journey, this clinic is holding happiness hostage.

"Given your age, I recommend IVF."

The doctor is matter-of-fact as she delivers her stump speech, compassionate and polished. Using a selection of depressingly sloped graphs, she takes us through what amounts to glaring evidence of a criminal conspiracy between Mother Nature and the Patriarchy. Although other issues are mentioned in passing, there really only appears to be one salient point when it comes to fertility. They should translate it into Latin and engrave it in stone on the building's facade:

ANVS NON POSSVNT INFANTES
CONCIPERE SINE IMPENDIO.
(*Old Women Can't Make Babies Without Paying.*)

We write the clinic a check for the entirety of our savings and embark on a scary lonely journey at the bleeding edge of where Frankensteinian science meets human life.

Our bathroom quickly starts to resemble an amateur production of *Drugstore Cowboy*, littered with empty syringes and the smell of desperation, as I spend months injecting ten thousand dollars' worth of performance enhancers into my ovaries. (In the ultimate metaphor for global gender injustice, Neil's assigned role is to enjoy the clinic's buffet of free porn and provide a sperm sample.)

We set a financial and emotional limit at three attempts at IVF. If it doesn't work after three cycles, then we agree we will resign ourselves to having an only child. I try to convince myself that this is a lucky position to be in, given how many people aren't able to have any children at all.

I am over the moon to be pregnant from the first cycle, but then it ends with a soul-crushing early miscarriage. Then the same thing happens with the second attempt. When I find out that I am pregnant again from our third and final cycle, I will the baby along with gut-twisting worry and many, many hours typing incoherent strings of blood test results into Google with the desperate suffix "will this work???"

Somehow the baby manages to hang in there. The pregnancy is fraught with complications, requiring hospital trips three times a week to be strapped up to monitors. But eventually, a few days after making a heady, guilt-fueled cake in the shape of the entire Bay Area Transportation system for Solly's third birthday, our longed-for second son Zephaniah arrives, every part of him exquisitely, breathtakingly sweet.

My kids were a photo finish with the end of my fertility, and they will always feel like a scarce and precious resource. There is no question in my mind that my life is happier with Solly and Zeph in it.

FUNNILY ENOUGH, DESPITE everything it took to get him, I'm much more relaxed with Zeph than I ever was with Solly. In an unexpected twist, our anchor baby is Californian to his core. I may not be an attachment parent, but he is definitely an attachment baby, refusing to sleep anywhere except in my bed, his little attachment lips clamped to my nipple all night, binge-guzzling breast milk like a tiny Elvis knocking back hamburgers. But most of the time, I'm so happy just to have him, and so busy making sure that his brother doesn't feel jealous or pushed out, that I don't have the time or energy to hyperparent him. We spend most of the early days of Zeph's life sitting on our front step listlessly, with me blissed out and trapped in an endless loop of breastfeeding and Solly waiting eagerly for emergency vehicles to drive past, rubbing his hands with glee every time one does, like a personal injury lawyer.

FREED FROM THE self-imposed crushing belief that my child's entire future happiness hinges on my own performance, motherhood second time around is much more enjoyable. When Solly was a baby, parenting always felt a little as though I was continually taking my driving test, on hyperalert, an imaginary stern public official monitoring and evaluating my every move. With Zeph, I'm not even trying to optimize him and instead can just enjoy him.

I'm not alone in feeling happier as I let go of some of my parenting vigilance. The almost universal adoption of the intense hyperparenting

style by the American upper-middle classes has been shown by research to account for a fair chunk of the rise in parental unhappiness.

Over the last few decades, the expectation of what a parent's role
should involve has been constantly inflating. Time use surveys show that
a mother in 2010 spent an average of four extra hours with her children
every week than her 1965 counterpart, while college educated mothers
put in an extra *nine hours*, despite being far more likely to work outside the home.[8] Much of this time is spent in what sociologists call "con-
certed cultivation" (think scrambling over a jungle gym two inches
behind a four-year-old while maintaining an unbroken educational
commentary about the park's flora and fauna).

But recent research suggests that the more intensely we approach
the job of parenting, and the more strongly we believe that our child's
development and happiness is dependent on our own actions as parents, the more unhappy we become.

Surveying a large group of mothers of children under five, an unusual study published in the *Journal of Child and Family Studies* in 2013
attempted to measure the "intensity" of participants' approach to the
job of parenthood, by asking how strongly they agreed or disagreed with
a range of statements such as "You the mother should always provide
the best, most intellectually stimulating activities to aid in your child's
development." and "It is harder to be a good mother than a corporate
executive." After controlling for confounding factors, the study showed
that the more intense a mother's approach, the unhappier she became
and the greater her risk of depression, with the most intense mothers
experiencing a rate of depression more than three times the level in the
general population.[9]

The continual ramping up of the intensity of American parenting
is a manifestation of a culture that places profound faith in individual
responsibility. The idea that a parent can somehow, through their own
grinding effort, turn out a flawlessly happy child speaks to deep-seated
Calvinist beliefs about hard work and meritocracy.

The narrative that parenting should be an almost entirely individual endeavor can be a hefty emotional burden for parents to shoulder. And as long as we are prepared to do so, society is let off the hook for taking any collective responsibility for children's well-being or for offering any tangible practical support for families.

Because, despite American politicians' frequent sentimentalizing of the family unit, it can often feel as though life is stacked against parents here.

Without a universal system of health care coverage, even the most basic birth in the United States can run to tens of thousands of dollars, and it is typical to start the journey of parenthood heavily burdened by bills or debt. After my uncomplicated C-section plus three nights in hospital with Zeph, we received a bill for more than fifty-five thousand dollars, and our insurance company refused to confirm until much later whether or not they would cover it (eventually they paid for most of it, but the experience was hideously stressful). Although back in London I complained about the inedible food and Victorian plumbing in the run-down National Health Service hospital when I gave birth to Solly, I took it for granted that our care would be unlimited and free.

While in the UK it is typical to take around six months' maternity leave with each baby (most employers offer this and for those that don't, the government steps in), the United States is the only country in the developed world with no federally mandated maternity leave at all, and many of my American friends returned to the office with six-week-old babies at home.

There are few concessions in the workplace for American parents, and little flexible or part-time work available, and so many of these same friends ended up dropping out of the workforce altogether. While all but one of my British friends with children have maintained some variation of their previous jobs, most of my American cohort who are mothers either don't work at all or have massively scaled back their careers since having their children. With no state subsidy or support, childcare is patchy and hugely expensive.

Given these hurdles, it is no accident that American parents are some of the unhappiest in the developed world in comparison to their childless peers. A growing body of research demonstrates that the stronger a country's welfare system and social safety nets, the happier the parents of that country are in comparison with nonparents.[10] If a fraction of the time and emotional energy poured into agonizing over whether children make their parents happy was diverted toward giving practical support to those parents, then net happiness would almost certainly increase.

BUT PERHAPS IT isn't our children's job to be making us happy anyway. Somehow in the midst of all this agonizing, the decision to enter parenthood has become a question of personal gratification, another option in a happiness marketplace overloaded with competing options, filed under *P* between parachute jumps and Pilates.

If this mind-set continues much longer, it won't be the revolution that brings down the bourgeoisie. The middle classes will die out as a species when we all collectively decide that Bikram yoga gives a better happiness return on investment than procreation. But really, if our own children don't make us happy, then rather than rethinking our children, perhaps we should be rethinking our very understanding of happiness.

The more we chew over and over the same questions as to whether having children makes us happy, the more we somehow expect our kids to deliver us our own personal happy-ever-after, to be a source of constant transcendent bliss rather than a normal part of life with the highs and lows of any human relationship. The yawning gap between this fantasy and the more humdrum realities of daily childcare can be hard to bridge.

BUT IF EVEN children, valued throughout human history as our main wellspring of joy and meaning, don't make modern Americans happy, then what does? Is there any foolproof lifestyle or value system that does guarantee a happy life in twenty-first-century America? If so, I want to know what it is. And I'm starting to get the uneasy feeling that the answer might lie somewhere in a family event we have coming up, the thought of which is gripping me with terror.

6.

GOD'S PLAN OF HAPPINESS

Both sets of grandparents are perched nervously in our living room, bitching about the quality of the bagels, not quite as good as those other mythical bagels they used to get from Bakery Utopia in Somewhere-else-ville. The small talk is forced and uneasy, the product of that uniquely suburban Jewish combination of pastel blue cupcakes and imminent genital slicing.

Our families are over from London for Zeph's bris, the formal circumcision ceremony that Jewish boys go through on their eighth day of life. I am love-addled and exhausted, still bleeding, oozing hormones and inexplicably weeping at laundry detergent commercials. Barely more than a week ago, this longed-for baby was still inside my body. In approximately ten minutes time, a stranger will come to our house and sever a section from his penis. I profoundly do not want to be here.

So why are we doing this? The motivation isn't exactly religious, at least not in the strictest fear-of-God sense. As a family, we are what you might call Jew-*ish*. My husband, Neil, has the kind of hyper-Semitic look that means that the instant he puts on any kind of hat—whether baseball cap, Stetson, or bishop's mitre—he is instantly transformed into a Hasid. But he ditched the religious part of his religion the moment he had squawked his way through his bar mitzvah portion, retaining only a lingering all-purpose sense of guilt and a love of discussing his health complaints at the dinner table. I am technically only half Jewish, and we are, at most, agnostic. (Neil calls it "atheist." I only stop short as a hedge against lightning strikes.) So we could have opted out, invoking my Methodist grandmother or crying "child mutilation" like many of our mixed-marriage friends.

But, to my surprise, my atheist husband—the same man who, when asked to be godfather to a friend's child, renamed his role "Dawkins-father" (I wasn't impressed. If anyone's running a more sexist ship than God, it's Richard Dawkins)—felt strongly that he wanted his sons to be part of the tribe. Apparently, the uneasy truce we have reached with the mash-up of our genes and beliefs is that our kids get a Christmas tree every year but must pay for it with their foreskins. Because for Neil, this peculiar infant hazing, a ritual stretching back in time to Abraham, and toughed out by virtually every Jewish boy since, is the ultimate act of welcome, the mark of belonging.

And although Neil's path to this decision was obviously more "instinctive tribalism" than "positive psychology journal," in one left-field but important way, he is right. Everything I have learned so far about happiness points toward community identity and strong social bonds being the single biggest factor. And apparently I'm convinced enough by this fact that I am prepared to stake my son's penis on it.

The doorbell rings, and there stands the mohel, wheeling behind him a suitcase so large it looks as though his cutting tool of choice must be a samurai sword. I cling to my sweet baby and fight the urge to run.

After a few more bagels and a little more bitching, I reluctantly hand Zeph to his grandpa, who holds him tight on his lap. I look away. There's a hideous minute, a flurry of newborn fussing, a prayer, and then it's over. Afterward, I hold the very newest member of the tribe tight, and we all sing "*Siman tov u mazel tov*" to him as tears stream down my face. Ever so briefly, I understand the bright magic of belonging.

·   ·   ·

LOGIC HAS NO torturer like the self-justifying mother—and perhaps I'm just constructing a fancy rationalization for what really just amounts to fear of what my in-laws think—but the more I look into this topic, the more I start to feel that maybe we really have given Zeph a happiness head start in life.

There's an oddly consistent pattern in the happiness research that I'm finding increasingly hard to ignore. Study after study has shown that there is one distinct group of people consistently found to be happier than any other group, reporting higher levels of well-being across all measures. This is a finding that holds true across race, gender, social class, and income, and the difference is significant. That group is religious people.

Surveys by the Pew Research Center, Gallup, and the National Opinion Research Center agree that religious people are significantly more likely to report being "very happy" than nonbelievers.[1] A wide range of other studies has shown repeatedly that identifying as part of a religious community is a predictor of greater life satisfaction, higher self-esteem, more social ties, and an ability to cope better with difficult life events.

Perhaps this link between religion and happiness goes partway toward explaining the curmudgeonly nature of the British people. Back in the UK, showing any overt or excessive signs of religious belief is generally just "not done." In certain sections of liberal London, it is more socially acceptable to come out as an alcoholic than a Christian. Unlike American politicians who are apparently unelectable without a high-profile leg up from the Almighty, former British Prime Minister Tony Blair treated his devout Christianity almost as a dirty secret while in office, potentially more embarrassing to a British statesman than, say, the revelation that he was screwing his intern or the accidental tweeting of a photo of his penis.

So when my husband tells me that he has made friends with a devout Mormon at work, I am desperately curious. Stephen lives in Salt Lake City and has four children, which, as he tells Neil, is a small family by Mormon standards. His wife, Laura, is a stay-at-home mom and, since marriage, has never worked outside the home. Married at twenty-one, they are anti-sex before or outside of marriage, anti–gay marriage and anti-abortion, all of which are virtually unheard-of positions among our social circle.

At Christmas, Stephen and Laura send us a card that is more like a full brochure of their family, bursting with pictures of gleaming blond children engaged in wholesome activities, accompanied by a round-robin letter unashamedly spattered with Bible quotes and unironic references to "thankfulness" and "Christ." For us, in our world of snarky liberals and obligatory postmodern irony, they seem like a rarity, as though they must hold the keys to the magic kingdom of happiness.

And statistically speaking, this might well be true. Not only are religious people in the United States generally significantly happier than nonreligious people, but if the studies are to be believed, Mormons are the happiest of all.[2] On almost every measure, Mormons appear to be outpacing the rest of America. Around 90 percent of Mormons rate their communities as excellent or good, compared with just 70 percent of Americans generally.[3] Mormons have some of the lowest rates of unemployment in the country; and according to Gallup polls, Provo, Utah, where close to 90 percent of the population identifies as religious Mormon, is officially the happiest town in America.[4]

So is it that simple? Could all the books in the personal development section of the bookstore be condensed into one single three-word e-book? *How to Be Happy: The Definitive Answer:* Become a Mormon. The end.

Mormons certainly look happy, at least if certain corners of the Internet are anything to go by. Mormon housewife and mommy blogs have proliferated in the last few years. An idyllic vision of an alternative life, the 1950s made flesh, where large numbers of children remain clean and eagerly perform chores, mothers burst with fulfillment at staying at home and doing elaborate craft projects, and no one ever gets resentful or guilty or tortures themselves about how to express their true identity. The picture couldn't be further from the tormented my-children-are-making-me-miserable think pieces in the liberal press. With their complete absence of inner turmoil, these blogs are strangely addictive. I read them sneakily on my phone while breastfeeding Zeph as the laundry piles up around me, and secretly wonder whether maybe, just maybe, I might have backed the wrong horse.

Mormons, as a group, are highly conservative. They don't drink tea or coffee, let alone alcohol. They overwhelmingly vote Republican. The church advocates strict traditional gender roles, with men out providing and women at home looking after the (many) children. Black people were not permitted to hold the highest religious honors within the church until 1978. Women still aren't.

It all throws up a strange cognitive dissonance for me, like one of those logical paradox tricks that somehow mathematically prove that your name is Brian or that you are a giraffe. The statistics seem to point clearly to the idea that I would be much happier doing a lot of things that don't sound as though they would make me very happy at all. Spending lots of time in church. Having several more children. Giving up alcohol. (These last two seem particularly mutually exclusive.) Submitting to the patriarchy. Joining the Republican Party. Would I really be happier if I were a Mormon?

Then again, I have to admit, in the last few months, my way hasn't exactly been delivering the goods. So far, my lived experience of parenting two children is a lot closer to "tortured feminist think piece" than "Pinterest-perfect Mormon mommy blog." Since the arrival of his new brother, Solly is finding the sudden transition from cloyingly overparented to devastatingly underparented a nasty shock, and is giving voice to his dissatisfaction in an almost unbroken series of tantrums. Zeph will still only sleep when physically attached to me, dependent on my body like an iron lung. Our apartment is a swamp of baby paraphernalia and overwhelm, and Neil and I are ragged with exhaustion.

Happiness researchers draw a distinction between "life satisfaction," meaning the deeper overall assessment of a person's well-being when taken as a whole, and the more fickle moment-to-moment happiness of our changing moods. The latest thinking goes that these two kinds of happiness work independently of each other, and it is possible to have one without the other. Now, for the first time, I can understand this phenomenon. Without a doubt, my boys bring me the deep kind of happiness, but sometimes, around dinnertime, staring down the barrel of the evening ahead, with urgent simultaneous child need in piercing stereo, that happiness can feel like it's buried so deep it would take a specialist team of navy divers to locate it.

So when Stephen and Laura hear about my secret ten-a-day Mormon mommy-blog habit and invite me to come and stay with them in their home in Salt Lake City to get a taste of the real thing, I am excited and deeply curious. I am desperate to ask them (and especially her): "Is your life really like that? Do you never feel bored or pissed off or ambivalent or resentful?"

I have seen my fair share of magazine features and documentaries about Mormonism over the years, but they always seemed to feature the same family, headed up by a polygamist child abuser who is now in jail (in reality the church disavowed polygamy in 1890). I can understand how this has happened. During my years working in TV production, I also made my fair share of documentaries that involved tracking down the Weirdest Person on Earth and then insisting that they were representative of some pressing social phenomenon needing urgent discussion. But really, I am fascinated by Stephen and Laura's life not because they are fringe weirdos on the margins of society but because they are in many ways, just like us—a similar age, life stage, and education level. But at the same time, their lifestyle feels like something that my mother fought to escape and everything my own belief system (in as much as I have one) rejects.

So I'm hoping that while I'm in Salt Lake City, I'll find out what it is that makes their life, at least statistically speaking, the happiest on offer in America.

· · ·

WHILE I WAIT for Zeph to lessen his alarming dependency on my boobs so that I can leave him overnight, I take a trip to our local Mormon Temple in Oakland for some background research.

I've wanted to visit this place ever since we first arrived in California, so it's good to have an excuse to go. A vast Disneyland-style fantasy castle rising up on the hill, its ornate golden turrets spiking the heavens, the temple is a notorious local landmark, apparently even used by pilots to navigate into the airport at night. A stately ornamental lake leads up to the temple's front door, lined with towering palm trees. Several three-tiered fountains form an intricate water feature, gushing out scarce California water.

The temple itself is off limits to non-Mormons, but I've been told that the adjoining visitors' center is both welcoming and comprehensively diligent in explaining the Mormon belief system to the nonbeliever (who, they presumably hope, is merely a pre-believer).

The moment I walk in the door of the visitors' center, I find myself face-to-face with Jesus Christ. This is not metaphorical or the beginnings of a conversion revelation. The entrance hall is completely dominated by a giant statue of Jesus, at least twice my height, his huge hands outstretched proudly toward a panoramic domed fresco of the night sky as if to say, "My dad made all this." I'm just admiring this impressive effect when suddenly, to my alarm, Giant Jesus starts talking.

"Behold, I am Jesus Christ," he says, in booming surround sound. His voice is uncannily similar to the wonder and awe "Origin of Creation" voice-over at the planetarium. I suppose this must be deliberate. After all, I guess they are direct competitors.

I wait for Jesus to finish talking, then walk past him to a museum-style display of exhibits and leaflets to read up on Mormon doctrine.

I learn that Mormonism, officially known as the Church of Jesus Christ of Latter-day Saints, is technically a branch of Christianity but also subscribes to a gripping sequel to the Bible called the Book of

Mormon, featuring Jesus Christ, two hundred years after he is resurrected, taking a trip to America.

The contents of this book were apparently engraved on some golden plates, hidden for several hundred years, and then found by a man named Joseph Smith, after receiving a vision from an angel called Moroni, revealing their secret location. Unfortunately for theological scholars, Smith gave the gold plates back to the angel Moroni before anyone could verify their existence, but this didn't stop him founding a new religion based on their teachings, attracting tens of thousands of followers before being killed by an angry mob at the age of thirty-eight.

I'm just browsing a display entitled "Our Heavenly Father's Plan for Families," when two wholesome-looking teenage girls in long skirts approach me. They introduce themselves and tell me that they are sister missionaries, which sounds like a niche category of pornography but apparently means that they are on an eighteen-month-long proselytizing mission, something that Mormon teenagers are encouraged to do after leaving high school to spread the gospel across the world. (Or at least, girls are encouraged. Boys are required.)

"Would you like to know about God's Plan of Happiness?" one of the sister missionaries asks me.

Having spent the last year or so complaining about the poor credentials of many of the leading happiness experts, this feels like significant progress.

"Yes, please," I say.

THE SISTER MISSIONARIES lead me into a purpose-built movie theater to watch a video that they tell me will reveal God's personal secret to a happy life.

(Spoiler: It's family.)

According to the Mormon Church (acting in its role as God's spokesperson on earth), the key to happiness is to be heterosexual, married, and to procreate.

The video stars an impeccably cast mom with just the right mix of pretty and careworn, and a dad who does DIY after nightfall so he can devote his days to "wholesome recreational activities" with his children. Every time the voice-over refers to any form of fun, it uses the entire phrase "wholesome recreational activities," which I assume is designed to head unwholesome thoughts off at the pass, but seems to have the complete opposite effect on me. Every time the narrator says the word *recreational*, for the first time since giving birth, all I can think about is drugs.

The film cuts to a flashback scene in which the couple's first child is a newborn and they are putting her to bed in her pastel-hued nursery. The mom lays the baby down in her crib, and she instantly drifts off into a deep, peaceful sleep without a murmur, behavior which is so markedly different from my own wailing, thrashing, never-sleeping infant that animal behaviorists would probably classify them as two separate species.

Are all Mormon babies like this? I wonder. No wonder they're all so happy. Whatever the doubters may say, Joseph Smith certainly can't have been any more of a charlatan than the ridiculously overpriced sleep consultant to whom we recently donated a month's salary. I instantly decide to convert.

THE FOUNDING FATHERS may have agonized over the best way to preserve and institutionalize individual liberty, but in my mind there is no doubt. The truest expression of personal freedom that this life can offer is the experience of giving birth to children, raising them, and then traveling without them.

Carrying a tiny case—which contains no diapers, bottles, spare underpants, or crumbled ghosts of animal crackers, and with no one crying or whining or giving me a detailed rundown of the individual attributes of each train in the Thomas empire—waiting in the airport security line feels like a spa break. I wonder for the millionth time how

Laura and her friends do it, with four or more children at home full-time, and no job to retreat to for a bit of mental space. I pick up a rental car and drive out of Salt Lake City airport, breathless with liberty.

Like many American cities, Salt Lake is a kind of man-made iden-tikit dreariness superimposed onto a backdrop of spectacular natural majesty. The highway is lined with drab motels and fast-food billboards, but behind them, the magnificent tips of snow-capped mountains rise out of the mist, like a child's drawing of where God lives. I am so busy staring at this awe-inspiring effect that I take the wrong exit off the freeway and find myself hurtling toward Las Vegas. The further from Salt Lake City and closer to Vegas I get, the more anxious, stressed, and unhappy I feel; and the allegorical nature of this feels crashingly unsub-tle, as though I'm a character in a Sunday school morality tale about to come to a sorry end.

Stephen and Laura live in a well-heeled, heavily Mormon suburb, on a street with the same utterly mystifying numbering system of streets all over America, whereby on a tiny suburban lane of thirty houses, you find yourself desperately searching for house number 14,039. After driving up and down the street three times, eventually I find their place, and ring the doorbell.

I think Stephen might be the only person I have ever met who apol-ogizes for how tidy things are when he opens the door. "It's not normally this clean," he says in the exact inverse of my own standard door-opening apology. (Over the course of the weekend, I will come to re-alize that he is lying. It *is* normally this clean. You can't fake it for that long.) Inside, the house looks magazine perfect, recently remodeled with a fully matching interior and spanking new smell.

Stephen himself is about my age, trim from many hours of com-petitive cycling. Clearly highly intelligent—he studied law at an Ivy League university and is now a highflier in the business world—he is disarmingly open, telling me that I should feel free to ask any question and that he will try to answer as honestly as he can.

I know that Stephen and Laura's four children are home, but as well as being unusually clean, the house is also uncannily quiet. If I didn't know that there were kids living here, I would assume it was an adult-only household, with the atmosphere of quiet order and the striking total absence of sports gear and school papers and landfill-busting piles of colored plastic. The kids themselves, one boy and three girls—all modest skirts and *Little House on the Prairie* braids—are impeccably behaved. They don't disturb the adults and come in and out only occasionally from their bedrooms to get something or draw quietly at a table.

I think back to our apartment with its tangles of laundry, metastasizing Cheerios, disintegrating confetti of preschool art that I am paralyzed to either keep or throw out, and two boys constantly teetering on the precipice of total meltdown. Laura has clearly not only got on top of domestic chaos but has whipped it into meek obedience, like a Mormon dominatrix leading an investment banker around on a dog leash.

She doesn't seem remotely scary though. Warm and instantly likable, Laura is sitting at the dining room table, looking relaxed dressed in sweats and glasses, behind what looks like an impressive array of specialist hole punchers of different sizes. In front of her, the table is covered in several hundred blue and gold cardboard circles. After we introduce ourselves and make a bit of small talk, I ask her what she is doing.

"I'm making garlands," she says.

After coming to Salt Lake City secretly hoping to expose Mormon reality as Nothing Like a Mommy Blog, hearing the word *garland* just minutes after arriving feels like a significant setback.

"What are they for?" I ask.

"I'm hosting a bridal shower here tomorrow. It's a luncheon. I've invited about seventy people."

I look at her. "*Seventy?*"

"I've invited most of the women in the ward. Or at least anyone who could conceivably be interested." She looks a bit embarrassed.

Laura is acting like all this is nothing, and not a stagy, chest-clasping "this old rag?" kind of "this is nothing," but a genuine feeling that it is actually No Big Deal to single-handedly sew two thousand cardboard circles into garlands and then cook lunch for seventy people with four children to take care of.

And you're doing all this without alcohol? I think to myself. I briefly wonder whether the real question behind the entirety of our religious and lifestyle difference is whether I am using drinking to compensate for my lack of garlands, or whether Laura is using garlands to compensate for her lack of drinking.

"Who is the bride?" I ask instead.

"Her name's Annabel. I used to teach her in Sunday school a while ago. She's an undergrad at the university."

"How old is she?"

"Twenty-one."

Twenty-one? An image of the boyfriend I had at twenty-one flashes into my brain, and I feel a brief and overwhelming gush of relief that we are not now married and living in Utah with our five children. Making a final and binding decision about a lifelong partner so early in life feels instinctively lunatic to me.

"Wow! That seems so young to get married," I blurt out.

It's the wrong thing to say. Stephen bristles. I realize, of course, that Stephen and Laura got married at twenty-one too, and that this is a very typical age for Mormons to marry. I immediately start apologizing.

"I'm sorry. I guess that was offensive." I backtrack.

"Not offensive, but a bit condescending," Stephen replies. It's a good response. For a certain kind of secular liberal, when discussing religion, "offensive" has become almost a point of pride, a mark of debating rigor. But it's hard to find anything good about condescending. But for some reason, I feel compelled to press on.

"Would you be happy for your daughters to marry at twenty-one?" I ask. "You wouldn't just think 'Noooooooo!!! You're too young!'?"

"Not even remotely," says Stephen. "I'd be more worried about them getting too old. Most of the women I know from work are in their thirties and wanting to get married, but with no clear idea of how to meet anyone. Or if they are living with their male partner, he shows no interest in getting married. Why would he? He already has the dedicated sex and he's too juvenile to realize that marriage is so much more than that. When I was working in New York I honestly didn't know anyone who wasn't in a situation like that, and I had twenty plus women working for me."

I mull this over. I can't help thinking that the whole "bitter childless feminist who left it too late to get married," is just as much of a lazy stereotype as "oppressed Mormon wife with more children than opinions." Quite aside from the question of whether marriage should be seen as such a defining life goal, when I think about my friends, pretty much anyone who ever expressed any interest in the idea is now married, and with the exception of one woman in my birth group who had her first child at twenty-seven and got treated like a teenage mother, we all managed to pull off this apparently impossible feat in our thirties.

Probably fortunately, we are interrupted from continuing the discussion by the doorbell ringing. It's a neighbor dad, who has come to ask if Laura would mind babysitting for three of his young children for a few hours tomorrow night, while the rest of the family is at a baptism preparation class. This would raise the total number of children in the house to seven, which sounds like a terrifying prospect to me, but to my surprise, Laura agrees enthusiastically and generously, and doesn't even bitch about it after the door closes behind him.

After that, the doorbell doesn't stop ringing for the entire rest of the evening. Every half hour or so, someone shows up on an errand or for a chat or to drop off some kind of baked dessert. A woman comes over to show Laura a historic flyer from the church's women's group and to discuss the next meeting. A neighbor stops by with a jar of chocolate spread as a birthday gift for one of Stephen and Laura's three daughters. (I had barely even registered that it was her birthday—unlike in our house where all human activity is suspended and diverted toward the glorification of the birthday child, she and her siblings have been quietly amusing themselves the entire evening.) A whole family of neighbors rings on the doorbell, and then bursts into a spontaneous chorus of "Happy Birthday" in enthusiastic harmony on the doorstep. A woman turns up to give back a pie dish that she had borrowed, returning it complete with homemade cookies inside.

I try to remember the last time anyone popped over to our house unannounced who wasn't trying to either sell us something or convert us to something, and come up empty-handed. The whole thing is so warm and generous and community spirited, it's hard not to like it.

IN AN INDIVIDUALISTIC culture, in which we are primed to see happiness as the result of a private internal journey, people often see the magic ingredient in the link between religion and happiness as the personal sense of meaning that a religious faith brings. But when researchers have drilled down into the reasons why religious people are happier, it turns out that the opposite is true. It isn't the inner journey of private religious belief that is making religious people so happy but the community and social connectedness that comes with a religious lifestyle.[5]

Religion is a uniquely powerful community builder. Research by Robert D. Putnam, author of *Bowling Alone* and *American Grace*, shows that people who regularly attend religious services are more likely to give to charity, do volunteer work, help the homeless, donate blood, help out a neighbor, and spend time with someone who is feeling depressed.[6] Almost all the studies that show that religious people are happier than the nonreligious also show that they tend to have a greater number of social ties and stronger and more supportive communities. When the studies control for these increased levels of social connection, the link between religion and happiness almost always disappears.

Now, at Stephen and Laura's, seeing this super-strength Mormon community-spirit in action, this research makes complete sense.

. . .

ALTHOUGH I HADN'T expected it to be quite this constant, I had half expected to see this kind of neighborly goodwill here in Salt Lake City.

What I'm more surprised to find out is how on top of this informal community building, there is another whole layer of detailed structured support and volunteer networking organized and tightly controlled by the Mormon Church.

All evening, both Stephen and Laura have been dropping offhand references into our conversation about different types of volunteer work that they do for the church and the Mormon community. Every time I think I have a rough handle on how many hours they are putting in each week, they keep adding something else.

When I do finally ask them to pin it down to some actual numbers, I am honestly staggered by the amount of unpaid labor they are clocking up on a weekly basis for church and community-related causes.

Stephen tells me that the church officially assigns every adult member a specific calling, or designated volunteer job within the church structure that can be anything from bishop (the Mormon Church has no paid clergy) to Sunday school teacher to cleaning supervisor. Depending on the job, it can take from a few hours to ten or more each week. Laura tells me that she once had a calling organizing a Christmas crèche that in the winter months took up to twenty-five hours a week.

Then on top of their calling, every man in the church is assigned a handful of families that he must visit every month to teach Scripture, and visits are typically at least half an hour long. (They will also receive similar visits at home each month from someone else.) Women have a similar requirement to teach other women. All church members are required to help clean church buildings, adding on another few hours every quarter. Every Monday night the church stipulates that families should stay home, have dinner together, and discuss church-sanctioned topics. Then, in addition, most active Mormons take on several hours of additional volunteer work, raking leaves, visiting sick ward members, and helping out on various church-related projects. This is all, of course, on top of three hours of church every Sunday.

It makes me feel both exhausted and kind of ashamed listening to it all. At Solly's preschool, each family is required to contribute fifteen hours of volunteer work per *year*, and it is only the risk of being found out that stops me putting it up on TaskRabbit. A typical Mormon can easily clock that much up in a couple of weeks.

And alongside all this more-official unpaid labor—listening to Laura talk, especially for women—there is also the clear expectation that people will also help one another out informally too, babysitting one another's kids, making potluck dishes for neighborhood social occasions, and hosting parties for one another's milestones.

If the average American spends less than four minutes a day "hosting and attending social events," Mormons seem to be doing so much to bump this average up that everyone else in America must be actively sabotaging social events.

THE INTRICATE VOLUNTEER economy of the Mormon Church doesn't just mean that everyone in the community stays well stocked with casseroles and Bible verses. I am surprised when Stephen tells me that the Mormon Church is also running perhaps the most detailed and comprehensive welfare system in the country, short of the federal government's.

EVEN WITH MY atrocious sense of direction, Welfare Square is hard to miss. A vast industrial complex in downtown Salt Lake City, with a cluster of factories and a towering grain silo and elevator rising a hundred and seventy feet into the sky, the hub of the Mormon Church's nationwide welfare program is visible from quite a distance.

When Stephen first mentioned this place, I had visualized something along the lines of a soup kitchen or the Salvation Army, somewhere the needy could turn up and get a hot meal or a secondhand winter coat. But even from the outside, it's clear that this is an operation on an entirely different scale from anything I could have imagined.

Another pair of sister missionaries meets me at the entrance to give me a tour. I'm starting to think that the boys must get given all the high-prestige missions off converting the natives in Africa, leaving the girls behind showing old ladies round the visitors' centers of Utah.

It doesn't appear to bother them however. Even though I'm the only person here, they take me on an enthusiastic and detailed tour of the whole site, an area covering several acres.

First they explain the basics of the system. Every month, each member of the Mormon Church is encouraged to skip two meals and donate the money that they would have spent on that food to the church's welfare program, with many church members choosing to pay significantly more that amount (this is in addition to the 10 percent of their total income that all Mormons are required to tithe to the church). Although the church doesn't publish figures, with more than fourteen million church members worldwide (six million of those in the United States), these so-called fast offerings must push the annual church welfare budget well into the billions, funding a full-scale welfare program for any church member in need as well as many non-Mormons seeking help.

First stop on the tour is the bishops' storehouse, a 570,000-square-foot warehouse, filled to the brim with food and household basics, buzzing with forklifts lifting and loading. I stare down the sweeping rows of shelves, piled high with vast pallets of boxed food rising to the ceiling and as far as the eye can see. Beef stew. Applesauce. Toilet paper. I make a mental note of where to come in the event of the Apocalypse.

This storehouse is one of a network of more than a hundred similar ones across the entire country. What I am surprised to learn is not that the church stores food to donate to those in need but that they have taken control of the entire food chain, from growth to processing, packaging to distribution. The sister missionaries tell me that much of the food in here, spanning virtually every type of commonly eaten household staple, is grown at church-owned farms; processed, canned, and packaged at church-owned industrial plants; and distributed across the country by a church-owned trucking company.

Our next stop is a full-scale industrial cannery, with a fleet of highly professional-looking volunteer workers in white coats and hairnets, churning out cans of tomatoes and soup and spaghetti. Then we see a similarly scaled bakery, making thousands of loaves of bread and other baked goods out of grain from the vast silos towering over the complex. There's an industrial dairy plant, bottling the milk of a herd of seven thousand Mormon cows out in Provo, as well as turning it into surprisingly tasty yogurt, cheese, chocolate milk, and puddings. (They give out free samples.)

Then there's the grocery store, where welfare recipients come to shop for their products, using special chits given to them by the bishop, and the hub of the church's trucking company, with a large fleet of trucks distributing all this food to the sub-storehouses across the nation. There's a clothes store, which accepts donations of used clothes and then sells them, that looks more like a Walmart than a Goodwill, and a fully serviced on-site employment center. It's hard not to be impressed at the sheer scale of the operation.

Over the course of the tour, I lose count of how many times the sister missionaries use phrases like "self-reliance" or "not a handout." The motto is posted everywhere, on signs and display boards: "Foster Self-Reliance." The clear philosophy is that Mormon welfare is about "helping people to help themselves," and welfare recipients usually do volunteer work at the Welfare Square site in return for their benefits. This is a deeply American take on welfare.

The Mormon welfare program potentially explains a significant chunk of the happiness advantage of this community. In international comparison studies, people living in countries with strong government-run social welfare systems consistently rate as happier than citizens of countries with less comprehensive safety nets.[7] It is not hard to see why.

Living with the background fear that if you fall, there will be no one who will pick you up can produce a happiness-sucking constant low-level anxiety. Compared to most of Europe, America's safety nets for welfare and health care are thin and threadbare. But visiting Welfare Square, it's easy to see how an active member of the Mormon Church is likely to feel as protected and cushioned as they would in Scandinavia.

This level of protection doesn't just make people feel cheerier, it genuinely provides more opportunities and better life outcomes. Despite the deep-seated faith in the American dream, a number of studies show that the United States has one of the lowest rates of social mobility in the developed world, with a child born to a poor family in America more likely to remain poor than they would in almost any other comparable country.[8] But Utah, and particularly Salt Lake City with its strong Mormon communities and robust alternative welfare system, bucks this trend. A child born poor in Salt Lake City is more likely than any poor child in America to make it to a position of economic security in adulthood, with the city's social mobility levels on a par with Denmark's—the best in the developed world.[9]

THE NEXT DAY is the day of the bridal shower, and back at Stephen and Laura's I wake up at 7 a.m. after the best night's sleep I've had in four years to an uncanny quiet. I stumble into the bathroom, hoping to slip past unnoticed and get back to bed, only to find all four children hard at work, industriously scrubbing the shower and mopping the floor in highly choreographed formation, like a lost scene from the *Sound of Music*.

I head upstairs instead. I can't drink coffee—caffeinated hot drinks are forbidden to Mormons and I'm not sure whether that extends to visitors. I sneak some tea that I have stashed away in my bag, burying the tea bag in the garbage like a used needle. I'm just gulping it down guiltily when the whole family files in together for their morning Scripture reading and prayer. They tell me that they do this every day, including during the scramble of getting four children out of the door to school on time. (Stephen does his own private Scripture reading every morning before the family one when he gets up at 4:30 a.m.)

Strangely, the whole thing makes me miss my noisy, messy boys, and the chaotic and unpredictable swirl of life at home. After feeling so overwhelmed by the loss of control that came with a combination of two children and my own parenting shortcomings, I am surprised to find this level of controlled orderly virtue a little oppressive. I realize just how many of my life's greatest joys have stemmed from a basic guiding philosophical combination of "screw this" and "oh, whatever."

BY NOON, WITH everyone helping, the bridal shower garlands are hung, the salads are prepared, the individually hand-painted white and silver cookies are wrapped, and the guests start to show up, leaving their shoes at the door to protect the pristine floor.

As I wander round making small talk with the guests, I start to get an odd sensation. The conversations I am having are giving me the uncanny impression of a movie in which a series of different actresses play the same character at different ages and stages of life. The guests are all women, aged from eighteen to eighty-one, but age seems to be pretty much the only point of diversity. Everyone here seems to be at different points on the time line of the exact same life.

Apart from a rather highly strung–seeming former first lady of Utah—whose husband went on to serve in Bush's cabinet—who is flitting skittishly from person to person, making maniacally high-pitched small talk, everyone I talk to is either a stay-at-home mom, a student soon planning to become a stay-at-home mom, or a retired stay-at-home mom. All those with children have a minimum of four. Their husbands are highfliers—lawyers and doctors and even an architect who works designing the fantasy-princess-castle temples for the Mormon Church.

Everyone looks relaxed. Stella, who has just had her fourth child a couple of months ago and is carrying the baby with her in a car seat, looks about twenty-five years old, fresh faced as though recently back from a restful vacation. I talk to one woman of about my age who has seven children, the youngest of whom is exactly the same age as my son Zeph. Although she has a slightly jumpy, darting-eyed nervous energy about her, she doesn't seem to be actively Losing Her Shit, which is what I feel like doing just from the idea of seven children. A few people mention another friend who hasn't made it to the party because although she already has eight children, she is currently in China, adopting another one.

I ask the question "How do you do it?" over and over again. I do not mean it rhetorically. I am actually hoping for a minute-by-minute break-down with instructions, and ideally a home-consultancy visit. One of the women I ask, a kindly and wise elder of eighty-one, with eight children and numerous grandchildren and great-grandchildren, responds by throwing the question back to me. "You have two children, don't you?" she asks.

"Yes."

"And they take up all of your time?" I nod vigorously.

"Well there's no such thing as more than all of your time. So eight children can't take up more of it."

Logically bamboozled, I later find out that while raising her eight children she also published seven books on homemaking skills. Laura gives me one of them to take home later. There's a section in it about "every woman's mending basket." It is not a euphemism.

My attempts to dig up any self-justifying simmering low-level un-happiness or domestic bitterness among this group are totally unsuccessful. Instead I get a series of slightly bemused looks and responses along the lines of "It's such a blessing" or "I am so thankful I am able to be home with them."

I talk to the bride's best friend, Becky, a student at Brigham Young, the Mormon university, who tells me that she has organized a surprise bachelorette party for Annabel for that night. "Where are you going?" I ask, wondering what's left for a bachelorette party that can't involve alcohol, strippers, or staggering around bad nightclubs in a dildo tiara.

"We're going pole dancing," she says.

"Really?" I ask, intrigued. "Is that allowed?"

She chooses her words carefully. "Pole dancing isn't specifically addressed in Mormon doctrine," she says finally.

IN COMPARISON WITH most of my cohort who hobbled down the aisle in our mid- to late thirties in Spanx and antiaging cream, Annabel, with her shiny brown hair and eager smile, seems like a child bride. I want to tuck her in and read her a story. She is brimming with happiness and excitement.

Part of me wants to grab her and shout "No!! Don't get married just because this is the only way you can have sex! Go out, meet lots of boys, sleep around! Get a career, travel, have fun. Don't shackle yourself to a man and a brood of kids when you are this young and beautiful."

But then again, I have to admit, that the women I've met today, who are living the exact same life that Annabel is about to embark on, at least on the face of it, certainly seem happy and fulfilled.

I've been thinking about what Stephen was saying yesterday, about the women he knew in New York leaving marriage too late, and, much as I hate to admit it, I wonder whether there might be a grain of truth in that whole picture. Although most of my friends do now have children, it was an uphill struggle for many of us to get there. Neil and I weren't the only ones who ended up spending tens of thousands of dollars on IVF, and we were lucky. I know a fair few people who never got the second or even first child they longed for. And then, after annihilating our ovaries and our bank accounts attempting to conceive our children, we then apparently spend the entire next decade of our lives whining about how unhappy they make us. Maybe if we had them at twenty-two, we wouldn't feel quite so keenly that they were robbing us of our freedom.

I wonder if the women I met today might be happier precisely because they don't feel paralyzed by choices, by having to think every last decision through from first principles and never feeling fully committed to any path, always keeping one foot in the Land of Infinite Options. Perhaps having a strict blueprint for how to live actually removes the anxiety from the search for happiness, and my own gut instinct that Annabel should have a decade of freedom and sex and cocktails before getting stuck into domestic drudgery is really just a self-serving prejudice.

I SUPPOSE WHEN it comes down to it, the real sticking point for me isn't so much the marrying young but the strict gender roles and inequality of status between men and women in Mormon culture.

Not all Mormon women are stay-at-home moms, of course. Especially outside of Utah, there are plenty who go out to work or who never had children, and to be fair, Stephen is certainly not a 1950s dad, kicking back with the remote control and a mocktail. He is clearly a very involved parent, and like Laura, is in constant industrious motion doing jobs. He takes pains to point out that women are not there to serve men, and that both men and women are serving together, equally valued in their respective roles.

But I just can't quite buy it. "By divine design, fathers are to preside over their families, and are responsible to provide the necessities of life and protection" declares the Mormon Church's Proclamation on the Family, the official document laying out their stance on family relationships and gender roles. "Mothers are primarily responsible for the nurture of their children. In these sacred responsibilities, fathers and mothers are obligated to help one another as equal partners."

I've heard the whole different-but-equal argument before in various incarnations, both in relation to gender roles and to race, and I've always found it a bit disingenuous. It's not just that in this particular document the "equal partners" is ever so slightly undermined by the telltale "preside" (and of course by the fact that Mormon women don't have the priesthood, the highest religious honor of the church). Of course there are many people of both sexes who, given a free choice, find full-time parenting deeply fulfilling. But wholesale assigning one sex all the low-status domestic responsibilities that involve meeting other people's needs while the other sex gets the chance to be self-actualized and financially independent in the wider world just doesn't quite stack up for me as just a different version of equality. And is genuine happiness really possible without equality? In a fundamentally unequal society, does half the community's happiness come at the expense of the other half's?

A lot of romanticizing goes on about what it's like to stay home with children (often by people not actually doing it), but there is a fair amount of evidence to suggest that stay-at-home mothers are more likely to be depressed than either working mothers or people without children, and they are significantly more likely to describe themselves as angry, sad, or isolated.[10]

I garble these thoughts to Stephen, after the party.

"I see what you're saying," he says, "but it's not that straightforward. We believe this is what God wants, and so it's not as simple as just saying 'believe something else.'"

For the second time this weekend, in the nicest possible way, Stephen tells me that he thinks my attitude is condescending and that Mormon women don't need people like me coming in from outside and telling them they are oppressed when they don't feel that way themselves. A little too churlishly, I reply that given that the entire Mormon leadership is made up of elderly white men, it's not as if Mormon women are exactly speaking for themselves within the church either.

Stephen tells me that I should meet an old acquaintance of his, a woman named Emily Holsinger-Butler, whom he met years ago on the Mormon University's study abroad program, one of a small but vocal band of Mormon feminist agitators. He texts her to ask if she will meet with me, and she texts straight back, inviting me to pop over to her house for a chat.

Emily lives in out in Provo, Utah, about a forty-five-minute drive from Salt Lake City, a community which, as well as being officially America's happiest city, also holds the dubious honor of being, by a wide margin, its most conservative, with the highest percentage of Republican voters in the entire country (another example of how happiness statistics point clearly to the fact that I'm living the wrong life). As I drive through Provo's *Truman Show*–style suburbs looking for Emily's house, it feels like perhaps the worst place in America to be a militant feminist activist.

When I do finally ring on the doorbell of her cozy but unremarkable suburban house, Emily tells me that it used to belong to multimillionaire Steven Covey, also a religious Mormon and author of the *7 Habits of Highly Effective People*, one of the bestselling self-help books of all time. She gives me a sneak peak of Covey's old study, left untouched since he sat there creating his billion-dollar personal development empire. The study is a weirdly claustrophobic 1970s basement man-cave. Perhaps the little known 8th Habit of Highly Effective People is to work out of a room with no windows, oppressive ski-chalet wood paneling, and Abigail's party-style shag carpeting.

Emily's three children are downstairs with her husband. When she introduces me to them, I realize how far my perspective has shifted in a single weekend. When one of my friends back in London had a third child it seemed like an almost unthinkable feat of domestic conjury. Here in Utah, a mere three kids makes Emily seem like one of the bitter childless New York career women of Stephen's darkest fears.

Emily is the first Mormon woman I have met on my visit who is not a full-time stay-at-home mother. Formerly a corporate lawyer, she now writes young adult fiction. One of seven children herself, with a family lineage dating back to Joseph Smith, Emily grew up in the church and is still an active member, attending services every week and reading

Scripture to her children every night before bed. But her views are well outside the Mormon mainstream.

"I'm a pretty committed feminist in all areas," she tells me, taking a sip of the herbal tea that is apparently a loophole in the no-hot-drinks rule. "I realized it in fourth grade. Most women in the church feel completely comfortable with the patriarchy. The conditioning is still 'a woman's place is in the home.' They glorify domesticity."

I ask Emily what she thinks about the whole idea that men and women are equal partners within the church, just with different roles to play.

"I know that many Mormon women feel very valued for what they contribute at home," she replies carefully, "but equality is not a feeling. It's something that you can actually quantify. You might feel valued, but you are not equal.

"When my kids were baptized, my husband blessed them, I did nothing but make the programs and play the piano." Emily pauses for a moment, and slumps back into the sofa. "It fills me with anguish."

It's strange listening to Emily talk. I can't quite work out what's keeping her in the church, given that her views on such fundamental ideas are so at odds with Mormon teaching. I ask her about this.

"These are my people," she replies. "This is my tribe. I have a sense of belonging. I need to belong. That's really valuable, the older you get. I have that connection that would be really hard to sever. We disagree with each other on a fundamental level, but if something bad happened, I would have people to rely on. It's like being in a marriage that's really difficult and you just get hurt a lot."

I ask her if she would ever consider leaving the church.

"I might," she says. "But it's more likely I'll be 'invited' to leave the church. If you are too belligerent about your beliefs you can be invited to leave."

Emily is right. There have been a couple of high-profile excommunications recently of campaigners voicing views outside of the mainstream. Podcaster John Dehlin was recently excommunicated from the church, in part for advocating for same-sex marriage on his radio show. Feminist activist Kate Kelly, who campaigned for Mormon women to gain the priesthood, the religious honor given automatically to virtually all boys and men over the age of twelve, was also kicked out of the church. Clearly part of the success of the Mormon community is keeping a strict level of control over people's views and behaviors.

As I DRIVE out of Provo, America's happiest town retreating in my rearview mirror, and head back to Stephen and Laura's, Emily's words are still rattling round in my head. "Equality is not a feeling." It's a moment of clarity. Surely if not everyone is equal, then not everyone has the chance to fully thrive; and without that, not everyone has an equal shot at happiness. The Mormon Church's stance on gender roles feels like a deep fault line of injustice right at the heart of the system.

It makes me wonder what Laura thinks about all this. With all the party preparation, I haven't had much of a chance to sit down and talk to her properly this weekend. As a stay-at-home mom, maker of garlands, enthusiastic church volunteer, and bridal shower hostess, she has certainly lived out the life as idealized in the Mormon Church's imagination. But I have had a couple of clues this weekend that her views might not be quite that simple.

When we were all getting ready for the party, rushing around hanging decorations and chopping vegetables, the conversation had turned briefly to the topic of abortion. It had almost felt like a formality, as though it would be impossible for a liberal feminist and a member of the American religious right to spend an entire weekend together without at least a nod to the subject. Stephen had reiterated the official Mormon doctrinal position that terminating a pregnancy for any reason other than rape, incest, or a threat to the life of the mother was morally wrong. I hadn't pushed it. I disagree with Stephen's view, but actually think that at least it is a coherent and even honorable one. Given what a sacred cow the whole pro-life position is to many religious people, I had thought the chances of changing his mind on the matter were virtually zero, and felt it was totally pointless getting into some kind of drawn-out debate about it.

But then, to my surprise Laura had chimed into the conversation, saying that she thought that abortion might be morally acceptable just as a matter of personal choice, up to about twelve weeks gestation. I knew what a highly controversial position this was for a religious Mormon woman to take, and Laura had obviously shocked Stephen with the revelation too. He was clearly put out, and kept returning to the topic over and over again during the course of the day, as though it was a paper cut that wouldn't stop smarting.

It made me wonder whether there might be more to Laura than meets the eye. I'm intrigued and want to hear what she has to say about the church's take on the family and gender roles more generally.

"I grew up thinking that men were the preferred gender," she tells me, when we finally get a chance to sit down and talk. "I wanted to be a man. I felt a lot of pain about that for a lot of years.

"Our marriage—for the first several years, it was very hard for me. I felt too young when we did get married, I really struggled. For women, you go from being completely chaste, having to keep your body covered and be modest, straight to having sex on your wedding night with nothing in between. That's very hard. And the boys have waited so long, there's a real problem with them thinking 'you owe me.'

"I felt like all the women I knew were saying 'I'm married to my best friend' or 'I love being married.' And I was thinking *really?* He's your best friend? We're fighting all the time. I felt like if you don't say those kinds of things, then people think you aren't trying hard enough. Sometimes we hated each other for days. Four months in I went and told my father-in-law I was going to divorce Stephen."

Laura tells me that when she and Stephen were first married, she applied to go to theater school and was accepted. But while she was waiting for the semester to begin, she found out that despite being on two types of contraception, she was pregnant.

"I felt like everything had been taken away from me," she says, her voice suggesting that twenty years on, the pain of this loss still has ragged edges. "I was on birth control. I thought I had ten years. I wanted to go to theater school and then become a teacher. I felt very resentful. For *years*."

When their first daughter, Emma, was born, the transition to motherhood was not as instinctive for Laura as the Mormon Church might lead women to believe. "Motherhood didn't come naturally to me," she admits. "When Emma was born, they put her on my chest and I didn't feel a connection," she tells me. "I had postpartum depression.

"I remember one time, when she was a baby, I had to go to the store, and I looked at her and I started crying. You know that kind of angry crying, because I knew I either had to take her to the store or find someone to watch her, and both options seemed intolerable. It wasn't until she was about a year old that I looked at her and thought, this could be something that I would find fulfilling."

For someone who struggled with the realities of motherhood, having four children and then staying home with them full-time seems like a lot to take on. I ask Laura about this. "It's about expectations," she says. "Having four kids here is standard. If I had not been raised Mormon, I would have had a career and been a working mom. Being a stay-at-home mom was not a natural choice for me.

"It's been a struggle for me in many ways. There's that motherly expectation and if that is your only profession, your only vocation in life, it's hard to admit that it isn't always natural. If I had a profession, I'd be thinking 'I've also got this.' But this is your identity, this is how you're identified by other people in your religious culture, and that is hard."

Instead of a career, Laura started taking on extra volunteer work as an outlet. "I did get into some excessive volunteering," she says. "It was like it was 'permissible work.'"

"Permissible to who?" I ask.

"To me and to Stephen."

"Would Stephen have minded you working?"

"The idea wouldn't have bothered him," says Laura, "but the actuality would have made home life more stressful and I don't think he would have been happy about that."

I ask Laura if she wishes she had done things differently, if she wishes that she had waited to get married, or gone out to work instead of staying home with the kids. She thinks for a minute. "I'm glad I made the choice I did," she says finally. "It's a choice I kept making. Now the kids are older, I don't have the tears-in-my-eyes hopelessness anymore. I see the friends who I knew that went to theater school. I envied them for years, but now they are forty and single and there are no good guys around and they look at me and say, 'You are so lucky you already have your family.'"

LAURA TELLS ME that she has struggled with depression on and off for years. And she also points me in the direction of some surprising and confusing research that puts a whole new spin on the issue of Mormon happiness.

The data show up a mysterious anomaly. Despite Mormons consistently ranking as among the happiest people in America, Mormon Utah also has the highest rate of antidepressant use in the United States, with records released by prescription drug companies showing that the rate of prescriptions for depression medication in Utah is around twice the national average.[11] (This is part of a wider trend whereby the more religious states tend to have higher-than-average rates of antidepressant use.) A study by the group Mental Health America also suggests that Utah has the highest rates of depression in the country,[12] while surveys carried out by the Centers for Disease Control suggest that Utah residents report having more suicidal thoughts than anyone in the entire United States.[13]

It's a strange and unexplained paradox how Mormons can be both happier and more depressed at the same time. Maybe both things are genuinely true—a community with clear boundaries and expectations might well bring extra happiness to the majority of its members who naturally fit the mold, but for the minority who don't, could easily lead to alienation and depression. Maybe people are only reporting as happier because of the drugs. Or maybe there's something else going on.

When the research about the high levels of depression in Mormon Utah was first published, many experts speculated about whether, particularly for women, there might be unique pressures and anxieties associated with being an active part of the Mormon community that might be contributing.

When Curtis Canning, the former president of the Utah Psychiatric Association, was asked by an ABC journalist about his view on why people in Utah might be so disproportionately depressed, he speculated:

In Mormon culture, females are supposed accept a calling. They are to be constantly smiling over their family of five. They are supposed to take supper across the street to an ill neighbor and then put up with their husband when he comes home from work and smile about it the whole time. There is this sense that Mrs. Jones down the street is doing the same thing, and there is this undercurrent of competition. To be a good mother and wife, women have to put on this mask of perfection. They can't show their tears, depression, or agony.

This idea that Mormon women feel under pressure to put on a constant happy front, even when they don't feel happy, is echoed on a number of anonymous online forums. On the 22,500-strong support group Exmormon on the site Reddit, the social unacceptability among Mormon women of acknowledging unhappiness or emotional struggle comes up frequently.

"Young Women are literally told that they should present themselves as cheerful," writes one commenter. "It can be stressful to put on that face, pretending that you're cheery, but inside you're in pain. It's actually asking people to behave dishonestly by asking them to behave differently than they might actually feel. I have had to put on a smiling face when I did not feel like smiling. I found it to be draining."

"I think it's because the church teaches that living the gospel brings happiness," suggests another commenter. "So if you're unhappy, it must be because you're not doing something right. As one who suffered from clinical depression as a missionary, I was afraid to write home how miserable I truly was. If I was, must have been because I was a shitty missionary."

It all makes me wonder if perhaps Mormons aren't actually happier than anyone else at all, but simply saying that they are when pollsters call them, because they feel that is the righteous response.

LATER, I ASK Laura whether she has ever felt this cultural pressure to put on happy front when things were a struggle.

"Oh, yes," she says. "Pretending to be happy is a virtue in and of itself in Mormon culture. Like, you should always be happy even in the midst of horrible things happening to you. It's like you always have to ascribe meaning to every bad thing that happens, which can be really crappy. I think it's my personality—I would compare myself to other people and feel that way even if I weren't religious, but within a religious culture, it's almost an imperative to feel that way. It's an extra layer of 'This should be your goal.'"

DR. KRIS DOTY, a professor of social work, and chair of the Behavioral Science Department at Utah Valley University, has studied this topic in depth, carrying out a year-long research project interviewing Mormon women suffering from depression to try and pin down the root causes behind it. Her research showed that one of the key factors was a mind-set that she describes as "toxic perfectionism."

Doty, an active member of the Mormon Church herself, used to work as a clinical social worker and therapist, both in private practice and as a crisis worker in a busy emergency room. When I catch up with her on a phone call, she tells me that during her time working in the ER, she had seen a worrying pattern emerging. On Sundays, after church hours, women would turn up at the emergency room overwhelmed by feelings of depression, inadequacy, and anxiety.

"They were comparing themselves with other women at church who all seemed to be perfect mothers or have perfect bodies or be perfectly happy," she tells me. "I remember once on Mothers' Day, a woman turned up with acute symptoms of depression, saying that the Relief Society meeting at church had been all about how wonderful everyone's mothers were. She just sat there listening, feeling totally inadequate."

When Doty entered academia, she focused on Mormon women and depression as her research specialty. Her interviews showed that these types of feelings of inadequacy in the face of overwhelming expectations were a recurring theme.

"We have this idea in our mind of what we should be: to be a perfect mom or whatever," said one woman she interviewed as part of her research. "Being a stay-at-home mom is very difficult for a lot of people, myself included . . . then you also have these expectations of what you should be doing to be the Molly Mormon or the perfect little homemaker . . . I think that's a lot different in other cultures."

Doty is keen to stress that this is a cultural phenomenon rather than something the church itself is pushing on people. "The church isn't saying we have to be perfect," she says. "There's a culture, especially among young women that no one sees them making any mistakes.

"People put on a public mask and don't show what's really going on behind the scenes. Their walk-in closets are full of skeletons, but they're keeping the doors closed. They're stopping them from getting up and walking out."

CLEARLY IN MANY ways the high expectations and clear boundaries of the Mormon community are the secret to its strength and

coherence. But for those who don't or can't stick to the script, the results can be devastating.

When I had first told a few people back in California that I was coming to Utah to learn about Mormonism, an acquaintance, Dan, had told
me that he had been raised in the Mormon Church but had left in his
early twenties. When I ask him why, he told me he had found it oppressive and stifling. He doesn't really elaborate, but gives me the number for his friend, Gary, telling me that if I talk to him, I'll understand
what he means. Last year, at the age of forty, after being married to a
woman for fifteen years and having four children together, Gary came
out to the world as gay.

Gary, who is now separated from his wife, but still living in Salt
Lake City, has agreed to meet me for a coffee before I go back to California. He suggested a café in the shopping plaza opposite the Mormon
Church's flagship temple, an architectural flight of fancy even more
splendiferously Disneycorp than the Oakland one I visited a few months
back. A statue of the angel Moroni blowing a trumpet rises up in the
background, a gilded threat.

"They call it Happy Valley here," says Gary, not long after I arrive,
"because everyone is on antidepressants."

The church's official stance on homosexuality is that the orienta-
tion itself is not a problem, as long as people don't act on it. Sex outside marriage is not permitted, and the church does not recognize gay
marriage, a neat piece of logical wizardry that allows church authorities to maintain that they are not homophobic while still banning gay
sex. For the individual, it can be a peculiar prison.

"I grew up in the church," Gary tells me. "Both sides of my family
go all the way back to Joseph Smith. Growing up, it's like it was my
whole life. We had Family Home Evening on Mondays, Wednesdays was
youth group, then Scouts was linked into the church, and then three
hours of church on Sunday. My parents weren't dictators. It wasn't like
they said 'You must do this.' It was just life."

The youngest of five children, Gary started feeling attracted to other boys during his teenage years but did everything he could to suppress it. "I lived that secret alone. I dated girls, I went on prom dates. I just mimicked my older brother and did what he did, but it felt more like besties than anything else. I knew I had to suppress those other feelings, because it didn't fit into the mold of who I was supposed to be."

Although Gary tells me that he knew pretty definitively that he was gay by the time he turned twenty-one; two years later, he married his first wife. The two of them were both singers and dancers in a college performing group and had a lot in common. "I thought that if I had sex with a woman it would all go away," he says.

Unsurprisingly, the attraction Gary felt to other men did not go away, and instead became more and more pressing. During their short marriage, Gary found himself going to watch pornography in adult arcades and occasionally going out cruising, seeking sexual encounters with other men. Wracked with guilt each time, eventually he confessed what he had been doing to his wife. "She was LDS too, but more liberal LDS," he tells me. "Her mom had a friend who was a lesbian. When I told her, she encouraged me to just go and be who I was. She said, 'You're gay. Go and be gay.'"

His wife called Gary's parents and told them what had been going on. But far from embracing the "go and be gay" idea, they were horrified. "My father said, it's okay, Gary, we can sweep this under the rug, and no one need ever know."

It's at this point as Gary is telling me his story that I assume the turnaround point will come. Growing up so steeped in the culture of American self-actualization, in which being "true to yourself" is considered our one incontrovertible life's calling, I find it genuinely hard to imagine a young American of my generation not at that point saying to his father some version of "This is who I am. Deal with it."

But it wasn't simply that Gary was too scared to stand up to his father. He actually agreed with him. "I just kept trying to work out how do I stop doing this? How do I not want this?" he tells me. "The whole thing was devastating."

Gary went to see the bishop to confess and seek counsel. The bishop was similarly keen to make the whole problem disappear. "He told me, maybe if you marry another girl, it will go away," says Gary.

"How could he possibly think that was a good idea?" I ask. "Isn't being gay a fundamental part of who you are?"

Gary's answer surprises me. "Yes," he says, "but so was the church. I loved the church. I still love parts of it. I was determined to make it work."

Gary took a job in Japan to get away and try for a fresh start, and three weeks after his divorce was finalized, started dating his soon to be second wife, Melanie. But even as they were dating, he was still seeking out physical and emotional contact with other men. "I desperately wanted to stop," he says, "but I couldn't. I kept thinking, I'm a bad person. I have to stop this."

Surprisingly, Gary didn't try to hide any of this from Melanie. "I was totally upfront with her from the start," he tells me. "She went into it with her eyes wide open. She was twenty-five years old, and in the LDS church. For a girl, that's well overdue to get married. You've gotta get going if you're a girl. She knew I was dating guys. She knew their names. She was saddened by it, but she sees me, a good LDS guy, with a good job and she was ready the second I was."

Desperate to live a church-sanctioned life, Gary and Melanie married. But Gary couldn't stop seeking out sex with men. Eventually, Melanie called his parents, telling them, "Your son is in trouble." At Gary's father's urging, the couple moved back to Utah, and had four children together. But even with the weight of the Mormon Church and the extended family around, Gary still couldn't suppress his urges.

Over the course of this period, Gary went to seek advice from the bishop several times. They advised him to join a program called Evergreen, which ran reparative therapy programs for "people who want to diminish same-sex attractions and overcome homosexual behavior."

Gary spent hundreds of hours and thousands of dollars on group and individual therapy, trying to force himself to be straight. But nothing worked. He would stay "clean" for a few months, then go out cruising, seeking out steam rooms or other places where sex with men was available. Then each time he would feel wretched and seek out the bishop to confess. "They just told me to keep reading, keep praying, keep trying again."

Eventually, Gary was excommunicated from the church for adultery, although after a period of abstinence he was rebaptized, though he never regained the priesthood. "To get the priesthood back, I would have needed to be sober sexually for years," he tells me. "I only ever made it to nine months.

"I felt like I deserved everything I got, that I was a bad person. My wife had the Proclamation on the Family framed in the hallway. I felt that I needed to fit into that box. I put so much pressure on myself. I really, really tried. It was a constant battle of suppress, suppress, suppress. Eventually it goes into depression. I had a bag of medication, the biggest ziplock bag you can imagine of different antianxiety meds and antidepressants."

Eventually, it all got too much for his wife. After she caught him lying to her, telling her he was out running on a trail, when really he had gone to a gay gym, she set up another appointment for the couple to see the bishop. It was at this point, that something snapped for Gary. "We were sitting there and the bishop started using jargon that I knew meant that I was going to get excommunicated again, that another church court was coming," he says. "I started to hear Charlie Brown voices in my head. I just somehow knew I was done. I knew I was walking away."

Gary has been separated from his wife for a year when I meet him. He hasn't taken any medication of any kind since. He has a new boyfriend and seems happy and relaxed, wearing a tight T-shirt, tanned and buff from the gym.

But to my surprise, he still looks back wistfully on his years in the church. "I still wish I could be part of the church," he tells me. "It will always be a part of my life. But there are too many wounds. I was trying to play on the team, but I'd been benched for too many years."

. . .

WHAT SURPRISED ME, talking to both Gary and Emily, was that even in the face of some real struggles, just how much warmth and affection they both had for the church and the wider Mormon community.

Gary's wasn't a straightforward story of a cartoonish oppressor church persecuting a man for his difference. Even at his lowest moments, he told me that he never felt as though the leadership was trying to shame him but rather, in its own, slightly twisted way, trying to help. Gary wasn't sticking around because he was scared of the church. He was sticking around because he loved it.

In a similar way, even though Emily disagreed with the church on some absolute fundamentals, what it offered her in terms of support and community and a sense of belonging was so compelling that she still felt she was more likely to be pushed out than to leave. The ties we choose are those that bind us most tightly.

As I drive back to the airport in my rental car, trying to make sense of it all in my head, I have mixed feelings. My time in Salt Lake has left me even more convinced about just how crucial community and other people are to our happiness. I have come away filled with genuine admiration and even envy for the intricate support structures and social bonds that the church has created, bonds that people will seemingly go to great lengths to preserve, even at huge personal cost.

But I'm still uneasy. Perhaps the Mormon community would never have prospered as it has without a highly prescriptive approach to its members' behavior and values, but for me, the whole thing feels a little too oppressive.

There will always be a tension in any community between the needs of the individual and the needs of the group, but when people feel compelled to bury their feelings and even to suppress their most fundamental selves to conform to the community's expectations, then it's not hard to see how this can lead to anxiety and depression.

And in Mormon culture, this pressure to conform outwardly is compounded by the perhaps even more stressful expectation to feel inwardly happy about it too.

In a bizarre way, this cultural emphasis on happiness reminds me slightly of Tony Hsieh's alcohol fuelled dystopia in Downtown Las Vegas. It's not surprising that people in both places have found the pressure to perform emotionally, stressful in and of itself. A wide-scale study conducted in Australia and Japan, led by psychologists at the University of Queensland, asked respondents in both countries to rate to what extent they felt outward, societal pressure to be happy and not to experience negative emotions. The same people were then asked how often they felt negative emotions such as stress, anxiety, and sadness in the past month, and how intensely they had felt them. In both countries, those people who reported feeling the strongest societal pressure to be happy also reported feeling negative emotions most frequently and strongly. They also felt lower life satisfaction than those who felt less outward pressure to be happy and were more likely to experience symptoms of depression.[14] The study's principal author, Dr. Brock Bastian, commented at the time, "In short, when people perceive that others think they should feel happy and not sad, this leads them to feel sad more frequently and intensely."

This may go some way toward explaining the high levels of depression in Mormon Utah, where happiness is also culturally wrapped up with virtue and achievement and religious piety. In this context, the feeling that everyone else is happy when you are struggling is likely to feel particularly shameful and isolating.

But the more I think about it, the more I realize that it's not just these particular communities that are creating a kind of mass public emotional fiction and anxiety-inducing expectation of total blissful happiness. It suddenly hits me that of course, we're all doing the exact same thing.

7.

I'M NOT A HAPPY PERSON,
I JUST PLAY ONE ON FACEBOOK

Not long after I get back from Salt Lake City, I run into my friend Alice in Trader Joe's, recently returned from a romantic weekend minibreak with her husband. I make the mistake of chirruping in my perkiest yay-vacations! voice—the California equivalent of "How was it?"—carefully grammatically engineered to eliminate the possibility of a negative reply: "Was it *great?*"

It was not. The word *disaster* features heavily in the torrent of discontent that follows, as does the phrase "totally fucking inconsiderate." Apparently Alice and her husband had spent the entire weekend arguing, culminating in a furious impasse, with each of them perched on the furthest reaches of the four-poster bed as far apart as possible, fuming and silently wondering whether true loneliness can only be experienced within the context of a failing relationship.

But when I get home, I log on to Facebook and up pops the social media version of the same trip. Without the remotest hint of strife are ten or so whimsically captioned pictures of an adorable couple in complementary sun hats, frolicking in front of a series of heritage sites. I "like" it, she responds, and neither of us ever acknowledges the conversation we had less than two hours previously.

This is social media's basic Faustian pact: you believe my Facebook fiction (and allow it to make you slightly envious and insecure), and I'll do the same for yours.

Happiness is the currency of social media and the loophole in the generally accepted no-bragging rule. In its short lifetime, Facebook has developed its own unique internal language and set of social norms, totally distinct from what is generally considered acceptable in real life. Somehow, without ever discussing it, we have almost universally decreed social media to be a kind of personal PR agency, a forum for us to assemble a set of glittering promotional materials for our own lives, all with the aim of making ourselves appear as improbably blissfully happy as possible.

Facebook is a parallel universe in which everyone is either stratospherically successful in their career, married to the "best guy ever," "enjoying every moment of motherhood," or in a state of single childlessness for which the only descriptive adjective permitted by the social media authorities is "fabulous." (Although when I started to edge toward the fortysomething demographic most often described as fabulous, I started to realize that fabulous is almost certainly just social media for "female human aging reluctantly.")

In a culture that both insists that we have complete control over our happiness and too often equates unhappiness with inadequacy, social media gives us an unprecedented ability to craft and present a happy front. This shifts the business of bliss away from how happy we feel, to the perhaps more culturally urgent matter of how happy we look. Facebook has made Mormons out of us all.

We live in the era of the curated life. At sixteen, this might mean taking a momentary break from feeling fat, ugly, and unlovable to post a barrage of confidence-throbbing, boob-thrusting bathroom mirror selfies. At thirty-five, when Facebook starts to flag your boobs as "offensive content," it might mean social sharing your pedicured toes on the sun lounger from your once-in-five years vacation or taking advantage of the brief moment that your newborn draws breath from his seven-week screaming-and-vomiting marathon to place him in an Easter basket and bury him in rose petals. (On Instagram, these nuggets of personal PR are now often flanked by the gloating hashtag #nofilter, to double up on the brag. No filter, except for the Giant Life Filter, that is.)

I'm just as bad. I am a heavy social media user (certain members of my family might prefer the term *problem user*). The Facebook button on my phone is like a mosquito bite, a constant low-level itch, for which scratching provides momentary relief but then only aggravates the need.

Living far from home, in many ways Facebook has been a lifeline. Social media allows me to keep up with the minutiae of hundreds of people's lives that I wouldn't see otherwise from one year to the next. Every September I love seeing every single child I know across the world sporting a brave smile and a backpack, off to start the new school year. There's something deeply life affirming about having a real-time feed of the proud moments and milestones of virtually everyone I've ever known.

But I regularly reach the end of the day sick with the stale self-loathing of a person who has Read the Whole Internet. I get sucked into bitter, unwinnable arguments about topics I know very little about, with people who I barely know, and then find myself inexplicably browsing through those same people's vacation photos.

I post far too many photos of my children, and keep my friends abreast of their cuteness way more often than anyone could possibly find interesting. A few times a year, after a particularly insufferable Facebook binge, I am struck down with the social media equivalent of a hangover, a low-level but ugly blend of overexposure, shame, insecurity, and paranoia.

And frankly, my online persona bears only a marginal resemblance to my actual life.

Facebook Me is like a little, much-prettier avatar of the actual me, representing me in some gloriously pimped-up approximation of my actual life. Her children look like mine would after a bath and some light eugenics. Sometimes Facebook Me even does the same thing as the actual me at the same time. While I was apple picking in the fall in a hot, uncomfortable orchard, with no restrooms and an incessantly whining toddler, my social media doppelgänger was simultaneously appearing online apple picking in a climate-controlled orchard, with lavish bathroom facilities and a cooperative and photogenic toddler.

Mercifully for everyone involved, I missed the selfie generation and, round about the time that Facebook hit its stride, I had already transferred pretty much every ounce of vanity onto my children. However this didn't stop me posting an early family photo after Zeph's birth in which Solly was looking the other way and Zeph was sporting a clearly identifiable diaper-filling grimace. But because it was quite possibly the best photo ever taken of me, in which lighting and placing and divine intervention all came together in a glorious one-time fiction of pretty that looked absolutely nothing like me, it was inevitably destined for the public domain. At least I had the good grace to bury it inside an album of kid pictures, but it says a lot about just how far social media's cultural norms have strayed from real life that I was too embarrassed to stick it up on the fridge.

When I scroll through my Facebook photos from the last few years, or when Facebook periodically decides to release one of its occasional corporate highlight reels of my own life's highlight reel (Check Out Ruth's Year! It's Been Another Great One!), my personal narrative looks pretty flawless. According to Facebook, I went seamlessly from fun-loving, cocktail-enhanced singleton to blissful new mother to cute family of four with only a brief blip around the shotgun, fat-in-wedding-dress marriage. All characters appearing in this work are fictitious, and any resemblance to real persons or events is purely coincidental.

It's a strange mix of oversharing and undersharing. Because although we increasingly share every aspect of the minutiae of our lives for public appraisal and critique, none of it paints a remotely representative picture.

All this is in stark contrast to more anonymous social media. Anyone yearning for a more realistic window into what other people's lives are really like should try logging onto a social network where people have anonymous usernames. The British parenting Web site Mumsnet attracts a broadly similar demographic to most of my Facebook friends, but while my Facebook feed is full of photos of adorably well-behaved children and declarations of incomparable happiness, Mumsnet is full of threads like "I regret having children," "My husband is leaving me," and "I just pooed on my skirt."

There have been a few scattered attempts to galvanize people into greater honesty on social media, like the Instagram account WomenIRL (Women in Real Life) showing photos of messy bedrooms and laundry piles, or the Twitter hashtag #totalhonestytuesday where people are supposed to post honest photos (although many of these are themselves at least 50 percent humblebrag). But social media's cultural language of curated perfection has been adopted with such wholesale universality, these projects never really seem to take hold on a mass scale.

EITHER I HAVE always carried around an undiagnosed hidden sore of low self-esteem, or Facebook has created in me an unhealthy need for constant validation.

The simple but genius scoring system of the Facebook "like" has to be one of the clear drivers of the network's stratospheric success. At some deep level, a like feels like shorthand for "I like you" or "I give the blue thumbs-up to your existence and the cuteness of your children," a tiny hit of affirmation. But the like is a constantly inflating currency.

When Solly was born in 2010, his standard newborn picture—fierce and wrinkled, all tiny fists and regulation hospital blanket—attracted just six likes. Six! And one of those was from my mom. At the time, I don't remember thinking anything much of it, but at current inflation rates, a mere six Facebook likes for the birth of a first child now would probably be considered a diagnostic indicator for some kind of social adjustment disorder.

When Zeph was born, an arguably identical baby, and I posted an unarguably identical picture (even I regularly fail the Pepsi challenge on my two sons' newborn photographs), the response showed just how rampant like inflation had become in the intervening three years. Although my online friend network was virtually unchanged from first time around, Zeph's picture attracted around a hundred likes, which I considered a generous but not excessive number. I've clearly become a validation junkie. Six likes used to give me a solid hit. Now I need fifty just to feel normal.

Living this way makes for an odd new relationship with reality, in which occasionally social media life can start to loom larger than actual life itself. It is now difficult to experience a happy moment without at least a fleeting thought about how the happy moment will play on social media.

While chatting to a group of parents after a toddler music class (I think it was music, it actually could have been anything—most organized preschool activities in this area from judo to ballet basically just involve waving colored scarves around until an overwrought adult steps in and starts singing the "Clean Up, Clean Up" song with barely disguised relief), one of the moms starts talking about plans for a baby shower she is organizing for a friend that weekend, telling us in detail about the decorations, the gender-neutral color scheme, the whimsical games, and the high-concept cupcakes.

"I just hope we don't have to cancel it. She'll be so disappointed," she says.

"Why would you have to cancel it?" I ask.

"Because the weather forecast says it might rain. Of course we could have it inside instead, but then the photos will look terrible, and I'm really trying to build up my Instagram at the moment."

Most of us have walked the thin line on social media between "sharing proud moments" and "totally warping reality." It's an odd cycle of buy-in and amnesia. We all post our carefully edited best moments and, although at a rational level we know that other people are doing the same, we somehow believe that everyone else's life is Really Like That.

We are all complicit in creating the fiction, yet we still have faith in its veracity, like a dad in a false beard, filling his kids' stockings, then hanging out his own for Santa.

But this shared archive of perfection has been assimilated into the background hum of our expectations, and increasingly, we are taking our cues for how happy we are "supposed" to be from the curated perfection of social media. In turn, our expectations of what contentment should look like are constantly inflating, creating a whole new level of happiness anxiety.

IT WASN'T ALWAYS like this.

When I first signed up for Facebook, back in 2007, before the International Lifestyle Whitewashing Treaty, no one seemed to be quite sure what they were supposed to be posting on social media. There was an awkwardness to people's posts, and updates in general were much less surefooted, the general tone much more individualized and varied.

In those days, the difference between the jaded, cynical Brit and the perky life-embracing American on my Facebook feed was stark. Back then, you could blindfold me and read me the status updates of my friends without their names, and I could tell you which were American and which were British.

Americans would post links to inspirational memes and parenting blogs packed with life lessons. (British parenting blogs tended to be packed with despair and vomit.) My American friends would post heartwarming "you go, girl" messages of support to each other and often to themselves, while my British cohort's status updates tended to be some variation on "this is rubbish."

While American Facebook instantly took on the feel of the Oscars, with everyone in sparkly gowns, clutching bunches of roses and gushing out their thanks to the universe (with occasional nods to the plight of people in Haiti), the average British Facebook feed felt more like wandering round IKEA on a rainy holiday weekend. You might have caught a glimpse of a life in which the curtains matched and everything was tidied away into cute storage tubs, but the overall impression was more of a place where people gathered to argue with their loved ones and complain about being inconvenienced. If Facebook had originated in the UK, it would almost certainly have offered a dislike button.

But after a couple of years living in the States, I have noticed that this cultural difference has slowly started to narrow. Little by little, it sneaked up on me that my British friends' Facebook feeds are becoming indistinguishable from my American ones.

I first notice it when I realize that British friends who have never previously shown any religious leanings are now declaring on Facebook that they are "feeling blessed." This was a phrase I had never actually heard a British person say in real life, so it takes me a while to realize that this wasn't a sign of the spread of a new religious cult but actually a preset option from a new drop-down menu of emotions, complete with matching emoticons provided by Facebook. (Oddly this appears to be the only option anyone ever uses. I have never seen anyone, American or British, drop-down declare that they are feeling "overwhelmed" or "old," or "meh," even though these are also entrées on the emotional menu.)

Before I know it, my British friends are sharing inspirational virtual photo cards of sunsets proclaiming that "Happiness comes from within," and making public declarations of adoration to their spouses and their preliterate children. It feels like the international creep of a kind of McHappiness, a universal global emotional tone.

Then one day, General Pollyanna's advancing army scores a decisive victory on virtual UK soil. Up pops a bright red number 1 on my Facebook header, alerting me to the fact that I have been tagged in something called a Gratitude Challenge. And to my surprise, it is by a British friend.

The most efficient mechanism for social control ever invented has to be the Facebook tag. Forget tear gas, the Islamic State, or a Midwest traffic cop equipped with the entire US nuclear arsenal, a simple request on social media will have us scurrying to haze ourselves with lethal frat-boy alcohol combinations, grow ill-advised dictator mustaches, and tip buckets of ice water over our heads.

Happiness challenges are among the most popular, providing impressively efficient disseminators of positive thinking culture. As well as The Gratitude Challenge, there is also 100 Happy Days, The Happiness Challenge, and The Positivity Challenge.

They are mainly variations on a similar theme. The idea is to give ourselves a happiness bump by focusing on the positive aspects of our lives and expressing thanks for life's gifts. (The supplementary benefit is to make sure that our entire social network knows just how happy we are.)

The challenge itself comes in various levels of labor intensiveness. Anything from the lowest effort, "express something you are grateful for in your Facebook status right now," to a "one thing a day for a week" or a "two things a day for five days." My challenge is an Olympic level, three things a day for seven days. (Although I later come across a hundred-day Gratitude Challenge, so the fact that I escaped that one gives me the first day's gratitude offering right there.)

It's virtually impossible to say no. Ignore a tag in the Gratitude Challenge, and you're effectively replacing your profile picture with a sign saying "I am an overprivileged ingrate who hates her own kids."

But when I start thinking about what to write, I start to feel increasingly awkward. The whole thing seems like a minefield of potential insensitivity.

In real life, people tend not to brag about their possessions to those who can't afford them, about their career achievements to their colleague who has recently been laid off, or about their newly discovered pregnancy to their friend who has just suffered a miscarriage. But social media blunts our ability to make these distinctions. Our updates are like mass marketing, hitting the news feeds of a couple of hundred people at a time, all in the midst of different life circumstances.

I need to come up with twenty-one separate things for which I am grateful, none of which sound as though I am doing victory laps of my own happiness at the expense of my friends' feelings. Even discounting the obvious braggy-brag ones—"I'm thankful to be on a wonderful tropical beach vacation," it's still virtually impossible to come up with something that doesn't clash horribly with another person in my social network's misfortune.

The obvious choice would be my profound gratitude for my children, for example, but I'm sure that the handful of my Facebook friends currently going through IVF might be less keen to explore every nuance of that particular joy with me. My happy marriage? Our good health? But as I mentally scroll through my friend list, I think of one friend who is going through a divorce and another who is in the middle of a nail-biting wait for the results of a genetic test that will determine whether she has inherited the gene for a virulent hereditary form of cancer. Best to stick with things that everyone can enjoy. But twenty-one separate expressions of gratitude for sunshine and autumn leaves? That starts to feel like Kindergarten Harvest Festival.

The Gratitude Challenge is essentially a more concentrated and intense example of social media's basic cultural language, throwing its more obnoxious pitfalls into laser-sharp focus. It makes me wonder what the wider social impact is of all of this. Does this type of gratitude grandstanding raise our happiness at the expense of other peoples'?

THE RESEARCH WOULD suggest so.

In 2013, a group of psychologists at the University of Michigan went looking for an answer to the pressing question of whether Facebook makes people happier or sadder. They were looking at two types of happiness—both the moment-to-moment sensations of our changing moods and the deeper more general feeling of overall life satisfaction.

Taking a group of young people, before the study started, the researchers surveyed them about their overall levels of general life satisfaction. Then over the two-week study period, they measured their daily Facebook usage, and then five times a day texted them to ask about their happiness in the current moment, with questions like "How do you feel right now?" "How lonely do you feel right now?" and "How worried do you feel right now?" At the end of the study period they repeated the same overall life-satisfaction survey they had done at the beginning.

The results were stark. The more people used Facebook during the study period, the lower their moment-to-moment happiness and the more their overall life satisfaction dipped over the two-week time span. These findings were true across the range of participants irrespective of gender, self-esteem, loneliness, number of Facebook friends, and perceived supportiveness of these friends. At first the researchers speculated that a phenomenon called reverse causation might have been at play, meaning that rather than Facebook making people unhappy, people who were already unhappy just tended to use Facebook more. But the data didn't support this theory, showing no evidence that people used Facebook more when they already felt bad.[1]

In contrast, when the people studied had had face-to-face meetings or phone contact with other people, they immediately felt happier. There was clearly something about Facebook itself that was making people unhappy.

What this study didn't do was pinpoint exactly why and what it is about Facebook that was leading to these negative effects. But more recent and detailed research suggests that the problem lies not with Facebook itself but with the cultural norms and etiquette we have collectively adopted for how we use it and the kinds of things we post. It seems that the competitive happiness posturing and widespread culture of lifestyle spin-doctoring might be playing a big part.

Another influential and large-scale study on the link between Facebook and unhappiness by a team of academics in Germany pinned this idea down.[2] Surveying a group of more than six hundred Facebook users, the researchers confirmed the previous link between Facebook use and general unhappiness, and then pinpointed its cause as a phenomenon called social comparison, defined by the researchers almost poetically as "an unpleasant and often painful blend of feelings . . . caused by a comparison with a person or group of persons who possess something we desire."

Social comparison theory is a concept in psychology, long predating the invention of social media, which suggests that we determine our own self-worth by assessment of how we stack up against others. Unsurprisingly, when we observe the successes of our friends and find our own lives wanting in comparison, our happiness drops.

Social media means it has never been easier or more convenient for us to benchmark ourselves against our peers. At its most cloyingly braggy, it takes this preexisting, but relatively marginal aspect of human nature, and places it front and center, then dances round, taunting and goading it to the breaking point.

If at a real-life party, a guest starts carpet bombing the conversation with observations about how wonderful, hot, and expensive his last vacation was; the dazzling accomplishments of his children; and the unblemished happiness of his marriage, all right-thinking people will, quite appropriately, hate him. If he pulls the same stunt online, apparently instead we hate ourselves.

According to the German study, the most common cause of Facebook envy and social comparison was seeing other people's vacation photos. But in close second place was a new phenomenon. The people surveyed claimed that their biggest source of anxiety when they looked at their online friends' profiles was not anything specific but a more general envy and insecurity about their friends' overall happiness and how their own lives stacked up in comparison. Oddly, when the same researchers carried out a parallel survey of causes of envy and social comparison in real life as opposed to online, this generalized "happiness" insecurity did not feature at all. It seems as though social media has created a whole new type of happiness anxiety.

The same researchers in the German study also identified a phenomenon they called the envy spiral in which, when confronted with painful feelings of jealousy or inadequacy in response to their friends' Facebook postings, the people in the study went on the defensive with something that the researchers euphemistically called "impression management," embellishing their own profiles to even glitzier happiness heights. Then, of course, the cycle would continue.

With thirty billion pieces of content shared every month, most of them with at least undertones of bragging if not full-on gloating, Facebook can sometimes feel like the anxiety-inducing wholesale mass production of social comparison.

THESE STRANGE NEW social norms can have more damaging effects than mere passing jealousy. For some young people, the impact of being bombarded with their peers' instagrammed perfection can give rise to some worrying consequences.

We know that anxiety among college students has been rising steadily over the last few years as part of a wider trend, but more steeply in the very recent past. The 2013 survey of college counseling centers suggested that the number of their clients with severe psychological problems had increased by nearly 10 percent in the previous two years, a time period that has coincided with the explosion of use in sites like Facebook and Instagram. Many elite universities have seen suicide clusters.

The relationship between social media and mental health is a complex one, and it certainly can't be inferred from this that social media alone causes depression or other mental health problems. Social networks can clearly bring some strong positive benefits to students too, with studies showing that Facebook users have higher social capital and more social connections than nonusers. In many cases, online social networks have given students information about and access to mental health support services.

But experts who work with university students have expressed real concern over the cultural norms of how college kids use social media.

When *The New York Times* ran a piece about the rising anxiety and mental health issues among elite college students, touching on the suicide of a successful and popular Penn freshman, Madison Holleran, the third suicide in a series of six at the university over a thirteen-month period, they noted that Madison's Instagram feed showed a series of images of smiling, party-fueled perfection, including one posted on the morning of her death.

The College Dean's Advisory Board at the University of Pennsylvania organized a panel discussion, partly in response to Madison's suicide, on a phenomenon known as "Penn Face," the mask that Penn students feel they need to put on in order to hide their distress and appear effortlessly happy. The online advertisement for the event explained: "Many a time individuals at Penn feel that those around them seem to be leading a life close to perfect. We live under the illusion that others . . . are on top of it all, causing us to feel overwhelmed. . . . We want to shed light on the fact that everyone at Penn, . . . however perfect their life may seem on social media, have to struggle with the same issues."

It' s not just at the University of Pennsylvania. When the *New York Times* reporter asked Gregory T. Eells, the director of counseling and psychological services at Cornell University, for his take on the recent increase in serious mental health problems among college students, he said that he believed "social media was a huge contributor, creating the misperception among students that peers aren't also struggling." "'When students remark during a counseling session that everyone else on campus looks happy,' he tells them: "I walk around and think, 'that one's gone to the hospital. That person has an eating disorder. That student went on antidepressants.' As a therapist, I know that nobody is as happy or as grown-up as they seem on the outside."[3]

As Meg Jay, a Virginia-based therapist specializing in young adults, wrote in an article in *Psychology Today*, "Over the past few years, my office has become a place where day after day one twentysomething after another drops onto the couch and groans: 'According to Facebook,

I'm the only person not saving orphans after graduation' or 'Every time somebody changes their relationship status on Facebook, I panic' or 'I'm convinced Facebook was invented to make single people feel bad about their lives.'"[4]

SOCIAL MEDIA'S CULTURE of curated positivity and sanitized happiness is now filtering beyond our personal lives. A third of Americans now receive the majority of their news and information about current events from Facebook, which has led to a subtle but significant shift in the content and tone of the news itself.

In March 2012, three social media rising stars, Eli Pariser of MoveOn .org, Peter Koechley of *The Onion*, and Chris Hughes of Facebook, launched a new news Web site called Upworthy. The site quickly became the one of the fastest growing media powerhouses on the Internet, soon logging more than eighty million unique visitors in a single month.

Like many successful news organizations in the digital age, Upworthy is as much a data-science project as a journalistic labor of love. The secret of its stratospheric success is the laboratory-level focus it brings to maximizing viral shareability. Every piece of Upworthy content is meticulously crafted with the explicit aim of going viral.

Through painstaking research and rigorous testing, Upworthy has become masterful at pinpointing the characteristics that the most viral news stories have in common and using that information to develop content that compels us to click the share button. The upshot of all this research? We are keen to avoid coming across as negative online. In much the same way that we hide the downers and share only the shiny and happy from our personal lives, we apparently do the same with what we choose to share of the news.

"When we started, the prevailing wisdom was that snark ruled the Internet," said Eli Pariser in an interview with *Time*. "And we just had a really different sense of what works. You don't want to be that guy at the party who's crazy and angry and ranting in the corner—it's the same for Twitter or Facebook."[5]

A strange phenomenon was emerging from Upworthy's research, and that of its competitor BuzzFeed, which also started life as a laboratory to study viral sharing. Just as in our personal lives, where people carefully create an online image of unblemished positivity and happiness, researchers noticed that they were doing the same thing in selecting which news stories they chose to share with their friends online.

Although their data showed that people would click on and read both positive and negative stories in roughly equal numbers, people would share far greater numbers of positive stories, and it was almost exclusively positive stories that would go viral. Broadly speaking, the more heartwarming positivity that can be packed into a story, the more likely we are to want to be associated with it and to click the share button.

In the same way that we instagram the millisecond of toddler cooperativeness between the two terrifying tantrums that bookend it, we share the "wondtacular" news and keep the more challenging, difficult, or unpleasant to ourselves. Who we want to appear to be is not quite the same as who we actually are.

With the stated mission to be at the junction of the "awesome," the "meaningful," and the "visual," Upworthy's genius is in having identified this strange phenomenon and exploiting it to the max. What makes the site differ from its predecessors in the viral Internet business is that rather than merely hunting down traditionally feel-good or uplifting content—the flash mob sing-alongs and puppies on Roombas—it takes the existing news agenda, the dreary, the geopolitical, the tragic, and even the genocidal and with impressive sleight of hand manages to somehow rebrand virtually every story, no matter how entrenched, unjust, or complex, as capital U uplifting.

And as Upworthy is surprisingly upfront about acknowledging, it is not just chronicling the news for the sake of public awareness or the spread of knowledge and information, but instead co-opting it in service of online personal PR.

"Part of what we're trying to do with Upworthy is give people the tools to express a conscientious, thoughtful, and positive identity in social media," said Eli Pariser in the same *Time* magazine piece, sounding uncomfortably as though he might be offering up war-torn Syrians and Ebola victims as a personal branding alternative to sun lounger selfies or instagramming our sushi.

In a SlideShare presentation entitled "The Sweet Science of Virality," in which the Upworthy editors share their secrets, they home in on the looming presence behind their editorial philosophy.

SLIDE 45, THE SWEET SCIENCE OF VIRALITY

Let's Talk About Your Mom, Dude.

FACT: No one likes to disappoint their mom.

DOUBLE FACT: Middle-aged women are the biggest sharers on the Interweb.

ERGO: If you frame your content to not make your mom shake her head, you have a better chance of winning.

In a later piece for *Quora* magazine, Adam Mordecai, one of Upworthy's editors, explains in more detail the exact techniques for how their team goes about rebranding global politics to avoid disappointing their moms.

1. Don't depress people so much that they want to give up on humanity. Negative headlines breed negative shares.

2. Don't use terms that overwhelm, polarize, or bore people.
I never use *Social Security,* the *Environment, Immigration,
Democrats, Republicans, Medicare, Racist, Bigot,* etc. You can
talk about issues without giving away what they are. Most
people aren't going to want to look at an immigration video.

When the news is rinsed of anything negative, boring, polarizing,
or that our moms wouldn't want to share, what are left are oddly sanitized headlines like:

"WHEN HE WAS DEPLOYED TO AFGHANISTAN, HE DID ONE THING
AND ONE THING ONLY. MAKE PEOPLE HAPPY."

"SUPER FUNNY HONEST REACTIONS FROM 5-YEAR-OLDS THAT ARE
BETTER THAN THE MEDIA'S REACTIONS TO EBOLA."

"THE VIDEO ABOUT ISRAEL-GAZA YOU CAN SHARE WITH YOUR
FRIENDS THAT (HOPEFULLY) WON'T OFFEND THEM."

"THIS KID JUST DIED. WHAT HE LEFT BEHIND WAS WONDTACULAR."
(UPWORTHY'S BIGGEST EVER HIT.)

By stripping the stories of negativity and complexity, and picking out
the least controversial elements and placing them center stage, Upworthy's content is all designed to elicit the same emotional response,
a kind of glossy, cigarette-lighter-waving "We Are the World" feel-
goodathon.

AND AS WE start to get the majority of our news via social media, this
becomes a self-perpetuating cycle. Facebook's basic unit of precedence
is the "like," with Facebook's 1.6 billion users clicking the like button

more than 6 billion times every day. Facebook CEO Mark Zuckerberg has publicly ruled out the possibility of ever instituting a dislike button. In 2013, when he was asked in a company Q and A if it was something he would consider, he replied, "That's not something we think is good for the world. So we're not going to build that."

It's hard to overstate Facebook's influence in determining the nature and tone of the news to which we are now are exposed. The social network has already been accused of political bias through editorializing of the content that appears in its "trending topics" sidebar, with former employees claiming that the site deliberately suppressed stories of interest to conservatives and artificially promoted other stories that were not organically trending at all.

But beyond this controversial element of human curation, even the basic algorithm itself, with its hefty reliance on the like button, tends to skew the type of news that we consume, perpetuating the culture of manufactured positivity in the types of stories we share.

And because increasingly for news organizations like Upworthy and its competitors, the key goal for a story is no longer simply to attract clicks or readers, but to secure Facebook likes and shares, this stripping out the substance from the news becomes self-perpetuating.

But "liking" is one of the most unchallenging and anodyne of all the human emotions. *Like* is the word teenagers use to strip love or sex or crushing unrequited devotion of its power to humiliate them. *Like* rinses the news of challenge and complexity.

This hits me when a Facebook friend shares a link to a local newspaper story with the headline "School District Denies Second Graders Free Lunch," about some Latino children who had been refused the school lunch they were entitled to, I obviously can't click like in response, as that would be declaring my personal political beliefs to be a combination of hungry children and institutionalized racism.

But in a snatched, guilty prebreakfast look at Facebook on my phone while simultaneously trying to prevent Zeph from upending the garbage can, I don't have the time or the brain capacity to craft a nuanced comment in response, unpicking the legacy of funding cutbacks, discrimination, and the countless petty humiliations and injustices of poverty. So of course what I do, is nothing. Had the headline read instead "The School District Refused to Give This Kid Her Lunch. Now Watch Her Epic Comeback," then they may as well have dragged my finger straight to the like button themselves.

But life isn't always awesome, stories don't always have magical arcs with Hollywood endings, and most hungry second graders struggling with the exhausting daily realities of poverty don't have the personal resources needed for epic comebacks. Real-world news events are usually complex and entrenched and uncomfortable, and one of the responsibilities of good journalism is to expose and challenge this. Negativity may be a bummer, but genuine critical thinking and analysis can't happen without it. But in a system in which *like* is the main driver of success, the schmaltzy and uplifting naturally rise to the top, and the complex, challenging, or uncomfortable grind to a halt.

Upworthy has set the standard for a slew of copycats and competitors to bring a tone of nonstop feel good to the news and wider culture. BuzzFeed's books editor, Isaac Fitzgerald, on accepting the job, announced he wouldn't be publishing any negative reviews. "Why waste breath talking smack about something?" he said, then declared that in a public rejection of what he saw as the snarky negativity-fest of old-school mainstream cultural outlets, from then on his editorial role model would be Thumper, the rabbit from the movie *Bambi*, with his much quoted motto, "If you can't say something nice, don't say nothing at all."[6]

Upworthy's founders argue that the methods they use enable them to bring important issues and world events to vast numbers of people who would not otherwise be aware of them. This is undoubtedly true, but, then again, like a charity campaign that raises "awareness" but no actual cash, if their content is neutered of any substance or specificity, then it's hard to see quite where this awareness is actually heading. If even the words *Democrat* and *Republican* are considered too much of a downer in an Upworthy world, then it's hard to see how people would make the leap from merely clicking on a video to meaningful engagement with the issues or participation in the political process.

IN A STRANGE way, social media's squeamishness about the more complicated or unpleasant aspects of our lives and worlds feels oddly similar to the parenting trends that attempt to eliminate all negativity from our children's lives. And, like with our kids, it seems that relentless positivity and a world wiped clean of shades of gray or difficult questions creates its own anxieties.

It makes me wonder whether there is any way out of this positivity arms race, and if so, how that might ever happen.

In the meantime, however, I'm more worried about a pressing issue closer to home.

8.

POSITIVE PSYCHOLOGY (OR IF YOU'RE NOT HAPPY, IT'S YOUR OWN FAULT, YOU LAZY SCHMUCK)

In the spring, our friends living in the apartment below us move out, and an elderly couple moves in. I start off full of good intentions about getting to know them. Ever since learning of the links between community involvement and happiness, and especially since spending time with the Mormons in Utah, I've been intent on becoming more community spirited myself. On the plane home from Salt Lake City, my plans became increasingly ambitious, and by the time we touched down in Oakland I had mentally sketched out a full-blown rural idyll, full of barn raisings and village dances, like something out of 1950s Kansas (although ideally without the cold-blooded killing). But since I've been back, I've done virtually nothing to put any of this into practice, so socializing with the new neighbors feels like a good place to start.

Unfortunately, the problem with socializing with the neighbors turns out to be the actual neighbors. It soon becomes clear that living directly underneath two marauding, overindulged toddlers is not how they pictured their golden years unfolding. I can hardly blame them. As Placid Baby Zeph transforms seamlessly into Willful Toddler Zeph, and his big brother takes up the challenge with some high-energy attention seeking of his own, even my husband starts to describe the experience of looking after our children as "like being a waiter at a fraternity party."

I spend way more time that I would like yelling at the boys to be quiet, and my neighbor spends way more time than I would like yelling at me to be quiet. It gets to the point where I dread seeing her in the mornings. Unfortunately we share a washing machine, and frosty silence is a difficult mode to pull off when you're regularly handling each other's underwear.

This slightly stressful set of circumstances is compounded when she sets up a home-based business as an alternative healer, an enterprise that apparently requires total silence. I look up her Web site. Apparently her method is designed to "harness the powerful placebo effect." I doubt that regular socializing would bring either of us much of a happiness boost.

All of this hammers home a somewhat obvious point. Any generalizations about happiness, or universal recommendations about how to increase it, do little to describe the complexities of human experience.

Studies may tell us that we would be happier if we were Mormon or childless or invited our neighbors over for canasta, because on average, people with these characteristics are happier. But cohorts, like corporations, are not actually people. Studies show, for instance, that married people are, on average, happier than singletons, but that average includes both blissed-out newlyweds and couples who can barely stand the sight of each other. An average level of moderate happiness across a nation might mean that everyone living there is reasonably happy, but it might also mean that half the population is in the throes of ecstasy and the other half in abject despair. Either way, on an individual level, these statistics can often seem all but meaningless.

Happiness is so individualized and complex, so dependent on a myriad of factors—of circumstances and life events, upbringing, culture, relationships, preferences, and personality quirks—that anything averaged out over a group is unlikely to do much to describe the lived experience of any one person. And when it comes to happiness, perhaps individual experience is really all that matters.

Cohort studies may be a blunt instrument to understand something as nuanced and idiosyncratic as human happiness, but in the last fifteen years or so there have certainly been an awful lot of them.

Happiness studies, or positive psychology as it's called in academic circles, is a relatively new field of research. In 1998, the American Psychological Association appointed a new president, Dr. Martin Seligman of the University of Pennsylvania. Up until this point, Seligman was best known for his work in the 1960s administering electric shocks to captive dogs,[1] but in his new role as president, he was now changing tack. Seligman used his inaugural speech to the association to declare the grand opening of a whole new branch of psychology, to be known as "positive psychology."

This brave new discipline would cast aside the shackles of old-school negative psychology, with its party-pooping tendency to dwell on downers like depression and pathology. Instead, this new, upbeat psychology would focus exclusively on "the most positive qualities of an individual" with a particular focus on happiness. Happiness would no longer be left to chance or private experience but would be measured, assessed, documented, and then controlled and manipulated through precise clinical techniques and interventions.

There would be prizes. Seligman announced a series of hefty new cash awards for positive psychology research, sponsored by a quasi-religious organization called the John Templeton Foundation, a group previously dedicated to efforts to put religion on an equal footing with science in society. Sir John Templeton, the organization's founder, a prominent right-wing billionaire philanthropist, declared that the money was to encourage "scientific investigation of the benefits produced by optimism, thanksgiving, and the power of positive thinking," sounding a little as though he had decided the outcome of the research before it had even begun.

At the height of the economic boom, this new feel-good science captured the public mood; and in the intervening years, positive psychology has exploded, quickly becoming one of the fastest-growing and best-funded specialties in academia.

As the field's thought leaders scowl through their beards attempting to crunch the numbers into a definitive happiness algorithm to needlepoint on a throw pillow, Happiness Studies courses are now offered at more than a hundred university campuses across the nation, including most of the Ivy League. Harvard boasts its own dedicated Happiness Lab, and positive psychology professors have been signed up to coach everyone from the bigwigs of corporate America to the US military. Even governments are getting on board, with positive psychology professors now at the heart of public policy, advising prime ministers and presidents on how to secure the happiness of their citizens.

Like some kind of *Brave New World*–style parable of joylessness, in its short life span, the positive psychology movement has generated more than sixty-four thousand scientific research studies attempting to unpick and codify the roots of contentment.[2]

The studies fall broadly into two categories. The first tries to work out who is and isn't happy already. Which country or American city is the happiest? (Spoiler: Denmark and Provo, Utah, respectively.) Are married people or rich people or Republicans happier than the single or poor or progressive? [Answers: (A) yes, (B) obviously, yes, and (C) for some weird reason, yes.]

Others in this category focus on personality traits. Studies show that optimistic people are happier than pessimistic people! Positive Pollies are happier than Negative Nellies! People who talk about good jobs, exercise, and spiritual meaning on Twitter are happier than people who use lots of words like *bored* or *tired* (this last, part of a research project from Martin Seligman's positive psychology center at the University of Pennsylvania[3]). These lines of enquiry can sometimes seem peculiarly obvious or even tautologous, essentially fancy ways of saying "Happy people are happier than unhappy people."

But where the real money lies is in the second strand of studies—

those that don't just attempt to understand the human condition but to advance the dream of improving it. These studies test out interventions for boosting happiness that can then be packaged and sold.

The jolt of academic respectability and flood of cash breathed new life into the personal happiness movement. Buoyed up by the claim to scientific rigor, it quickly expanded from a purely academic endeavor to an exciting commercial proposition.

So in demand was the new happiness science that positive psychologists were soon superstars in their own right, able to command tens of thousands of dollars for appearances and speaking engagements. (Martin Seligman's agents list his price range for a single speech as "$50,001 and above.")[4]

Now the discerning happiness seeker, formerly reliant on a few unregulated self-appointed self-help gurus, had the full miracle of science at his or her disposal. Academic positive psychologists have taken full advantage of this business opportunity, quickly creating a thriving industry of books, apps, coaching, consultancy, and courses.

An online positive psychology course with two residential weekends taught by ex-Harvard positive psychology professor Tal Ben Shahar will set you back $5,500 (plus accommodation).[5] A certificate in "applied positive psychology" from the Open Center in New York comes in a little cheaper at $2,950.[6] In comparison, UC Berkeley's Greater Good Science Center's weekend retreat at the famous beachside Esalen Institute in Big Sur, California, Putting the Science of Happiness into Practice, at between $421 and $1,766 (depending on accommodation) seems like a bargain.[7]

For those on a budget, the positive psychology movement has also spawned an entire new generation of happiness advice books, aimed not at an academic audience but at the general reader. A cover story in *Psychology Today* reports that in the year 2000 just fifty popular nonfiction titles on the subject of happiness were published. By 2008 that number had grown to four thousand.[8]

While positive psychology professors are often openly snobby about old-school self-help, in many ways the field has become self-help's more respectable cousin. In one article, *New York* magazine went as far as to say that "positive psychology functions as a (research arm) of the self-help industry."[9] The books sit on the same shelf of the bookstore as their less august predecessors and are often virtually indistinguishable in tone and substance.

Positive psychology has done a great job of washing away the tiny but apparently indelible stain of failure that old-school self-help always carried with it. While a person on the subway underlining passages in a self-help book will always carry the vaguest whiff of tragedy, a positive psychology book almost seems like a status symbol.

Part of this is a branding issue. Traditional self-help books tend to have a slightly overwrought nineteen eighties greed-is-good feel about them, all shouty capitals and unnervingly white teeth. In contrast, positive psychology books have a gentler aesthetic, with whimsical fonts and pictures of sunflowers or dandelions. (These two flowers are clearly the international symbols for Happy Thoughts. Out of the top thirty picks on Amazon for positive psychology, seven of them have either sunflowers or dandelions on the cover.)

To further distance itself from self-help, an average positive psychology book will mention the word *science* on its cover and introductory pages many, many times.

"[T]he star of *The How of Happiness* is science," writes Sonja Lyubomirsky in the introduction to her positive psychology bestseller, one of the most influential books in the field, "and the happiness-increasing strategies that I and other social psychologists have developed are its key supporting players. My story is that of a research scientist, not a clinician, life coach, or self-help guru."

This is not, apparently the spoilsport sort of science that cautions moderation in its conclusions or might feel compromised by a hefty consumer promise. Positive psychology books pack a similar marketing punch in the titles as their self-help competitors: *The How of Happiness: A New Approach to Getting the Life You Want; Authentic Happiness: Using the New Positive Psychology to Realize Your Potential for Lasting Fulfillment;* and *The Happiness Advantage: The Seven Principles of Positive Psychology That Fuel Success and Performance at Work.*

IT'S NOT JUST the rampantly consumerist tone of positive psychology books that feels reminiscent of self-help. The more of them I read, the more I start to realize that they also share a deep underlying philosophical similarity.

Ever since I started delving into the world of the commercial happiness machine, one of the most consistent messages coming out of the industry as a whole, from the Landmark Forum to the mindfulness movement, is the insistence that how happy we are is essentially something that is under our own control and that our life's circumstances are all but irrelevant. Now I'm realizing that the exact same message is also coming through loud and clear from the positive psychology movement.

Clearly anyone in the happiness trade has a strong financial incentive to at the very least play up the amount of agency we have over our own well-being and to play down the elements that we are unable to change. And, like the self-help industry, positive psychology almost defiantly downplays the role of our life circumstances in our happiness. In contrast, it emphasizes to the max the ability of the individual to radically alter his or her own levels of contentment by sheer effort and force of will.

THE OMNIPRESENT INESCAPABILITY of this narrative is probably expressed most clearly via a rather unappetizing-looking cherry pie.

This pie is the cover star of *The How of Happiness*, by Dr. Sonja Lyubomirsky of the University of California, Riverside, a prominent and influential figure in the movement as a whole. (Different editions of the book have different pies—the lemon meringue pie on the paperback edition looks slightly less "gas station chiller cabinet" than the cherry.) Lyubomirsky herself is an academic, with her own "happiness laboratory" at the university and a million-dollar research grant to come up with techniques for becoming happier. *The How of Happiness* aims to distill this research along with other findings from positive psychology into actionable advice nuggets for the armchair happiness seeker.

The pie is a recurring trope in the book, a pie chart infographic designed to show the relative importance of the different factors affecting our happiness. It is divided into three slices, to represent genetics, circumstance, and our own voluntary contribution—that is, the amount of our happiness over which we have control.

The largest slice of Lyubomirsky's pie, 50 percent, is allocated to genetics. She explains that research carried out in the late eighties on sets of twins showed that around half our happiness can be attributed to our genes. Each of us has a genetic set point to which, like a high-achieving homing pigeon, we tend to return.

The genetic aspect of happiness is relatively uncontested in the literature. But where things start to get more controversial is in the other half of the pie. The second slice is a measly, Weight Watchers–style sliver of just 10 percent for what Lyubomirsky calls "circumstance," that is, the factors that we are either born into or the other aspects of our lives and worlds that we cannot control. She never defines exactly what she is including and excluding from this category, but there seems to be a lot thrown in there—our demographics (such as our race, age, sex, income, marital status, and level of education) plus some other chance variables, such as our appearance and health, plus our relationships and the events of our lives.

To underscore her insistence that our life circumstances have a negligible impact on our happiness, Lyubomirsky also provides a long and slightly bizarre list of things that, she claims, will *not* make us happier. This peculiar inventory includes: "cure from a chronic illness or disability," "more supportive and loving parents," "more money," "knowing what

you really want to do with your life," "a relationship," and "more time."
As she claims definitively, "None of these things will make you sub-
stantially happier," going on to stress that "if we can accept as true that
life circumstances are *not* the keys to happiness, we'll be greatly em-
powered to pursue happiness for ourselves."

This empowerment will come, she assures us, in the form of the
entire rest of the pie, a sugar coma–inducing giant wedge of 40 percent
that represents the amount of our happiness that Lyubomirsky claims
is under our own control, "in our power to change through how we act
and how we think."

This 40 percent figure is much quoted in the positive psychology
literature in both academic and popular texts, and it represents the
field's great marketing opportunity. This is the 40 percent that anyone
with a book to sell, a course of coaching to offer, or a happiness technique to market is hoping to co-opt.

Lyubomirsky herself has several. The rest of the book is devoted to
the happiness exercises and "interventions" tested in her lab and developed by the other positive psychology research, techniques that she im-
plies will have the power to increase our happiness by up to four times
as much as the sum total of our life's circumstances.

Considering the hefty expectations placed on them, the happiness
recommendations themselves are a little underwhelming. (To be fair,
Lyubomirsky is upfront about this, admitting that they are the kinds
things your grandmother might have suggested. Although my actual
grandmother, who lived a happy and vigorous life well into her nine-
ties, preferred a couple of vodka tonics and a good bitching session.)

There's a slightly peculiar section on enhancing your relationships
with other people that advises practicing "acts of kindness" but not too
often, because apparently Lyubomirsky's research shows that kind acts
make you happier, but only if you limit them to once a week.

Then, aside from a bit of padding about "taking care of your body"
and mindfulness that seems to have little to do with positive psychology,

the main thrust of the advice is various different takes on the theme of positive thinking, including exercises to cultivate a sense of gratitude, instructions to "count your blessings," and techniques to increase your levels of optimism.

This deft rebranding of actual problems into "problematic ways of thinking" is a common theme in the happiness industry. "You're thinking the wrong thoughts" seemed to be the general theme underpinning much of Valerie's yelling at the Landmark Forum. When Eckhart Tolle wrote that the "primary cause of unhappiness is never the situation but your thoughts about it," he echoed a long line of happiness gurus, who insist that the real problems in our lives are never discrimination or poverty, bad relationships or unfair bosses or being the only person in the house who knows how to use the washing machine, but our own failure to adopt whatever the latest Big Happiness–endorsed thinking style might be, to think positive or practice mindfulness, to "take personal responsibility" or count our blessings.

The whole "think-different-thoughts" school of happiness advice reminds me a little of how I felt when I moved into my first apartment after college, a place whose previous owners can only have been either Egyptian pharaohs or serial killers. The walls were encased in heavy gold-flocked wallpaper. The carpet was patterned with churning orange and brown swirls like a sociopath's take on a Rorschach test, and the whole apartment smelled of decay and onions. When I complained to a friend about the effort likely to be involved in turning it into somewhere that a person could live without losing her mind, she replied, "Why don't you just change your taste? It would be a lot easier."

The idea that our circumstances are trivial to our happiness, that what we really need to do in order to be happy is to think positive, and that keeping a gratitude journal or counting our blessings can potentially have quadruple the impact on our happiness than the love of our parents, whether we live in affluence or poverty, or whether or not we suffer from a debilitating chronic illness seems like a stretch at best. I wonder how I would feel about this message if I were, say, a poor African

American single mother on welfare, dealing with systemic injustice and struggling to get by. The idea feels particularly inflammatory when put forward by a privileged, white, well-compensated academic.

Ever since I first dipped my toe into the world of the consumer happiness industry, I have struggled with this basic narrative. With its almost belligerent denial that structural obstacles to happiness exist, it seems to promote a dangerous level of social and political disengagement about tackling the injustices of the wider world. On a more personal level, I find it unforgiving and dismissive of others' often very real problems and all too liable to veer into victim blaming. Most important, it seems to undermine the very idea of a supportive community in which we all take responsibility for one another's welfare, something that is at the very foundation of happiness.

But if the claim that circumstances don't matter and that happiness is a simple question of individual effort is somehow not just an ideology or a belief system but a scientifically proven fact, then whatever distaste I happen to feel about the idea is neither here nor there. So I want to dig a little deeper and track down the research on which this notion is based. Are our circumstances really irrelevant to our happiness? Do we all have an equal shot at contentment?

IN HER FOOTNOTES, Lyubomirsky cites the academic paper that she says forms the basis for her pie chart and her claim that circumstances are of minimal importance to our happiness, while "intentional activity" is king.

The paper is an old one, from back in 1999, written by Professor Ed Diener (the third male academic I have come across so far who is credited with being the "father of the positive psychology movement." Positive psychology's mother obviously had a fun few years.). Diener's paper summarizes all the research up until that point about the different factors affecting human happiness, citing a wide range of different studies.[10]

It's a dry read, and it takes me a while to get through. But when I do, it soon becomes clear that the paper doesn't really back up Lyubomirsky's neatly segmented pie chart with any such certainty.

The picture Diener paints is way more nuanced and complex than Lyubomirsky's pie would suggest. As it turns out, the estimates for the relative importance of the various factors affecting our happiness vary massively from study to study. The real takeaway from this paper would probably best by summed up by the phrase "nobody has much of a clue."

First, on the genetic component of happiness, estimates are wildly contradictory. The researchers of the major study of twins and happiness at first concluded that between 40 to 55 percent of our happiness is genetic (broadly in line with Lyubomirsky's figure of 50 percent). However according to Diener, a later analysis of the *same data* concluded that when it comes to long-term happiness, the figure was actually more like 80 percent, a finding which prompted Diener to write the following sentence, "based on the later heritability estimate, it could be said it is as hard to change one's happiness as it is to change one's height," an observation that is hard to square with the idea that we can transform our happiness by 40 percent by thinking positive and counting our blessings.

As for the "circumstance" slice of pie, the estimates from the studies in Diener's paper run anything from 10 to 20 percent, with most settling just under 20 percent, putting Lyubomirsky's 10 percent on the absolute bottom end. But crucially the studies Diener quotes define circumstance in a much more limited way than Lyubomirsky does in her pie chart. These studies limit their definition of circumstance to a few very basic demographic variables—age, sex, income, race, marital status, and education—whereas Lyubomirsky's definition appears to include *all* life circumstances and events beyond our control.

Even if we were to take Lyubomirsky's 10 percent estimate as a fair reading of Diener's paper, it is a huge conceptual leap from this to the idea that "everything else" is under our own control via intentional activity. The handful of demographic factors he mentions takes absolutely no account of the vast majority of life events that are fully or partially beyond our control—lost jobs, bad marriages, unfair bosses, bereavement, divorce, rent hikes, broken-down cars, miscarriages, illness, hostile family members, or your toddler carefully smearing mashed banana into every page of the library books. Instead, he takes pains to point out that whatever cannot be attributed to genetics and demographics is a complex and unknown mix of environment, culture, circumstance, fortune, and adversity.

In short, you can read Diener's paper, pick out whichever studies from it that support your own point of view or agenda, and use them to back up pretty much any conclusion you want. I could easily take this exact same paper and write a self-help book featuring a pie comprised of 80 percent genetics and 20 percent demographics and absolutely no intentional activity at all (although admittedly it probably wouldn't sell very well).

THE MORE I look into it, the more it seems that the claim that circumstance matters little to happiness might be based on some serious cherry-picking of the evidence.

As a general rule, the disadvantaged are significantly less happy than the privileged. The CDC estimates that rates of depression among poor Americans are roughly three times that in the general population.[11] White people in America consistently report as significantly happier than African Americans, irrespective of income, with the percentage of African Americans reporting that they are "not too happy" roughly double that of white Americans saying the same.[12] Men are significantly happier than women,[13] and the women who do the most "women-y" type things, stay-at-home mothers, are the least happy of all.[14]

Similarly, the much repeated and oddly moralizing claim that money has minimal impact on happiness also turns out to be based on a distorted interpretation of the evidence. (It is also notable that the people stressing the irrelevance of material wealth often tend to be the same people who have never gone without it.)

One much-misquoted study is a famous piece of research by Nobel Laureate Daniel Kahneman into the relationship between income and happiness.[15]

This study is almost always reported in both the academic literature and the popular press as showing that money makes no difference to happiness above an income of $75,000 a year.

But the study does not show this. What Kahneman's research shows is that money makes a big difference to all measures of happiness up to an income of $75,000. As he writes, "the effects of household income are almost invariably both statistically significant and quantitatively important."

Above that point, money still makes a significant difference to what most people would consider the most important measure of happiness—a person's satisfaction with his or her life when taken as a whole—and this trend never levels off in the data, no matter how high up the income scale you go. Above an income of $75,000 what does level off is any improvement in the kind of mood that the person was in the day before.

Even leaving aside the fact that the study doesn't say what people says it does, it is a mark of the privileged bubble, in which many journalists and academics operate, that this finding is often reported as "Money can't buy happiness, over $75, 000 a year" or even "once basic needs are met," as if $75,000 was an amount so trifling as to be barely worth mentioning.

In reality, only the top third of Americans have a household income of this much, and only 12 percent of individuals do,[16] so perhaps a more accurate reporting of the link between income and happiness would be that, for the vast majority of the country, the financial situation people find themselves in is of crucial importance to all measures of happiness. Unsurprisingly the further down the income scale you go, the more important it is.

THIS RELENTLESS FOCUS on individual effort, and denial that circumstances matter to happiness, has an ideological flavor to it, a kind of neoliberalism of the emotions.

And perhaps this philosophical bent isn't surprising, given the highly conservative nature of the key financial backers of the academic positive psychology movement.

Since the discipline's inception, one of the biggest private funders of academic positive psychology research has been the Templeton Foundation, an organization that has to date doled out tens of millions of dollars in prizes and grant money to positive psychology professors, at some point providing at least some funding to most of the major positive psychology university departments in the country.[17] Sonja Lyubomirsky herself is the recipient of both a Templeton Positive Psychology Prize and a research grant, and the foundation has provided millions in funding for Martin Seligman's Positive Psychology Center at the University of Pennsylvania.

Until his death in 2015, the Templeton Foundation's president was John Templeton, Jr., an evangelical Christian, high-profile political conservative, and generous donor to right-wing causes. His other personal funded projects have included the deeply conservative pressure group Let Freedom Ring, whose mission is to promote conservative social values and small government, and Freedom Watch, a group that declares on its Web site that its aim is to stop the politicians who want to "turn our nation into a socialist Euro-style welfare state." Templeton, Jr., donated millions of dollars to the Republican Party and the campaigns of numerous conservative political candidates over years, as well as donating substantial sums to various anti–gay marriage initiatives.[18]

It is rare that a single private financial backer has such a sweeping

202 AMERICA THE ANXIOUS

influence over an academic discipline. Although the Templeton Foundation claims to be politically neutral, and this is almost certainly technically accurate in a party political sense, in its choices of what types of research to fund, it seems to have played a huge role in shaping the philosophical direction that positive psychology has taken.

Right from the start, the research projects that have received Templeton cash have been those that focus on the primacy of individual effort and character strengths, with no attempt to even consider how social justice or systemic policy change might influence well-being. Right out of the gate, this has set the terms and intellectual scope of the discussion. And as more research gets conducted to confirm this initial bias, this view simply gets restated over and over.

Martin Seligman himself has done much to promote this neoliberal view that circumstances don't matter to happiness. "In general, when things go wrong we now have a culture which supports the belief that this was done to you by some larger force, as opposed to, you brought it on yourself by your character or decisions," he claimed in one interview in the early years of the positive psychology movement. "The problem about that is it's a recipe for passivity. . . . [W]hat you do matters a great deal. . . . A lot of your troubles were brought on by yourself. You are responsible for them."[19]

"IT'S THE MESSAGE we get constantly—it's so insidious, it's woven into the fabric," Linda Tirado tells me over the phone. "If you were just more grateful for what you have, if you just had a more positive attitude, if you just wouldn't focus so much on your problems. And you think 'Yeah, but my problems are pretty immediate.'"

I approached Linda for an interview after reading her book, *Hand to Mouth, Living in Bootstrap America*, an account of her life as a low-wage worker in middle America, mainly in the fast-food and chain-restaurant industry. She writes about working up to ninety hours a week at two or more jobs to make ends meet; about constant pain from a mouthful of broken teeth that she can't afford to get fixed, about exhaustion from walking the hour-long trek to work after her car breaks down and there's no money for a mechanic, and the gnawing worry about having no health insurance and doctor visits for her kids that were a luxury way out of reach. She describes jobs that demand workers be available at all times but guarantee no hours; about colleagues being fired on a boss's whim with no legal recourse; and the many, many daily humiliations, injustices, stresses, and sheer, bone-aching unfairness of living this way.

"I wouldn't even mind the degradations of my work life so much if the privileged and powerful were honest about it," she writes. "Instead . . . we're told to keep smiling, and to be grateful for the chance to barely survive while being blamed for not succeeding."

Linda is clearly skeptical about the idea that circumstances matter little to happiness. "Not all poor people are chemically depressed," she writes, "but a lot of us are situationally depressed at any given time. And that's because our lives are depressing. I realize that might at first sound simplistic, but I don't think it's a lot more complicated than that."

Linda's financial circumstances have changed since she published her book, but she is still unapologetically angry, not just about the routine degradations of life in low-income America but also about what she sees as a pervasive narrative that the poor might somehow be able to magic away their problems with a change of attitude.

"Positive thinking isn't just useless, it's counterproductive to my self-esteem," she tells me, when I ask whether she thinks that things might have seemed brighter with the help of a few gratitude exercises. "It makes things worse. You cannot kick me and expect me to say thank you for kicking me with a smile on my face."

Linda tells me about a time when she was working in a particularly miserable job in a chain restaurant, with wages that were barely enough to live on, no benefits or health insurance and a boss who she describes

as brutal; and all the staff were required to watch an employee training video about positivity, with a particular emphasis on smiling and
maintaining a positive attitude.

"We were all watching this video about positivity and keeping a
smile on your face at all times and how we were all one big happy family,"
she says, "and this guy who was *brutal* to his staff kept coming into the
room while this was playing to change over the video. It was surreal.

"We were underpaid, exhausted, and overworked. Then they tell us
we have to smile all the time, or else we won't be able to pay our rent.
It was all about putting a big shiny smile on your face and pretending
really hard. Everyone is suppressing everything all the time. But there
are studies that show, if you fake happiness, it starts to numb your
emotions."

"Did it numb your emotions?" I ask.

"Of course," she says. "It's soul killing."

I ask Linda if she's heard of mindfulness. She snorts. "I'm always
hearing these things about how the poor just need to practice mindfulness. It makes me think, 'Why would I want to be any more in the
present moment than I already fucking am?' The rational response to
a miserable situation is not pleasant mindful gratitude.

"They think, if they can just make people a little more chipper about
being oppressed. Problem is, if you just ignore all the hard shit in your
life, you'll never change anything. It's a way of making the poor bovine.

"It's a systemic disorder, not an internal disorder. It's much fucking
easier to be happy when you're not worried about the electric bill."

It's easy to dismiss Linda as an extreme case, but by her own admission, during the time period she writes about in her book, her income left her better off than around a third of Americans. It would take
a significantly higher income than Linda's to be free of all the kinds of
worries she describes.

Linda hasn't read *The How of Happiness*, so before we get off the
phone, I run her through the pie chart and the idea that things like
gratitude exercises and counting our blessings can potentially have four

times the impact on our happiness as the sum total of our life's circum-stances, and ask her what she thinks of the idea. For the first time since we got on the phone, Linda is quiet.

"The thing is so ridiculous I'm having trouble answering the ques-tion," she says finally. "The idea is so farcical on the face of it, I would want to go back to the dataset and see if those numbers were sound. If they proved to be sound, then I would go back and question my own sanity."

LINDA DOES INSPIRE me to go back to the data (at the same time wondering if the words *inspire* and *data* have ever been used in the same sentence before). I want to know just how sound the scientific evi-dence is for positive psychology's methods.

In *The How of Happiness*, Sonja Lyubomirsky certainly makes it sound impressive. In the introduction, she mentions a study by Martin Seligman that tested out a gratitude exercise on some severely depressed patients. Every evening, they were asked to write down "three good things that happened that day," such as "Rosalind called to say hello," or "the sun finally came out today." According to this study, apparently, the group who at the beginning had been so depressed "that they had great difficulty even leaving their beds," within fifteen days went from "severely depressed" to "mildly to moderately depressed" and 94 percent of them experienced relief.

This study sounds extraordinary, so I try to track down a copy to see for myself. The problem is, after a pretty exhaustive search, I find no evidence of it in any scientific journal anywhere, or on Martin Selig-man's extensive list of published works. In the end, I email Dr. Lyu-bomirsky asking if she knows where it might be. She replies, promptly and graciously.

"Hi—sorry Ruth—I am so swamped, I literally have barely enough time to brush my teeth," she writes. "I think the study was never pub-lished, but it was submitted when I was writing the book."

Something seems off. If the results were as impressive as they sound, why was the study never published? If it was never published, then it was unlikely to have been peer-reviewed. It seems particulary curious that Lyubomirsky would still be quoting it in her book, as fact, many years later (*The How of Happiness* is now on its fourteenth reprint) without qualifiers and no mention of its unpublished status.

Finally, I email Professor Seligman directly, asking where it is, and whether I might have access to a copy. He replies with a dashed off four word message, with no greeting or sign off:

"i never published it."

IT SEEMS PARTICULARLY curious that Dr. Lyubomirsky is relying on someone else's unpublished study as evidence for the stellar effectiveness of this type of technique, given that she runs her own "happiness laboratory" at the University of California at Riverside, carrying out trials of exactly this type of exercise, as well as other positive psychology interventions. I wonder what her own research has to say, so I pull up her published papers.

The results are significantly less spectacular.

Of the three studies I find by Lyubomirsky into these types of gratitude techniques, only one shows even the smallest benefit (although it is unclear whether this benefit was even statistically significant, because, despite citing the results many times in her academic and popular work, Lyubomirsky never published the actual study or the data itself, only a bar graph with an impressively large bar but an unlabeled scale). This benefit was also apparently only seen when people were instructed to do the task once a week. A group instructed to do it three times a week saw no benefit at all, which suggests that maybe the first group was benefitting more from the novelty than the gratitude.[20] Of the other two studies, one showed no statistically significant benefit at all for the group doing the gratitude task compared to a control group,[21] and the other showed that the gratitude group actually ended up feeling *worse* than the controls.[22] In the discussion section of this last paper, Lyubomirsky even writes:

> Our findings were unexpected, in that the practice of gratitude ac-
> tually *diminished* the well-being of dysphoric [depressed] par-
> ticipants from before to immediately after the intervention. . . .
> [W]riting the gratitude letter may have backfired if it led our dys-
> phoric patients to think they had little to be grateful for.

It's not just Lyubomirsky. When researchers from the Netherlands conducted a meta-analysis of published studies into the effectiveness of positive psychology interventions, they found that the overall effects of these techniques were small.[23] But a closer reading of the paper suggests that even this might be a generous interpretation.

The researchers found that the quality of studies across the board was low. When they first assessed the methodological rigor of the many published positive psychology studies in the literature to determine which ones they should include in the meta-analysis, *none* of them met the full criteria expected of a robust scientific trial. After discarding hundreds of studies that did not even meet the basic standards, they were left with just thirty-nine that could even be included in their as-sessments. Of this remaining thirty-nine studies, twenty were rated as low quality, eighteen of medium quality, and only one of high quality, and even this one didn't meet all the criteria.

Crucially, the studies with the lowest quality ratings tended to show the best results for the interventions, which might suggest that with more rigorous research methods applied, the small benefits noted in the meta-analysis might well become even smaller and might well disappear altogether.

NONE OF THIS is surprising to Dr. James Coyne.

I catch a glimpse of Coyne, avuncular and bearded, for approximately seven seconds before our Skype connection cuts to audio only, just in time for him to tell me the title of the lecture that he will be giving next week: "Positive Psychology Is for Rich White People."

Coyne, a psychologist and academic with a string of prestigious professorships to his name, has worked extensively in both academia and medical practice with a focus on psychosocial research. He is now one of the academic editors of the largest scientific journal in the world, *PLOS One.* Coyne considers himself part of an informal group called the Negateers, a name that conjures up a band of grumpy pirates but is actually a group of skeptics attempting to inject some caution into the juggernaut of positive psychology.[24]

Coyne grew up on welfare, in the projects. No one in his family had completed high school and yet he managed to get a scholarship to a four-year college. "For a while I was the poster child of the right wing and the idea that it's all about attitude and that anyone can make it," he tells me. "But after my freshman year, I rebelled. I realized it was rubbish to attribute this to attitude. So much of whether you make it in life is dependent on circumstance, or just on luck. The message that it's all about attitude is ridiculous. It neglects all complexities."

Although uncomfortable with certain elements of the basic philosophy, when Coyne had first started hearing about positive psychology research, he initially assumed that, given how heavily marketed the interventions were, they must have some benefits that could be helpful for his patients. At the time he was the director of the Behavioral Oncology Program at the University of Pennsylvania, specializing in ways to help cancer patients deal with anxiety and depression. So he set out to analyze the positive psychology literature to try to separate the proven claims from the hype.

"I had expected that positive psychologists out promoting their work and selling their products could surely come up with some unambiguous findings," he tells me. "I could then discuss *how* we could attempt to translate those findings into strategies for people's everyday lives and whether we could expect them to be sustained with any lasting impact on our well-being. Unfortunately, I didn't get that far. When I looked at the research, the findings turned out to be not particularly positive despite being presented as such.

"Most people would consider me a terrifying methodologist," he continues. But when he applied the same rigorous methodological approach that he uses for his own scientific papers, and to assessing the papers that he publishes in the journal he edits, to the positive psychology literature, he found that often the results were so low as to be almost negligible, or that they only showed up after a fair few statistical machinations. After reanalyzing the data in a couple of key positive psychology studies, and finding that the supposed results disappeared on closer inspection, he tried to submit these findings to a couple of academic psychology journals.

But each time his papers were rejected. "One editor told me that she didn't want to be part of a witch hunt," he tells me. "I asked what the appeals process was, and she told me that there wasn't one."

Coyne believes that positive psychology is a closed field, in which everyone is highly invested in showing the interventions in the best possible light and people are reluctant to criticize one another's claims.

"Positive psychologists tell me—'Our journals are a mutual admiration society,'" he says. "There is no critical thinking, no critical standards. If a bad paper is sent for peer review to another positive psychology academic, who is equally invested in making positive psychology look good, he or she would be unlikely to criticize it, because doing so would be bringing down the reputation of the field as a whole, and therefore his or her own reputation."

Coyne attributes this problem in part to what he sees as a serious conflict of interest right at the heart of the academic positive psychology movement. Clear evidence exists across various scientific and medical disciplines that when researchers stand to gain financially from a certain outcome of a trial or study, this often leads to skewed or

exaggerated results. Drug trials sponsored by pharmaceutical companies, for example, more often show favorable results for the drug in
question than independent research.[25]

Coyne points out that the issue of conflict of interest is particularly
acute and underacknowledged in the positive psychology field. As he
writes in an online article:

> We can't understand what passes for science in positive psychol-
> ogy unless we grasp the larger context of the positive psychology
> community, the multimillion dollar industry associated with posi-
> tive psychology, and incentives that the community and its indus-
> try offer to those claiming to provide the science of positive
> psychology.[26]

Although clearly not all academic positive psychologists are also in
the commercial self-help business, many of them are. If some of the
same people that are conducting the academic research are also out selling it to the public, they are likely to be heavily financially incentivized
to show clear results and to bury more lackluster findings.

BUT EVEN IF some positive psychologists are pumping up their results, claiming that their interventions are more effective than is really
justified by the evidence, what's the harm? Surely it's a good thing to
encourage people to be more thankful and positive in their lives? After
all, nobody's life was ever ruined by writing a gratitude journal. Positive psychology's recommendations are generally so anodyne and uncontroversial that raising any objection to them feels a bit like picking
a fight with a fridge magnet.

But positive psychology's heavily promoted message that circumstance is unimportant and that with enough individual effort we can
control our own happiness is a subtly toxic one, both for individuals

and societies. And this is particularly worrying as it is now taking hold right at the heart of public policy.

The happiness agenda is becoming increasingly influential in the corridors of power, with happiness floated in several countries as an alternative measure of national progress to GDP. Ironically, the cynical British have been at the forefront of this trend. Conservative British prime minister David Cameron is heavily influenced by the positive psychology movement and in particular the work of Martin Seligman. Soon after coming to office, he set up a National Happiness Index at a cost of two million pounds in order to conduct regular widespread surveys of the British people about their levels of contentment, with the aim of using this information to influence policy.

Given that the whole research tradition of academic positive psychology has been developed within a politically conservative framework and set of guiding assumptions, it is not hard to see why it appeals to right-wing, austerity-promoting governments like David Cameron's.

While throwing money at his happiness agenda, Cameron's government has presided over perhaps the most comprehensive dismantling of the welfare state in recent history, with deep cuts to health services and provision for the disabled, the elderly, and those with mental health issues. According to data from the Department for Work and Pensions, Cameron's policies plunged a million extra people in the UK below the absolute poverty line.[27]

This isn't just a bizarre disconnect between words and action, but part of the same intellectual framework. If circumstance is of little consequence to happiness, why worry if people are struggling?

ALREADY, POSITIVE PSYCHOLOGY'S techniques and narrative of individual responsibility have provided inspiration for a punitive reform of the British welfare system.

In a new scheme being trialled, the unemployed are subject to attitude profiling, whereby they must undergo a series of psychological tests to determine their level of positivity and motivation. Those displaying a more positive attitude will be allowed to continue to look for work on their own schedule, while those profiled as more negative will be placed on harsh regimes requiring that they spend thirty-five hours a week at the job center, on pain of having their payments cut.[28] Other claimants displaying a lack of motivation toward finding employment (although what constitutes motivation is not defined), are now diverted toward even more punishing workfare regimes in which they are required to provide thirty hours a week of unpaid labor for a range of private companies in return for their welfare payments.[29]

"Since our inception in 1989, we have inherently utilized the key concepts now attributed to positive psychology to inform and shape our service delivery," says the Web site of Ingeus, one of the corporate service providers with lucrative government contracts to deliver the government's newly privatized "Work Programme" for the unemployed. "Namely building on individuals' personal strengths, resilience, connecting to others, positivity and contributing to something bigger than the self. Indeed one of our earliest client workshops focused on 'Positivity in Action.'"[30]

Companies like Ingeus are now contracted to run positive-thinking-style motivational courses based along positive psychology's principles to transform the attitudes of the unemployed. Attendance is compulsory, and failure to show up can result in payment sanctions, whereby welfare payments can be stopped for weeks or months at a time, plunging some of the most financially vulnerable in society even deeper into poverty.

"I am shy and have difficulty speaking to people and I will not do play acting in front of a group of people I am very uncomfortable with [. . .]" writes one unemployed woman in a blog post about her course. "I was told I would be sanctioned if I didn't take part, so I said I would get up, but I am not speaking. [. . .] After that, we had to fill out yet another 'benefits of being assertive' sheet."[31]

In keeping with the philosophy of the wider positive psychology movement, the syllabus and tone of these courses also seems determined to deny the wider structural issues causing unemployment, instead blaming the individual for his or her plight.

"He [the trainer] laughed at my idea that we should deal with this issue as a society and he turned it all back on me."

"You've got all these hooks on you . . . it's your way of being . . . you need to shift the way you look at it. You've got all this anger and frustration and that's stopping you from getting a job," writes another welfare claimant, blogger Izzy Koksal, about her motivational course that involved a group of the long-term unemployed being instructed to "talk, breathe, eat, shit belief in yourself." "Does the government honestly think that sending unemployed people to these courses, where we are bombarded with pseudo psychology about positive thinking will actually make any difference at all to unemployment? I would argue that they are actively harmful to unemployed people who spend the time being blamed for the situation that we find ourselves in and being offered 'solutions' that will make no difference. . . ."[32]

BULLYING PEOPLE INTO positivity doesn't seem like a particularly clear path to a happy society, and this hostile, unforgiving substitute for a social safety net seems to have strayed a long way from any reasonable definition of happiness. If happiness is community, then a psychologically healthy society takes collective responsibility for the well-being of its most vulnerable members.

Consistently, the countries that do the best in international happiness surveys—the Scandinavian countries, Australia, and New Zealand—are those that buy into a wider social contract that everyone is responsible for one another's well-being via a robust welfare state. People are generally happier when everyone is well cared for. Research suggests that this phenomenon is no coincidence. Benjamin Radcliff, a political science professor at the University of Notre Dame and author of *The Political Economy of Human Happiness*, has conducted extensive analysis of the data and concluded that people living in more generous welfare states, where people both pay more in taxes and receive more in benefits, consistently report significantly higher levels of happiness.[33]

If we want to create a happy society, we need a new narrative of well-being that is inclusive, generous, and socially connected, in which rather than using questionable science to blame people for their own problems, we focus on solving them.

THEN BY SOME bizarre cosmic coincidence, just as I am writing these words, I see a young guy sitting next to me in the café reading a book, with a familiar-looking pie on the cover. The cherry one. It's *The How of Happiness*. We have a long chat. He tells me that he is a psychology student at UC Berkeley, and the book is a set text for his degree course. I ask him whether or not it bothers him that there might be questions about some of the research, and that some of the findings might not be as strong as they seem. He says no, and that he believes that people can just take what they need from it and ignore the rest. He had a hard start in life, and it's good to be positive and empowering to think that things can change. I ask him whether he would feel the same if, in theory, it could be absolutely definitively scientifically proven that things couldn't change. He tells me that it wouldn't matter to him. That he would still read, still try. Then I realize. The product isn't happiness. It's hope.

9.

STAR-SPANGLED HAPPY

The line for the women's restrooms at the Paramount Theatre in Oakland snakes out of the door and down the hallway. Women crowd around the mirror, chatting in Spanish and painting on thick stripes of eyeliner. Out in the lobby, a male vocal ensemble is performing a clipped close harmony version of "This Land Is Your Land," and a gray-haired Indian woman in a sari is singing along in heavily accented broken English. "This land is my land, from California to the New York iPad . . ." she improvises, plugging the gaps in her knowledge of the lyrics with optimistic phonetics. Technically, it won't be Her Land for another twenty-five minutes or so, but she's swaying her hips like it's a done deal.

This is a final pit stop before the official oath ceremony that will transform the natives of ninety-nine different countries from around the world into American citizens. My husband, Neil, is one of them. He's taken the plunge and has applied for dual nationality, the realization of a lifelong dream (and a year or so of soul-sucking bureaucracy). The atmosphere is a kind of guarded festiveness. Everyone is clearly wearing their best outfit, and the air is tight with hairspray and hope and best behavior.

Neil is waiting for me outside the bathroom, and I kiss him good-bye. During the ceremony, he'll be sitting downstairs near the stage with the rest of the aspiring citizens, while friends and family have been designated the seats upstairs in the balcony. Next time I see him, he'll be American. I wonder briefly whether he will be different, his teeth a shade whiter, his handshake firmer. I've always vaguely fantasized about what it would be like to sleep with an American man, about whether American exceptionalism translates to the bedroom. Soon, I'll get to find out, without even cheating.

Inside, the theater is packed. I pick my way through the crowds to a vacant seat next to a sprawling, extended Mexican family who are all taking turns trying to keep a pair of wriggly toddlers entertained with a single stuffed rabbit. On my other side is a middle-aged woman from the Philippines, who clutches her purse on her lap and peers nervously over the balcony in search of her husband, who will also be taking the oath. She tells me that they came to this country fifteen years ago. Next year she will be the one downstairs.

It's hard to know what to expect from this ceremony. This is the year that Donald Trump is running for the Republican presidential nomination, and the sound track to our summer has been his anti-immigrant demagoguery, pledging to round us all up and send us home and then build a giant wall to stop us ever coming back. Although I feel reasonably confident that Neil and I are not the exact Pantone skin shade of immigrant Trump has in mind, in recent months America hasn't felt like a hugely welcoming place for outsiders.

But then a government official walks onto the stage and in an instant, dispels all that. He tells us his name is Randy Ricks (I briefly wonder if this is a stage name concocted by a government committee to evoke maximum Americanness), then in a strikingly gracious statement of welcome, tells us, "We are here in recognition that our country becomes even better because of you. Thank you for becoming citizens."

Then Randy Ricks reads off a list of the ninety-nine countries represented in the room today.

"Afghanistan, Albania, Algeria . . ." he begins. Cheers rise for each country. Tiny for Denmark and Estonia, rabble-rousingly mighty for

China and Mexico. "South Sudan, Swaziland, Sweden, Syria. . . ." I look around the room and wonder about the stories lurking behind each of those country names, the different strains of aspiration and desperation that have propelled each person toward this moment, the infinite variations on the American dream.

Then the citizens of ninety-nine nations stand up together, raise their right hands, and in unison renounce all "allegiance and fidelity to any foreign prince, potentate, state or sovereignty of which they have heretofore been a subject or citizen." I wonder how this squares with the fact that Neil isn't actually renouncing his British nationality, just adding to it. Later the Internet tells me that the queen is secure in herself not to care what empty promises her subjects might whisper in the heat of the moment to a foreign power (although I can't help thinking that she's kidding herself, like a wife insisting that the back rubs her husband gives his secretary are a business requirement).

Then the nearly citizens promise not only that they will bear arms on behalf of the United States and "support and defend her against all enemies foreign and domestic" but also that they will do all this "without any mental reservation," a requirement that seems so genuinely impossible for any British person to fulfill that I wonder if it is the final secret test of the U.S. Citizenship and Immigration department. Able to perform a significant act of any kind without mental reservation? Congratulations! You are, by default, no longer British.

"You came into this theater today, the citizens of ninety-nine different countries," says Randy Ricks. Then he smiles broadly. "But you are leaving as the citizens of one country."

The crowd roars. My throat pricks. I glance over at the Mexican family beside me. They've given up trying to keep the toddlers quiet, and they are now running around in the back of the theater in outright mutiny. But the adults don't mind. They are home free. They all have tears rolling down their faces.

Every now and then, life gives us grand feelings—A-list feelings, a brief interruption in our default emotional range of irritation and boredom and guilt and "Can I Really Muster the Energy to Lean Over and Get the Remote Control"—and manages to punch through with an emotion that feels ancient and grand and noble.

We all feel it, a rare moment of sweeping, heart-thrilling all-the-feels togetherness, of shared humanity, and hope. And I realize that bit by bit, I have grown attached to this country, this crazy engine of human possibility.

HAPPINESS IS AT the very heart of the American project, the emotional ambition to mirror the economic. The idea that an entire nation can be founded on the principle that each person has the explicit right to a shot at personal fulfillment is endlessly compelling.

But when he wrote about the pursuit of happiness, Jefferson wasn't talking about self-discovery or the inner journey. The Founding Fathers' definition of happiness was intimately bound up with community and civic responsibility, with acknowledging that individual freedom and well-being depend on being part of the whole.

I had a glimpse of that grand sense of community and shared purpose in the ceremony. But all too often freedom and happiness, the two guiding tropes of the American experiment, have come to work against each other. Happiness has turned inward and become entangled with the idea of a personal journey and forging ahead alone.

Our narrative of happiness has become individualistic and punitive, totally divorced from social justice or wider responsibility.

If we genuinely want to build a happy society, we need a shift in thinking, and acceptance that happiness cannot be achieved by emotionally cloistering ourselves, that it needs other people in order to flourish.

We need to think of well-being as a shared responsibility, rather than an individual quest, and to develop a discourse of happiness that engages with people's problems rather than dismisses them. We need to acknowledge privilege and injustice and work against them, rather than blaming people for their own misfortunes, and to develop a vision of happiness that is inclusive and generous and socially aware.

Beyond that, I've realized over the last year or so of obsessing over this topic, that if we want to be happy, what we really need to do is to stop thinking about happiness.

At various points over the last year, I've managed to kvetch myself into a puddle of happiness neurosis. I am living proof of Dr. Iris Mauss's research that the more time you spend obsessively monitoring your emotional temperature, the less likely you are to be happy. I can confidently say that I am at my happiest when the topic of happiness is farthest from my mind.

And really, that's a liberating thought. For the slackers of this world, the idea that the harder we strive for happiness, the less likely we are to achieve it is good news. Now we can relax in the knowledge that if we concentrate on the life and liberty bits, if we focus on living a connected, fulfilling, and meaningful life, then if we're lucky, happiness might just hitch a ride.

LATER THAT NIGHT, my newly minted American husband and I order pizza and eat it out on our deck with the kids in the late evening sunshine. We talk about how awesome everything is, and mean it. We even sound strangely natural doing so. I post a picture of Neil on Facebook, grinning broadly, a slice of supersize Hawaiian in one hand, an American flag in the other. (I also post a close-up of the flag. It is printed with the words "Made in China.")

We're strangely American now. I drive an outlandishly large car, worthy of a Mormon soccer mom. I sprinkle exclamation marks liberally across my e-mails. Against my better judgment, I've even worn shorts.

This September, Solly will start at a local elementary school named after a dead president and will travel to it on the yellow school bus. He will call playtime *reeecesss* and if *Ramona the Brave* can be considered a reliable source, will pledge daily allegiance to a version of the same star-spangled banner that Neil is waving in the photo. Perhaps he'll even do it without mental reservation.

California has wormed its way into his bones. The other day, when his preschool class was due to perform a couple of songs to a group of the elderly at the community center, in the car on the way he announced to me that he "didn't want to sing to the seniors today."

"Why not?" I asked.

"Because it wouldn't be my self-expression."

At the other end of the spectrum, at age two, Zeph shows alarming signs of becoming a future Fox News–loving Tea Party member. One of his most enthusiastically deployed early words is *hate*. Between them our kids are covering the national extremes.

Over the four years we have been here, things have slowly shifted, and the clarity that I had in the beginning that England was home and America was a kind of pancake-themed fun park has blurred. We have real friends here now, not just mommy acquaintances, and we've seen each other through marriage and divorce, new babies and bereavements and serious illness and recovery. We've had a baby and seen him grow into a "spirited" toddler. I'm still homesick from time to time, but now it's more of a theoretical abstraction than a daily reality, and I know I'll feel homesick in reverse when we eventually do go back to England. Strangely, this is happiness. Because despite everything, I'm a sucker for a happy ending, and here it is.

ACKNOWLEDGMENTS

I'm not sure what good deeds I must have done in a past life to have had the profound good fortune and honor of working with Steve Ross, my agent, whose great kindness, wisdom, and incredible editorial vision have been so genuinely life-changing that "thank you" doesn't even begin to cover it. Unfortunately it's the best I've got without offering him my firstborn child. Also, thank you to David Doerrer and Kelsey O'Connell from Abrams Artists Agency, and to the impeccable Caspian Dennis from Abner Stein.

Thank you to Peter Catapano from *The New York Times* for publishing the original article that inspired the book and for an impressively rigorous editorial process.

My deepest thanks to Jennifer Weis from St. Martin's Press for her great enthusiasm and support for the project right from the beginning, for allowing me the editorial freedom to develop it in my own way, and for her incisive and impressive edits. Thank you also to Laura Clark, Tracey Guest, Staci Burt, and Sylvan Creekmore from St. Martin's Press for all their help.

I would like to thank the glorious Jocasta Hamilton for her editorial guidance, moral support, and for the all-round fun and hilarity, as well as the rest of the team from Hutchinson.

Thank you to the many friends, acquaintances, and colleagues who have read and commented on the manuscript and book proposal in its various drafts, including Tara Conklin, Alisa Pomeroy, Tamar Antin, Susie Meserve, Bill Bivens, Georgia Moseley, Rebecca Atkinson, Charlotte

Philby, Laura Martin-Robinson, Ana Balabanović, Nick Mamatas, Alf Lawrie, Susan Szafir, Adrienne Spangler, Michelle Feder, and in particular Colm Martin and Sarah Gregory. If anyone's reading this who I've forgotten that means I like you best.

I am extremely fortunate to know a brilliant, insightful bunch of people who have helped me in numerous other ways, sharing their own expertise in their respective fields, discussing the issues, and also providing various kinds of emotional and practical support. In particular, Judd Antin, Hanna Simmons, Steve Simmons, Jill Egan, Hannah Michell, Stephanie Mackley, Philip Levine, Jonathan Levine, Meghan Lopez, Sally Mason, Jeff Greenwald, Nick Mailer, Linda Woolf, Orla Katz Webb-Lamb, Wendy Ide, James Finberg, Jonny and Jane Girson, and my unique and amazing big sister, Sarah Vaughan.

A special thanks to the wonderful Leigh Carroll for being my on call American-English dictionary and cultural adviser on all things Americana, as well as providing much hilarity and friendship.

I was extremely fortunate to have help from the intellectual powerhouse that is Dr. James Coyne in decoding the academic papers and understanding the positive psychology literature.

Thank you to Cindy Bortman Boggess for her brilliant help in understanding some of the legal documents and related issues.

Matt and Jenny Asay and their family helped me hugely in understanding Mormon life and culture, and also happen to be some of the nicest human beings on the planet. My deepest thanks to all of them.

Thank you to Dr. Susan Willman, Jennifer Alvarado, and all the fantastic staff from the Reproductive Science Center of the Bay Area.

My deepest gratitude to Robyn Swan and Rina Moyal and the incredible staff of the JCC of the East Bay for taking such good care of the boychicks so I could work.

My eternal thanks to my mother, Constance Whippman, for her incredible love, inspiration, and support of every kind (and for not ruining my character by letting me have a Girl's World). One of the scientific findings that rang most deeply true for me (although never made it into the book) was that the single biggest factor affecting our long-term happiness and success is the love and warmth of our mothers. I couldn't have been luckier with mine.

Solly and Zephy Levine—under nobody's definition could either of you possibly have been considered the slightest help in writing this book. But without you two, I really wouldn't know a thing about happiness.

And Neil Levine, dearest love and best friend, I always thought that bit in the acknowledgments when the author said that she simply "couldn't have done it without her husband" was an empty platitude. Now I know that on every level, it really isn't. Thank you, and I love you. You are my happy ending.

NOTES

1. COMING TO AMERICA: OBSESSED WITH HAPPINESS, BUT NOBODY'S HAPPY

1 GfK MRI, *The Survey of the American Consumer*, 2003; *Oprah Winfrey Show*, income and education data.

2 House, *Report of the Committee on Appropriations*, 111th Cong., 1st sess., 2009, H. Rep. 111-220, itemizes a $900,000 earmark from the US Department of Education for social and emotional learning curriculum development and implementation in the Youngstown, Niles, and/or Warren City, OH, school districts. CASEL (Collaborative for Academic, Social, and Emotional Learning) Skills for Life Program describes the mindfulness aspect of this course, stating: "The unique aspect of this work is the integration of a researched based K-8 SEL program with nurturing the inner life of teachers, parents and students as well as students and teachers learning mindfulness practices."

3 Stephanie Warsmith, "Plain Township School Stops 'Mindfulness' Program After Some in Community Raise Concerns," *Akron Beacon Journal*, April 15, 2013, www.ohio.com/news/local/plain-township-school-stops -mindfulness-program-after-some-in-community-raise-concerns-1 .389761.

4 Marketdata Enterprises, "Overview & Status of the U.S. Self-Improvement Market: Market Size, Segments, Emerging Trends & Forecasts," November 2013, www.slideshare.net/jonlar/the-us-self-improvement-market.

5 Iris B. Mauss, Maya Tamir, and Craig L. Anderson, "Can Seeking Happiness Make People Unhappy? The Paradoxical Effects of Valuing Happiness," *Emotion* 11 (Aug. 2011): 807–15.

6 Gallup Positive Experience Index, 2014.

7 Ronald C. Kessler, Matthias Angermeyer, James C. Anthony, Ron de Graaf, Koen Demyttenaere, Isabelle Gasquet, Giovanni de Girolamo, et al., "Lifetime Prevalence and Age-of-Onset Distributions of Mental Disorders in the World Health Organization's World Mental Health Survey Initiative," *World Psychiatry* 6, no. 3 (2007): 168–76.

8 American Psychological Association, "Stress in America, Our Health at Risk," January 11, 2012, www.apa.org/news/press/releases/stress/2011/final-2011.pdf.

2. PERSONAL JOURNEY? IT'S NOT ALL ABOUT YOU

1 Food Marketing Institute Report, *U.S. Grocery Shopper Trends 2014.*

2 Miller McPherson, Lynn Smith-Lovin, and Matthew E. Brashears, "Social Isolation in America: Changes in Core Discussion Networks over Two Decades," *American Sociological Review* 71 (2006): 353–75.

3 General Social Survey, NORC, University of Chicago, gss.norc.org/.

4 US Department of Labor, Bureau of Labor Statistics, American Time Use Survey, 2013, www.bls.gov/tus/.

5 US Department of Health and Human Services, National Institutes of Health, National Center for Complementary and Integrative Health, "Use of Complementary Health Approaches in the US, National Health Interview Survey, 2012," nccih.nih.gov/research/statistics/NHIS/2012.

6 Kate Pickert, "The Mindful Revolution," *Time*, January 23, 2014.

7 Yoon Kim, "2014 Outlook for the Pilates and Yoga Studios Industry," Snews, www.snewsnet.com/news/2014-yoga-pilates-studios/.

8 Lauren Setar and Matthew McFarland, "Top 10 Fastest-Growing Industries," IBIS World, Special Report, April 2012, www.newstatesman.com/sites/default/files/files/Fastest%20Growing%20Industries.pd.

9 Marketdata Enterprises, "Overview & Status of the U.S. Self-Improvement Market: Market Size, Segments, Emerging Trends & Forecasts," November 2013, www.slideshare.net/jonlar/the-us-self-improvement-market.

10 Sam Harris, *Waking Up: A Guide to Spirituality Without Religion* (New York: Simon & Schuster, 2014): 12, 14.

11 Madhav Goyal, Sonal Singh, Erica M. S. Sibinga, Neda F. Gould, Anastasia Rowland-Seymour, Ritu Sharma, Zachary Berger, et al., "Meditation Programs for Psychological Stress and Well-Being: A Systematic Review and Meta-analysis," *JAMA Internal Medicine* 174, no. 3 (2014): 357–68.

12 McPherson et al., "Social Isolation in America."

13 Gretchen Anderson and Knowledge Networks and Insight Policy Research, *Loneliness Among Older Adults: A National Survey of Adults 45+*, AARP, September 2010, www.aarp.org/content/dam/aarp/research/surveys_statistics /general/2012/loneliness_2010.pdf.

14 Christine Carter, "Happiness Is Being Socially Connected," *Raising Happiness*, October 31, 2008,greatergood.berkeley.edu/raising_happiness/post /happiness_is_being_socially_connected.

15 Ed Diener and Martin E. P. Seligman, "Very Happy People," *Psychological Science* 13, no. 1 (2002): 81–84.

16 Ed Diener and Robert Biswas-Diener, "Happiness and Social Relationships: You Can't Do Without Them," in *Happiness: Unlocking the Mysteries of Psychological Wealth* (Malden, MA: Blackwell, 2008): 47–67.

17 John Zelenski, Maya S. Santoro, and Deanna C. Whelan, "Would Introverts Be Better Off If They Acted More Like Extraverts? Exploring Emotional and Cognitive Consequences of Counterdispositional Behavior," *Emotion* 12, no. 2 (2012): 290–303.

18 Julianne Holt-Lunstad, Timothy B. Smith, and J. Bradley Layton, "Social Relationships and Mortality Risk: A Meta-analytic Review," *PLOS Medicine* 7, no. 7 (2010), journals.plos.org/plosmedicine/article?id=10.1371/journal .pmed.1000316.

19 Brett Q. Ford, Julia O. Dmitrieva, Daniel Heller, Yulia Chentsova-Dutton, Ygor Grossman, Maya Tamir, Yukiko Uchida, et al., "Culture Shapes Whether the Pursuit of Happiness Predicts Higher or Lower Well-Being," *Journal of Experimental Psychology* 144 (2015): 1053–62.

20 Iris Mauss, Nicole S. Savino, Craig L. Anderson, Max Weisbuch, Maya Tamir, and Mark L. Laudenslager, "The Pursuit of Happiness Can Be Lonely," *Emotion* 12, no. 5 (2012), 908–12, www.ocf.berkeley.edu/~eerlab/pdf /papers/2012_Mauss_Pursuit_of_Happiness.pdf.

3. HAPPINESS FOR SALE: SELF-HELP AMERICA

1 Marketdata Enterprises, "Overview & Status of the U.S. Self-Improvement Market: Market Size, Segments, Emerging Trends & Forecasts," November 2013, www.slideshare.net/jonlar/the-us-self-improvement-market.

2 Landmark Education, "Fact Sheet," www.landmarkworldwide.com/about /company-overview/fact-sheet.

3 "The World's Highest Paid Celebrities: 2015 Ranking," *Forbes*, www.forbes .com/celebrities/list/#tab:overall.

4 There are many contemporary accounts of the est training, including *The Book of est*, a fictionalized but by all accounts accurate depiction of the training, by Luke Rhinehart. This book includes a foreword by Werner Erhard, in which he says, "[Luke Rhinehart] presents his experience of the training from his own point of view, while taking care to keep the facts basically accurate. . . . I support Luke Rhinehart totally." Other accounts of the training include *est: 60 Hours That Transform Your Life*, by Adelaide Bry, and "Pay Attention, Turkeys!; Est's Formula for Success: Charge Them $250, Bore Them to Death, Throw in a Few Insults, and They Love It," by Leo Litwak, *New York Times Magazine*, May 2, 1976.

5 Debbie Ford, of Challenge Day's Global Leadership Council, writes in her book, *Spiritual Divorce* (HarperCollins, 2001): "While attending school, I also began leading transformational seminars for Landmark Education. . . ."

6 Interview with Lynne Twist, the Social Entrepreneur, Empowerment Series, The Soul of Money. Twist (a member of Challenge Day's Global Leadership Council) says: "Everyone has milestones and epiphanies. Mine came in the est training which I took in 1974 with Werner Erhard." Available at wernererhardandest.wordpress.com/2011/05/29/lynne-twist/.

7 Steve Salerno, *Sham: How the Self-Help Movement Made America Helpless* (New York: Crown, 2005). This anecdote is drawn from Salerno's personal experience working at self-help publisher Rodale.

4. WORKAHOLICS

1 Sue Shellenbarger, "Thinking Happy Thoughts at Work," *Wall Street Journal*, January 27, 2010, www.wsj.com/articles/SB10001424052748704905604 575027042440341392.

2 Democratic Staff of the US House Committee on Education and the Workforce, "The Low-Wage Drag on Our Economy: Wal-Mart's Low Wages and Their Effect on Taxpayers and Economic Growth. An Update to the 2004 Report: 'Everyday Low Wages: The Hidden Price We All Pay for Wal-Mart,'" May 2013.

3 Michael Barbaro, "At Wal-Mart, Lessons in Self-Help," *New York Times*, April 5, 2007, www.nytimes.com/2007/04/05/business/05improve.html?_r=0.

4 International Labour Organization, "Americans Work Longest Hours Among Industrialized Countries, Japanese Second Longest. Europeans Work Less Time, but Register Faster Productivity Gains New ILO Statis-

tical Volume Highlights Labour Trends Worldwide," Statistical Study of Global Labour Trends, a cooperative effort of the ILO and the OECD, September 1999.

5 Oxford Economics, "All Work and No Pay: The Impact of Forfeited Time Off," October 2014, www.projecttimeoff.com/research/all-work-and-no -pay-impact-forfeited-time.

6 "Who Goes to Work to Have Fun?" *New York Times*, Dec. 11, 2013, www .nytimes.com/2013/12/12/opinion/burkeman-are-we-having-fun-yet .html?_r=0.

7 James Sweeney, "Happiness Coach Takes on Grumpy Reporter," *Plain Dealer*, February 9, 2008, blog.cleveland.com/lifestyles/2008/02/happiness _coach_takes_on_grump.html.

8 Patrick Flavin and Gregory Shufeldt, "Labor Union Membership and Life Satisfaction in the United States," October 2014, blogs.baylor.edu/patrick _j_flavin/files/2010/09/Union_Membership_and_Life_Satisfaction_10 .27.14-nlder4.pdf.

9 Bank of America Wage and Hour Employment Practice Litigation, United States District Court of Kansas, Case 10-MD-2138-JWL-KGS, document 653-1, Dec. 18, 2013, www.ksd.uscourts.gov/settlement-agreement-with -attachments-doc-653-2/.

10 National Labor Relations Board, case number 02-CA-037548. Starbucks lost the case on a number of counts. The company appealed the decision, and the case went back and forth several times. The quote used comes from Decision of the United States Court of Appeals, Second Circuit, *National Labor Relations Board v. Starbucks Corporation*, decided, May 10, 2012. "Starbucks mounted an anti-union campaign aimed at tracking and restricting the growth of pro-union sentiment. In the course of this campaign, Starbucks employed a number of restrictive and illegal policies. These included prohibiting employees from discussing the union or the terms and conditions of their employment; prohibiting the posting of union material on bulletin boards in employee areas; preventing off-duty employees from entering the back area of one of the stores; and discriminating against pro-union employees regarding work opportunities. In this Court, Starbucks does not challenge the Board's determination that this conduct violated the [National Labor Relations] Act." Available at caselaw.findlaw .com/us-2nd-circuit/1600558.html.

11 *Thomas Rosenberg et al. v. IBM Corporation*, settled for $65 million. *Michael Danieli et al. v. IBM Corporation*, settled for $7.5 million. *Whittington et al.*

v. YUM! Brands, Inc., Taco Bell of America, Inc., and Taco Bell Corp., settled for $2,490,000.

12 Chris Hedges, "Happiness Consultants Won't Stop a Depression," *truthdig .com*, July 27th, 2009.

5. "I DON'T CARE AS LONG AS HE'S HAPPY": DISPATCHES FROM THE PARENTING HAPPINESS RAT RACE

1 Diane Simon, "Breaking Up with Dr. Sears: How Attachment Parenting Nearly Killed Me," Mommyish.com, August 22, 2011, www.mommyish .com/2011/08/22/breaking-up-with-dr-sears-how-attachment-parenting -nearly-killed-me/.

2 Lori Gottlieb, "How to Land Your Kid in Therapy," *Atlantic*, July/August 2011, www.theatlantic.com/magazine/archive/2011/07/how-to-land-your -kid-in-therapy/308555/.

3 Robert P. Gallagher, "National Survey of College Counseling Centers 2013," International Association of Counseling Services, www.collegecounseling .org/wp-content/uploads/Survey-2013-4-yr-Directors-1.pdf.

4 American College Health Association, National College Health Assessment, Spring 2015 Reference Group Executive Summary, pp. 13–16.

5 Jean M. Twenge, Brittany Gentile, C. Nathan DeWall, Debbie Ma, Katharine Lacefield, and David R. Schurtz, "Birth Cohort Increases in Psychopathology Among Young Americans, 1938–2007: A Cross-Temporal Meta-analysis of the MMPI," *Clinical Psychology Review* 30 (2010): 145–54.

6 Daniel Kahneman, Alan B. Krueger, David A. Schkade, Norbert Schwarz, and Arthur A. Stone, "A Survey Method for Characterizing Daily Life Experience: The Day Reconstruction Method," *Science* 306, no. 5702 (2004): 1776–80.

7 Rachel Margolis and Mikko Myrskylä, "Parental Well-Being Surrounding First Birth as a Determinant of Further Parity Progression," *Demography* 52, no. 4 (2015): 1147–66.

8 Garey Ramey and Valerie A. Ramey, "The Rug Rat Race," National Bureau of Economic Research, working paper 15284, *Brookings Papers on Economic Activity*, Economic Studies Program 4 (Spring 2010): 129–99, www.nber .org/papers/w15284.

9 Kathryn M. Rizzo, Holly H. Schiffrin, and Miriam Liss, "Insight into the Parenthood Paradox: Mental Health Outcomes of Intensive Mothering," *Journal of Child and Family Studies* 22, no. 5 (2013): 614–20.

10 Arnstein Aassve, Stefano Mazzuco, and Letizia Mencarini, "Childbearing and Well-Being: A Comparative Analysis of European Welfare Regimes," *Journal of European Social Policy* 15, no. 4 (2005): 283–99.

6. GOD'S PLAN OF HAPPINESS

1 Research Center, Social and Demographic Trends Survey, November 28–December 5, Summary available at: www.pewresearch.org/fact-tank /2013/09/16/study-religious-people-more-likely-to-reject-the-idea-that -life-has-no-purpose/.
2012; Gallup -Healthways Well-Being Index, January 2, 2010–December 30, 2011.
Summary available here: www.gallup.com/poll/152723/religious-americans -enjoy-higher-wellbeing.aspx; General Social Survey, National Opinion Research Center, NORC at the University of Chicago surveys (1972–2014). gss.norc.org/. Smith, Tom W., Peter Marsden, Michael Hout, and Jibum Kim.
General Social Surveys, 1972–2014/Principal Investigator, Tom W. Smith; Co-Principal Investigator, Peter V. Marsden; Co-Principal Investigator, Michael Hout; Sponsored by National Science Foundation. NORC ed., Chicago: NORC at the University of Chicago [producer]; Storrs, CT: The Roper Center for Public Opinion Research, University of Connecticut [distributor], 2015.
2 Gallup–Healthways Well-Being Index, January 2, 2010–December 30, 2011. Summary available at: www.gallup.com/poll/152732/religious -higher-wellbeing-across-faiths.aspx.
3 Pew Research Center, Religion & Public Life, "Mormons in America— Certain in Their Beliefs, Uncertain of Their Place in Society," January 12, 2012, www.pewforum.org/2012/01/12/mormons-in-america-executive -summary/.
4 Gallup–Healthways Well-Being Index, 2014.
5 Michael J. Doane, "The Association Between Religiosity and Subjective Well-Being: The Unique Contribution of Religious Service Attendance and the Mediating Role of Perceived Religious Social Support," *Irish Journal of Psychology* 34, no. 1 (2003): 49–66.
6 Chaeyoon Lima and Robert D. Putnam, "Religion, Social Networks, and Life Satisfaction," *American Sociological Review* 75 (2010): 914–33.
7 Benjamin Radcliff, "Politics, Markets, and Life Satisfaction: The Political

Economy of Human Happiness," *American Political Science Review* 95, no. 4 (2001): 939–52.

8 Julia B. Isaacs, "International Comparisons of Economic Mobility," Economic Mobility Project, Pew Charitable Trusts, www.brookings.edu/~/media /research/files/reports/2008/2/economic-mobility-sawhill/02_economic _mobility_sawhill_ch3.pdf.

9 The Equality of Opportunity Project, a joint initiative by Harvard University and the University of California, Berkeley, 2014.

10 Gallup–Healthways Well-Being Index, 2012.

11 B. R. Motheral, E. R. Cox, D. Mager, R. Henderson, and R. Martinez, *Prescription Drug Atlas* (Express Scripts, 2002).

12 "America's Mental Health: An Analysis of Depression Across the States," November 29, 2007, prepared for Mental Health America by Thomson Healthcare, Washington DC.

13 Alex E. Crosby, Beth Han, LaVonne A. G. Ortega, Sharyn E. Parks, and Joseph Gfroerer, "Suicidal Thoughts and Behaviors Among Adults Aged ≥18 Years—United States, 2008–2009," *Morbidity and Mortality Weekly Report*, Centers for Disease Control and Prevention, October 21, 2011, www.cdc.gov/mmwr/preview/mmwrhtml/ss6013a1.htm.

14 Brock Bastian, Peter Kuppens, Matthew J. Hornsey, Joonha Park, Peter Koval, and Yukiko Uchida, "Feeling Bad About Being Sad: The Role of Social Expectancies in Amplifying Negative Mood," *Emotion* 12, no. 1 (2012): 69–80.

7. I'M NOT A HAPPY PERSON, I JUST PLAY ONE ON FACEBOOK

1 Ethan Kross, Philippe Verduyn, Emre Demiralp, Jiyoung Park, David Seungjae Lee, Natalie Lin, Holly Shablack, John Jonides, and Oscar Ybarra, "Facebook Use Predicts Declines in Subjective Well-Being in Young Adults," *PLOS One* (August 14, 2013), journals.plos.org/plosone/article?id=10.1371 /journal.pone.0069841.

2 Hanna Krasnova, Helena Wenninger, Thomas Widjaja, and Peter Buxmann, "Envy on Facebook: A Hidden Threat to Users' Life Satisfaction?" *Wirtschaftsinformatik Proceedings 2013*, Paper 92, www.researchgate.net /publication/256712913_Envy_on_Facebook_a_hidden_threat_to_users' _life_satisfaction.

3 "Suicide on Campus and the Pressure of Perfection," *New York Times*, July 27, 2015, www.nytimes.com/2015/08/02/education/edlife/stress -social-media-and-suicide-on-campus.html?_r=0.

4 Meg Jay, PhD, "Just Say No to Facebook Social Comparisons," *Psychology Today*, March 30, 2012.

5 Eliana Dockterman, "How the News Got Less Mean," *Time*, August 21, 2013, ideas.time.com/2013/08/21/how-the-news-got-less-mean/.

6 Isaac Fitzgerald, interview by Andrew Beaujon, "BuzzFeed Names Isaac Its First Books Editor," *Poynter*, November 7, 2013, www.poynter.org/2013/buzzfeed-names-isaac-fitzgerald-its-first-books-editor/228792/.

8. POSITIVE PSYCHOLOGY (OR IF YOU'RE NOT HAPPY, IT'S YOUR OWN FAULT, YOU LAZY SCHMUCK)

1 Martin E. P. Seligman, "Learned Helplessness," *Annual Review of Medicine* 23 (1972): 407–12.

2 As reported in *Psychology Today*, October 12, 2010.

3 H. Andrew Schwartz, Johannes C. Eichstaedt, Margaret L. Kern, Lukasz Dziurzynski, Megha Agrawal, Gregory J. Park, Shrinidhi K. Lakshmikanth, Sneha Jha, Martin E. P. Seligman, Lyle Ungar, and Richard E. Luca, "Characterizing Geographic Variation in Well-Being Using Tweets," *Proceedings of the Seventh International AAAI Conference of Weblogs and Social Media*, 2013.

4 All American Speakers, Martin Seligman profile. www.allamericanspeakers.com/celebritytalentbios/Martin-Seligman.

5 Wholebeing Institute, Certificate in Positive Psychology, West Coast USA. wholebeinginstitute.com/course-overview/cipp-overview/west-coast/.

6 New York Open Center, the New York Certificate in Applied Positive Psychology, www.opencenter.org/events/the-new-york-certificate-in-applied-positive-psychology/.

7 UC Berkeley, Putting the Science of Happiness into Practice, a weekend retreat at the Esalen Institute, greatergood.berkeley.edu/news_events/event/putting_the_science_of_happiness_into_practice#.VrpY6bkrK2w.

8 Carlin Flora, "The Pursuit of Happiness," *Psychology Today*, January 1, 2009, www.psychologytoday.com/articles/200901/the-pursuit-happiness.

9 Boris Kachka, "The Power of Positive Publishing: How Self-Help Ate America," *New York*, January 6, 2013, nymag.com/health/self-help/2013/self-help-book-publishing/.

10 Ed Diener, Eunkook M. Suh, Richard E. Lucas, and Heidi L. Smith, "Subjective Well-Being: Three Decades of Progress," *Psychological Bulletin* 125 (1999): 276–302, stat.psych.uiuc.edu/~ediener/Documents/Diener-Suh-Lucas-Smith_1999.pdf.

11 Laura A. Pratt and Debra J. Brody, "Depression in the United States Household Population, 2005–2006," NCHS Brief, no. 7, Centers for Disease Control and Prevention, September 2008, www.cdc.gov/nchs/data/databriefs /db07.htm.

12 Betsey Stevenson and Justin Wolfers, "Subjective and Objective Indicators of Racial Progress," 5th Annual Conference on Empirical Legal Studies, July 16, 2010, ssrn.com/abstract=1641491.

13 Betsey Stevenson and Justin Wolfers, "The Paradox of Declining Female Happiness," *American Economic Journal: Economic Policy* 1, no. 2 (2009): 190–225, www.nber.org/papers/w14969.pdf.

14 Gallup–Healthways Well-Being Index, 2012.

15 Daniel Kahneman and Angus Deaton, "High Income Improves Evaluation of Life but Not Emotional Well-Being," *Proceedings of the National Academy of Sciences* 107, no. 38 (2010): 16489–93, www.pnas.org/content/107 /38/16489.full.

16 United States Census Bureau, Current Population Survey: 2011, Annual Social and Economic Supplement.

17 John Templeton Foundation, www.templeton.org (Grant Search).

18 Federal Election Commission, Campaign Finance, 222.fec.gov/disclosure .shtml; Opensecrets.org, Center for Responsive Politics, donor lookup, "Templeton, John M."; Cal-Access, National Organization for Marriage California, Yes on 8, contributions page.

19 Martin Seligman, "An Interview with Martin E. P. Seligman, PhD," by Joshua Freedman, Walden Personnel Testing & Consulting, September 1999, www.waldentesting.com/salestests/sasq/seligmanint.htm.

20 Sonja Lyubomirsky, Kennon A. Sheldon, and David Schkade, "Pursuing Happiness: The Architecture of Sustainable Change," *Review of General Psychology* 9, no. 2 (2005): 111–31; see p. 125, sonjalyubomirsky.com/wp -content/themes/sonjalyubomirsky/papers/LSS2005.pdf.

21 Kennon M. Sheldon and Sonja Lyubomirsky, "How to Increase and Sustain Positive Emotion: The Effects of Expressing Gratitude and Visualizing Best Possible Selves," *Journal of Positive Psychology* 1, no. 2 (2006): 73–82, greatergood.berkeley.edu/images/application_uploads/sheldon -SustainPositiveEmotion.pdf.

22 Nancy L. Sin, Matthew D. Della Porta, and Sonja Lyubomirsky, "Tailoring Positive Psychology Interventions to Treat Depressed Individuals," in *Applied Positive Psychology*, eds. Stewart I. Donaldson, Mihaly Csikszentmihalyi, and Jeanne Nakamura, eds. (New York: Routledge, 2011): 79–96, son

jalyubomirsky.com/wp-content/themes/sonjalyubomirsky/papers
/SDL2011.pdf.

23 Linda Boiler, Merel Haverman, Gerben J. Westerhof, Heleen Riper, Filip
Smit, and Ernst Bohlmeijer, "Positive Psychology Interventions: A Meta-
analysis of Randomized Controlled Studies," *BMC Public Health* 13 (2013):
119, bmcpublichealth.biomedcentral.com/articles/10.1186/1471-2458-13
-119.

24 The informal group, the Negateers, is organized by Barbara Ehrenreich, author of *Bright-Sided: How The Relentless Promotion of Positive Thinking Has
Undermined America.* The group's Facebook's page says "The Negateers
joined forces in 2008 to fight the tyranny of positive thinking and the cult
of omnipotent agency."

25 Florence T. Bourgeois, Srinivas Murthy, and Kenneth D. Mandl, "Outcome
Reporting Among Drug Trials Registered in ClinicalTrials.gov," *Annals of
Internal Medicine* 153, no. 3 (2010): 158–66.

26 James Coyne, "More Sciencey Than the Rest? The Competitive Edge of
Positive Psychology Coaching," *Mind the Brain* (PLOS Blogs), August 11,
2015, blogs.plos.org/mindthebrain/2015/08/11/more-sciencey-than-the
-rest-the-competitive-edge-of-positive-psychology-coaching/.

27 Information Governance and Security Directorate, Department for
Work and Pensions, "Low Income and Material Deprivation in the UK,
11/12," June 13, 2013, www.gov.uk/government/uploads/system/uploads
/attachment_data/file/206850/first_release_1112.pdf.

28 Department for Work and Pensions, "Claimant Segmentation Trial Standards and Guidelines"; Matthew Holehouse, "Welfare Claimants to Get Attitude Tests, Employment Minister Reveals," *Daily Telegraph*, September
5, 2014, www.telegraph.co.uk/news/politics/11078359/Welfare-claimants
-to-get-attitude-tests-employment-minister-reveals.html (includes interview with Employment Minister Esther McVey outlining the new scheme).

29 Department for Work and Pensions, "Community Work Placements Pro-
vider Guidance," May 27, 2014: "Claimant Group 1.06—CWP will be
aimed at Jobseeker's Allowance (JSA) claimants who have completed the
Work Programme and have been identified by JCP as requiring CWP support due to the key barrier preventing them from moving into work, being
either insufficient work history or a lack of motivation."

30 www.ingeus.com/pages/leading_ideas/106/international_best_practice
_the_importance_of_wellbeing.html.

31 "The Joy of the Jobcentre Work Programme," Sothisismylifenow.blogspot

.co.uk, August 16, 2013; quoted in Lynne Friedli and Robert Stearn, "Positive Affect as Coercive Strategy: Conditionality, Activation and the Role of Psychology in UK Government Workfare Programmes," *Medical Humanities* 41 (2015): 40–47, mh.bmj.com/content/41/1/40.full.

32 Izzy Koksal, "Positive Thinking for the Unemployed: My Adventures at A4e," izzykoksal.wordpress.com/2012/04/13/adventures-at-a4e/.

33 Benjamin Radcliff, "Politics, Markets, and Life Satisfaction: The Political Economy of Human Happiness," *American Political Science Review* 95, no. 4 (Dec. 2001): 939–52.

INDEX

Gallup, 10
games, 58
Gawker, 89
gay marriage, 160
gender, 199
  equality, 149–50
General Social Survey, 10, 18
genetics, 194, 198
giving up, 15
God's plan, 134–35
Gold Spike, 82–83, 93
golden plates, 134
Google
  advice on, 14
  happiness searches on, 13
  meditation by, 21
  perks of, 93
  Zappos on, 73
Gould, David, 90
grandparents, 127
gratitude, 206, 207
Gratitude Challenge, 174–75
Great American Search for
    Happiness, 6, 9, 11, 49
group sharing, 56
guilt, 13, 45
gurus, 49–50

*Hand to Mouth, Living in Bootstrap
    America* (Tirado), 202–3
Happier at Home (Rubin), 2
happiness. *See specific topics*
happiness meter, 68–69
The Happiness Project (Rubin), 37
Harris, Dan, 21–22
Harris, Sam, 21
headlines, 183
headquarters, 6, 70
health, 28
high-end fantasy, 14
highlight reel, 169
Hitachi, 68–69
Holleran, Madison, 179
Holsinger-Butler, Emily, 150–52
home, 220
homosexuality, 160–63
honesty, 170
hope, 214

household income, 7
The How of Happiness (Lyubomirsky),
    192–93, 194, 204–5
Hppy, 68
Hsieh, Tony
  communal living of, 81–82
  Downtown Project of, 80
  employees of, 73
  mission of, 71–72
  priority list of, 72–73
  real estate of, 79
  social experiment of, 79
  of Zappos, 71
Hsieh residence, 81–82
human experience, 43, 45, 188–89

"I love you" principle, 65–66, 67
identity, 155
immigration, 216
impression management, 177–78
income, 199–201
independence, 24
individual achievement, 29
individual fault, 34
individual quest, 30
individual responsibility, 50,
    123–24
individualism, 24
  happiness through, 140, 197, 201
  in self-help, 50
  Seligman on, 202
industry profit, 32
inflation, 123
Ingeus, 212
inspirational meme, 17
intentional activity, 197
International Labour Organization,
    95–96
interpersonal relationships, 28
interventions, 61
interview, 53, 72
intimacy, 1
investment, 9, 26–27
inward journey, 18
isolation, 14, 16–17

Jay, Meg, 179–80
Jesus Christ, 133

242   *Index*

John Templeton Foundation, 189,
    201–2
Jorgensen, Dylan, 83–85
Journal of Child and Family Studies,
    123
journalist, 11
joy hunting, 6
justification, 129

Kahneman, Daniel, 119
kid negotiations, 111, 112
kids' reviews, 59
Kindlon, Dan, 114
Knoll, Kimberly
    approach of, 92
    of Downtown Project, 90
    on experiencing emotions, 92
    on suicide, 90–91

Landmark Education. *See also*
    Challenge Day; Landmark Forum
    in Britain, 48
    environment of, 38
    language of, 40
    in self-help industry, 36
Landmark Forum
    attendance reasons for, 35–36
    course by, 38, 43
    dreams about, 45
    effects of, 36
    facilitator at, 39
    free will at, 62
    group work at, 44
    history of, 39, 228n4
    interpretation of events by, 42
    kid version of, 51–52
    lack of self-awareness from, 50–51
    participant inauthenticity at, 42
    personal histories at, 41
    on personal responsibility, 46
    philosophy of, 40, 228n4
    physical effects of, 43, 46–47
    positive experience through, 43
    reputation of, 34
    transformations by, 33, 34–35, 38
    Valentine's Day at, 45–46
    Vanto Group as, 40
Landmark leader, 52, 228n6

Landmark technology, 47–48
Landmark's influence, 52, 228n5
Las Vegas Weekly, 89
lawsuit, 99
life
    blueprint for, 149
    choices for, 156
    circumstances of, 193–96, 198–99,
        202–3, 208
    failures of, 46
    priority of, 9, 105–6
    satisfaction for, 131–32, 200
    stories of, 42
lifeline, 168
lifestyle, 125–26
like button, 183–84
likes, 170–71, 184
loneliness, 2, 13, 26, 31, 35
lotus position, 24
love, 164. *See also* "I love you"
    principle
Love and Logic, 115
Lyubomirsky, Sonja, 193, 194, 204–5
    on gratitude, 206, 207
    on intentional activity, 197
    on positive psychology, 192
    techniques by, 195–96

Mandela, Nelson, 37
marriage, 138–39, 148, 154, 160, 162
maternity leave, 124
Mauss, Iris, 29–30, 32, 35
McDonald's, 68
meditation
    benefits of, 19, 21, 25–26
    for corporations, 63
    for depression, 25
    for emotional individualism, 24
    happiness increased by, 22
    human brain against, 5–6
    mindfulness with, 21
    perception of, 22–23
    of present moment, 5
    in public education, 7, 225n2
    silence in, 24–25
meditation meta-analysis, 25–26
mental focus, 22
mental health